COYOTE AT LARGE

COYOTE AT LARGE

▼   ▼   ▼   ▼   ▼

Humor in American Nature Writing

Katrina Schimmoeller Peiffer

THE UNIVERSITY OF UTAH PRESS

SALT LAKE CITY

Printed on acid-free paper

LIBRARY OF CONGRESS CATALOGING-IN-PUBLICATION DATA

Peiffer, Katrina Schimmoeller, 1969–
   Coyote at large : humor in American nature writing   /   Katrina Schimmoeller
Peiffer.
     p.   cm.
Includes bibliographical references and index.
   ISBN 0-87480-664-X
   1. American literature—History and criticism.   2. Nature in literature.   3. Natural
history—United States—Historiography.   4. American wit and humor—History and
criticism. 5. Comic, The, in literature. 6. Tricksters in literature.   I. Title.
   PS163   .P45   2000
   810.9'36—dc21

                                                                              00-009482

06   05   04   03   02   01   00

5   4   3   2   1

CONTENTS

ACKNOWLEDGMENTS

THIS BOOK HAS TRAVELED A GREAT DEAL ON ITS WAY TO PUBLICATION. I am grateful to all of the people who made the trip possible: Stephanie Sarver, for suggesting Louise Erdrich; Linda Morris, for her close reading and great editing; Gary Snyder, for proposing that I look to Coyote; and especially David Robertson, whose careful reading, fine judgment, and continued support truly carried the book along.

I am deeply grateful to Louise Chawla, whose friendship, hospitality, and cat gave me a nurturing place to type the manuscript. The interlibrary loan staff at the Paul Sawyier Public Library in Frankfort, Kentucky, and the Crawford County Public Library in English, Indiana, kindly filled all of my requests.

Dawn Marano and the other staff at the University of Utah Press have been enthusiastic and perceptive in their handling of the book. Dawn Woodring did an excellent job copy-editing.

The book also owes itself to my family's laughter, which I have been steeped in since the beginning, and my husband's talent for surprising me. Tim Peiffer, Charles and Laurie Schimmoeller, Chris Schimmoeller and Joel Dufour, and Mark Schimmoeller and Jennifer Lindberg are all readers, writers, artists, jokesters, and hard workers—I want to thank them for their endless love and inspiration.

Grateful acknowledgment is made to the following for permission to reprint:

Excerpts from *Beyond the Wall* by Edward Abbey, copyright 1984. Used by permission of Don Congden Associates, Inc.

Excerpts from "From a Few Words in Favor of Edward Abbey," "Why I'm Not Going to Buy a Computer," "Feminism, the Body and Machine," "Word and Flesh," "Waste," "The Pleasures of Eating," from *What Are People For?* by Wendell Berry. Copyright 1990 by Wendell Berry. Used by permission of North Point Press, a division of Farrar, Straus and Giroux, LLC.

Excerpts from *One Day On Beetle Rock* by Sally Carrighar, copyright 1944 and renewed 1972 by Sally Carrighar; copyright 1943, 1944 by the Curtis

Publishing Company. Used by permission of Alfred A. Knopf, a division of Random House, Inc.

Excerpts from *The Sea Around Us* by Rachel Carson, copyright 1950, 1951, 1961 by Rachel Carson. Renewed 1979 by Roger Christie. Used by permission of Oxford University Press, Inc.

Excerpts from *Under the Sea Wind* by Rachel Carson, illustrated by Bob Hines, copyright 1941 by Rachel L. Carson. Copyright renewed 1969 by Roger Christie. Illustrations copyright 1991 by Rob Hines. A Truman Talley Book. Used by permission of Dutton, a division of Penguin Putnam Inc.

Excerpts from *The Bingo Palace* by Louise Erdrich, copyright 1994 by Louise Erdrich; and *The Blue Jay's Dance* by Louise Erdrich, copyright 1995 by Louise Erdrich. Used by permission of HarperCollins Publishers.

Excerpts from "Buffalo Gals, Won't You Come Out Tonight," copyright 1987 by Ursula K. Le Guin; first appeared in *The Magazine of Fantasy and Science Fiction*; from *Buffalo Gals and Other Animal Presences*; reprinted by permission of the author and the author's agents, the Virginia Kidd Agency, Inc.

Excerpts from "Telling About Coyote," "Two Coyote Ones," and "How to Make a Good Chili Stew," from *A Good Journey* by Simon Ortiz, copyright 1984. Used by permission of Simon Ortiz.

Excerpts from "Through the Smoke Hole," "A Berry Feast," from *The Back Country* by Gary Snyder, copyright 1968 by Gary Snyder; excerpts from "The Call of the Wild" from *Turtle Island* by Gary Snyder, copyright 1974 by Gary Snyder. Used by permission of New Directions Publishing Corp.

Excerpts from "Coyote Man, Mr. President and the Gunfighters," from *Left Out In the Rain: New Poems 1947-1985* by Gary Synder, copyright 1986 by Gary Snyder. Used by permission of Farrar, Straus and Giroux, LLC.

PROLOGUE

▼▼▼

AMERICAN NATURE WRITING ON THE WHOLE IS PERCEIVED TO BE AN eminently serious pursuit, with its most famous writers achieving the status of guru or pilgrim—quasi-religious figures whose accounts of spiritual communion with nature have become the liturgical texts of their nature-loving following. Two such writers, Henry David Thoreau and John Muir, are read in context of both their religious-mystical awareness and their commitment to preserve wilderness; neither approach has lent itself to interpretations that identify humor in these writers' works. Ralph Waldo Emerson is also known for his serious philosophy, serious in tone and in magnitude of vision. This reputation of nature writers could be because they are, as a group, humorless, but that explanation oversimplifies this issue and dismisses too much of their work.

Although nature writers very often have serious aims, seriousness does not necessarily negate comedy or humor. Much the opposite is true: comedy must tweak the serious to achieve humorous results. Otherwise, Thoreau's image of a man pushing his inherited seventy-five-by-forty-foot barn before him in life would not be so hilariously accurate (8). The mistake—to cleave the serious and the comic—is a particularly dualistic one, corollary to the tendency in Western traditions to keep religion apart from humor, which would seem to profane it. Thus the religious and mystical aura that attends nature writing contributes to the general assumption that it partakes nothing of the comic. Ecocriticism itself has perpetuated this assumption, generating steadfastly serious interpretations of nature writing that emphasize its importance to us in learning to be better ecological members of nature. Our traditions and criticism thus have conspired to train us to perceive only the solemnity and seriousness in nature writing.

If we assume that no levity exists in nature writing, however, we lose fertile grounds for analysis. Even the briefest juxtaposition of comedy and nature writing yields provocative results. For example, parallel concern with perspective is important to nature writers in their efforts to look "into" nature and is fundamental to comedy in its manipulation of point of view and situation. Comedy as plot (the loss and recovery of equilibrium) and attitude (the acceptance of change and mystery) differs from humor (that which is funny) but cannot be extricated completely from it. I do not intend to force such a separation. My purpose is to demonstrate in nature writing a foundation in comedy and a potential field for humor.

Humor has long been thought of as the exclusive domain of the human. From classical times through the Renaissance and Neoclassical periods, writers identified humor's function as a social corrective, poking fun at the aberrant or ridiculous in order to reinforce social mores. With Romanticism, comedy's anarchic potential came to the fore, with humor serving to combat social restraint. Then, in 1900, Henri Bergson asserted that comedy involves only humans—that the subject of all humor is created by its relation to the appearance or condition of people. This anthropocentric tradition perhaps helps explain why critics have not looked for humor in nature writing, focused as it is on exchanges between the human and nonhuman worlds.

Yet solely anthropocentric theories of humor do not illuminate why the ineptly pursued rabbit my mother observed swerved and doubled back briefly to follow the tracks of the dog who was chasing it. Nor do these theories explain why the courting gopher snakes Edward Abbey was watching in the Utah desert came close to face him, the voyeur, before moving out again to privacy. They do not explain the wind that crops up in Louise Erdrich's *Tracks* exactly when Indian outsider Fleur needs it to topple the trees she has half-sawed in order to fell them around the loggers who have assembled to evict her.

Nor do the theories explain Coyote of Native American myth. To link humor only with the human excludes a vast territory where the comic may flourish. Although I do not intend to debate whether or not nature has its own sense of humor, I do analyze writers whose work suggests that nature is comic or that our experience of nature is comic. If one doubts the potential for reading humor into nature, imagine the possum completing another of its resurrections and waddling off on its bright pink hairless paws.

So why, then, have nature writers seemed largely to avoid this comic territory? The answer may lie partly in the moral burden that landscape has been weighted with. That humans have always ascribed significance and moral value to nature has been described by Neil Evernden in *The Social Creation of Nature*. Perhaps nature writers have been too busy trying to establish for themselves an explicable, known world—a moral world— to subject it to humor. In *The Mountains of California*, for example, John Muir labors to attribute to the water ouzel's behavior the characteristics of vigor and individualism that he undoubtedly values himself. Thus ennobling the bird, he limits his ability to see it, dooming the ouzel's antics in water to be significant in a particularly narrow way, curtailing its playful potential. Because seeing playfulness in the bird might subvert the meaning Muir has invested in it (the meaning he has invested himself in), he cannot afford to grant himself or the bird such humor.

The problem with moralizing nature (that is, attributing significance to it based on human values) is that people lose track of limits, irrevocably confusing where their projections end and nature begins and typically, then, reading only their own desires. However, a moral commitment to nature need not be devoid of humor. I believe that there can be a moral point of view that is also comic. The comic moralist, a rare breed, would not necessarily be funny but highly self-aware, conscious of the limits that her moral world projects. This comic moralist is a trickster of perspective, peek-a-booing around all angles that the limits suggest.

The writers studied in this book—Edward Abbey, Louise Erdrich, Wendell Berry, and Rachel Carson—are all in some way comic moralists, all interested in the limits they perceive to be created by their places. Their commitment to place thus provides the moral foundations of their worldviews. Berry's Kentucky farmland, Carson's Atlantic sea-coast, Erdrich's North Dakota reservation, and Abbey's American West each make these writers' perspectives moral and comic.

Central to both humor and nature writing is a concept of limits. Applied to humor, limits are the necessary control from which to generate surprise, incongruity, or absurdity; such limits are established by routine, personal expectation, social convention, and place. With regard to nature writing, the limits are those of the finite natural world, one now under pressure from a growing human population. There are boundaries, too, between species: the real and perceived limits that often prevent inter-species communication.

To juxtapose humor with nature writing suggests that the question of limits expressed in American humor might clarify the limits concerning our ideas and use of nature. At least one writer has approached this topic. Joseph Meeker reads in comedy, as a classical literary form, ecological principles. His 1974 *The Comedy of Survival* heralds the ecological plot as a comic one. He claims that comedy ensures balance and survival by accommodating necessity and avoiding moral design: comedy realistically portrays human problems, whereas tragedy egotistically inflates those problems and thus tends to overextend ecological limits. As Leo Marx has demonstrated, ecological limits are open to constant negotiation. In *The Machine in the Garden* (1964), he asserts that the pastoral design—wherein city and country counter each other—has had no limits in American history; that, furthermore, proponents of industrial and technological progress have continually reinterpreted the pastoral ideal to include (and even necessitate) the "machine."

The idea of limits has been critical in the development of American humor in particular. From tall-tale exaggeration to black or sick humor, from the woodsman hero of the "wonderful hunt" to the modern urban anti-hero, limits have consistently been used as foil, standard, and scapegoat. Although the social corrective function of humor is still employed, modern theories stress incongruity. In fact, the trend seems to be moving toward an increasing alienation between the self and any standards. Have we created black humor for the same reasons we have been unable to control the machine now driving in our garden? Are there still limits? How have we chosen to limit ourselves?

My concern with limits is shaped by Joyce Carol Oates' arguments in "Against Nature." She asserts that nature writers' literary responses to nature are limited to conventional awe, reverence, piety, and wonder; that such religious attention to nature is unwarranted and often pretentious; and that nature itself has no instructions for us. In short, Oates' contentions dismantle the moral significance of nature and deny it the potential of humor. Although I agree with her impulse to undercut romanticized nature, her critique seems unnecessarily to hoard all consciousness and humor into the human camp, excluding Mind from the world. The possum has more surprises for us than Oates would entertain.

So, apparently, do nature writers. When Rachel Carson writes about terrapins, a blue heron, and a rat on a sandy South Atlantic island in *Under the Sea-Wind*, her style has matter-of-fact grace, unadorned by awe, reverence, or piety. The young terrapins begin to wake after a winter hibernation. The heron hunts along the rising tide line. The rat searches out terrapin eggs and then snatches a young terrapin who is struggling in the high tide. Starting to eat this creature's soft shell, the rat loses track of the water rising around his tuft of ground. Carson concludes: "It was thus that the blue heron, wading back around the shore of the island, came upon the rat and speared him.(14)" The suspense and surprise conveyed here may be a narrative accomplishment—the effect of the writer's organization. But with it Carson flirts with nonhuman consciousness: she echoes the surprise that sparked the terrapin, rat, and heron. Despite Oates' dissension, the humor of humans springs from our awareness that the world does provide, in manifold and perhaps unfathomable ways, "instructions" for us and everything around us. In this book, I explore the extent to which Carson and others foster humor by reading the signs of cultural and natural limits.

The fact that Abbey, Erdrich, Berry, and Carson respond imaginatively to the limits they perceive in nature and culture demonstrates their potential as comic moralists. Each writer has a vision of how people might behave in order to live well in the places they have chosen, and each has chosen to convey his or her vision in a creative and literary rather than doctrinal fashion. Why? Why is each writer not merely a moralist? What purposes does humor serve?

First, humor compels us to expand or shift our perspective. Since these writers are trying to encourage us to see our place in the natural world with new understanding, humor is a perfect persuasive technique. Second, humor is often predicated upon loss; it provides a creative means for dealing with anxiety or fear. These writers need humor because they are, in a sense, embattled—coping with the loss or potential loss of wild places and place-based cultures. Third, humor is a means of both resistance and celebration. Via humor, these writers can oppose the attitudes, ideas, and forces they find destructive without themselves becoming bitter, without sacrificing the values that give them joy. Humor appeals to the wildest paradoxes of our existence—how we can simultaneously participate in our world and yet have a perspective of it that seems to place us outside of ourselves and nature.

The writers I am concerned with have each made choices that reflect the limits they perceive are necessary to their worlds. I am looking not only for what is funny in their work but for what demonstrates the moral groundwork for humor—how these writers have assayed the "instructions" that Oates claims are not provided for by any place. Attending to their attitudes toward human and nonhuman nature, I hope to extend the definition of humor in America and clarify the moral quality in nature writing.

Here Coyote of Native American myth emerges on the scene. He represents the nonhuman world, but he has cut, in his wayward adventuring, across human psychology and become a locus for humor. In this study, Coyote is an analogue for humor, as unpredictable and spontaneous as he is myth-laden and cultural; so humor, also culturally specific, arises universally, thus proving itself to be innate, a biological phenomenon. Humor, like Coyote, is wild. How we practice humor, I suggest, may direct the moral and biological development of our species.

ONE

Laying the Foundation for Humor in Nature Writing

A Wild Pair: Coyote and Humor

COYOTE TROTS IN THROUGH LEGEND, EMPTY-HANDED, TO A POTLUCK hosted by animals where he vies for the choicest food. Another time, he admires the pretty, fluttering cottonwood leaves, covets their experience of tumbling lightly to the ground, and negotiates with them to try it for himself—so he lands busted on rocks and dirt, his impact a solid reminder that the leaves and he enjoy different body types, which fall differently. Coyote dismisses again and again the limits of his body. He repeatedly gets smashed because he steps out of his expertise as *Canis latrans*, hunter of mice and grasshoppers and elk and urban garbage, and tries to play the games of the Beaver or Rabbit or Lizard—and he gets away with the risk, often by depending on the generosity of his fellow creatures to rebuild himself with spare scraps of the world, a piece of pine pitch for the eyes, a section of hide to quilt onto his own. For the thrill of theft or goodwill to humans, he torches his tail and dashes the fire down to people's camp—stolen goods—a hot item.

Coyote is prevalent in the stories of Native Americans, just as other tricksters appear in folklore around the world. Old Man Coyote has an ancient place in indigenous myths because he is a creature of the North American continent—endemic, related to the wolf by occasional breeding but an older native to this place than *Canis lupus*, who probably came across the Bering Strait when the land mass connected Alaska and Eurasia. Coyotes are opportunistic and flexible: able to scavenge as well as hunt, to hunt in packs as well as alone, and to respond perversely to losses from poisoning and trapping by increasing in numbers because their fertility survival mechanism is tripped by threats to their population. Although in the nineteenth century their range was primarily in the American West, coyotes have now spread into every state of the contiguous United States. They appear to have taken to the human population as if it were a challenge, with its Animal Damage Control Unit, its highways, livestock, rifles, suburban development, and farming serving as cultivators of the creature's capabilities. Though life on the continent changes, coyotes have not given up their place here as native; instead they have adapted with what we might call tenacity and quick wit, adapting perhaps even more successfully than humans have in coming to terms with our own technological feats.

It is no wonder that Coyote in legend takes risks and plays havoc with his own body; in reality, coyotes have what is called "biological reach," the *chutzpah* to move into niches that become available—filling, for example, the territory occupied by wolves since the early part of this century when the *Canis lupus* were largely extirpated in the lower forty-eight states. Whereas coyotes can move into the niche of wolves, in packs hunting large ungulates like elk, wolves cannot trade ranges with the coyote and thrive, as coyotes can, on rodents, lizards, fruits, and cactus (Wilkinson 58, 67–68).[1] As Frank Dobie writes, "the coyote's favorite food is anything he can chew; it does not have to be digestible" (107). So the coyote's generalist diet has been elevated in myth to his morphological flexibility.

If, as Gary Snyder proposes, creatures are called into being by the available food (*Practice of the Wild* 109), then the different foods that satisfy Coyote have resulted in the many personas of his character. In mythologizing him, people pay tribute to his biological wizardry, and they give him a place within human culture to communicate, for Coyote seems to have much to teach us. To tell Coyote stories opens the threshold of our house for Coyote's voice, making us alert to the coyotes we hear outside, to some texture in their tone that includes experience with us and embeds it in a howl bred primordially in this country, a range as lofty as our imagination and as quick as our cells, which instantly translate the thrill.

1. It is fitting that coyotes rather than wolves earned a trickster reputation, since wolves never learned (as a species) to cope with poisons and similar threats.

Coyote's ubiquitous presence in myth attests to the uncanny resemblance that people have found between the human psyche and Coyote's character. The creature's behavior seems to attract such identification—after all, people are fecund too, and curious. We are also opportunistic, creative, and flexible when pushed to survive. When biologist Bob Crabtree in Yellowstone found his traps pointedly unsprung yet overturned and defecated on by the coyotes that he wanted to radio collar, he was "bemused," as Todd Wilkinson records in his book about Crabtree's five-year study of coyotes in Yellowstone. With more freedom than the wildlife biologist to interpret the event, Wilkinson sees that Crabtree has encountered in the pack also the Coyote of myth, a trickster (31). The coyotes' gesture is an insult, returning in kind the rudeness of Crabtree's territorial invasion. In this case, myth, whose lexicon can include such subjective words as "insult," succeeds perhaps better than science in contextualizing the coyote and explaining its behavior. Old Man Coyote does become irked and does not hesitate to get even—to mess with the traps would be nothing new for him. Indeed, myth should have a comforting accuracy because it synthesizes and transforms stories that no doubt originated with experiences similar to Crabtree's. With a character complex enough to be insulted, coyotes are akin to human character, thus establishing a basis for folkloric identification.[2]

But as much as we read our mind into Coyote, the animal departs from it where we cannot follow. Coyote defies our mythologizing by showing up in our ordinary lives, where he passes through on prosaic business and thus deflates the possibility that we would have merely a mythic relationship with him. Oregon rancher Dayton Hyde had no precedent for understanding the coyote he eventually dubbed Don Coyote, who chose to den under the hulking farm tractor wherever it broke down or was stopped for the day's work. Hyde had something new on his hands, and it forced him into a unique relationship with the coyote. Hyde's encounters suggest a whole range of experiences and contacts that people have had with contemporary coyotes, ushering Old Man Coyote into the twenty-first century. The modern coyote has new skills and perhaps new tastes. We cannot control the coyote with stories any more than we can control him with traps, guns, or poisons. Coyote is wild.

He comes to us through the experience of Native American peoples,

2. William Bright's "The Natural History of Old Man Coyote" examines the connection between the biological coyote and the Coyote of myth; his essay acutely identifies ways in which human character can be revealed through Old Man Coyote.

whose knowledge of living on this continent has been at least ten thousand years in the making. Their myths manifest their cultural success in being partners with wild places, not diminishing them—proving so skilled, in fact, at cohabiting with nature that when Europeans first arrived in what was the ancient home of native peoples, they declared it to be "virgin" territory, unmarred. Old Man Coyote is a product of indigenous peoples' skill in being at home in the wilderness. Their myths show that all creatures were members of the most ancient household—the wilderness—and that this home had to have rules for getting along—an etiquette, as Snyder might say, as a way of keeping the house in order. There were Beaver People and Badger, Bison, Elk, Grizzly, Turtle, Squirrel, Cougar, Skunk, and Human. How were they all to live together? Because the tricksters were the ones most likely to unsettle the order, we can turn to Old Man Coyote to explore the etiquette appropriate to the wilderness and, in doing so, perhaps develop something of native peoples' skill in being at home.

Coyote as an Analogue for Humor
Divided between identification with the creature and bafflement over it, Native Americans have made Coyote into a trickster-figure hero who, in the classical tradition of comedy, up-turns the world and runs off until it falls again to rights and he can return. Or who, by virtue of bad choices, is himself up-ended or killed until the world sets him to rights.[3] In Navajo myth, for example, Coyote often wants to participate in the fun he finds his animal cousins having. Although the Lizards, sledding in desert sand, warn that if he slides down the hill on a big rock he will get crushed by it, and although the Beavers caution that he will not be able to regrow his hide if he loses it in the hoop and pole game, Coyote proceeds to careen downhill on the biggest rock—and be smashed under it—and to play with the hoop and pole until he loses and gets skinned. The Lizards resurrect him, and the Beavers suggest that Badger might give him a new skin.

Self-destructively curious and consummately lucky, Coyote cuts in and out of human psychology, as if he and people share the same psychic turf. To the extent that people have imaginatively followed the Coyote—and defied consanguinity in identifying with him—they have thought of this trickster as a taboo-breaker. So the stories show him to be a peddler of his

3. Coyote stories vary according to tribes in different areas. As William Bright points out, in California and the Great Basin, Coyote is most often the "prototypical mythic trickster" (347), whereas in the Southwest he is generally the loser or bungler (367).

own wit—getting in trouble, having fun, and even doing good. As a transport for humans into the nonhuman world, Coyote cavorts with Possum, Squirrel, Badger, and Bear, transgressing species lines with oblivious prelapsarian intimacy.

We track and perpetuate Coyote because it is a pleasure—both funny and dangerous—to break taboos with impunity and belong to the nonhuman world he represents, to join in its jokes. That Coyote has become a locus for humor in the process of his wayward adventuring reveals much about the nature and pleasure of humor. A wild creature both in and out of myth, he can do for us what we might not be willing to imagine ourselves doing. The ubiquity of Coyote (and the trickster figure in general) throughout folklore indicates that we want to imagine or to participate vicariously in waywardness, and so it is our pleasure and Coyote's usefulness that have driven him broadly across myth. To read Coyote inevitably unearths this pleasure and our own psychology.

This book is not about the Coyote of Native American lore but about Coyote at large—how he has traveled into contemporary literature and thrived there, how he is emerging anew in the modern world.[4] In this study, Coyote is an analogue for humor, as unpredictable and spontaneous as he is myth-laden and cultural; so humor, also culturally specific, arises universally, thus proving itself to be innate, a biological phenomenon. Humor, like Coyote, is wild. Humor is wild particularly in eluding definition, being capricious enough to render inadequate all of the theories that attempt to explain it. The character of humor—biological, ineffable, and befuddling as it is—is better described through analogy than by definition: therefore, I use wild Coyote as a template for humor, allowing humor the incredible range that Coyote enjoys.

---

4. The spread of his character has been under way since the 1950s, impelled at first by writers interested in Native American tradition. Patricia Clark Smith cautions that the appropriation of Coyote by non-natives may be too facile, ungrounded by "any real knowledge of or sympathy for either coyotes or Coyote" (194). Even for true aficionados or scholars of the creature, what we do not know about Coyote always seems to be larger than what we do know. Indeed, Barre Toelken's extensive three decades of research on Navajo Coyote stories yielded to him knowledge that he was not willing to pursue for fear of compromising Navajo culture and his place in it. Namely, Toelken learned that the stories have more than entertainment and moral values: they may also be used for healing or for witchcraft (388–401). These topics go more deeply into the power of Coyote stories than I do. Those of us who pursue Coyote in our writing or research or lives inevitably trail behind, forever shy of the full story.

Humor and Wildness

But what is wild? Roderick Nash has traced the word to its origins in the Teutonic and Norse meaning of "will," particularly in the sense of "self-willed," spontaneous and uncontrolled. Through Old English it is associated with animals not under control, that is, undomesticated ones, with *wilderness* meaning the place of the wild animals (*Wilderness and the American Mind* 1). Gary Snyder also points out possible connections to the Latin *silva* and *ferus*, and he notes that the *Oxford English Dictionary* and dictionaries in general tend to define *wild* negatively—according to them, *wild* is undomesticated, unruly, uncultivated, uncivilized, unrestrained, destructive, rude, insubordinate. To get a different look at the word, Snyder generates a positive list, words that he says closely resemble the Chinese description of the *Dao* (or the Way of Nature), including the following: self-propagating, self-maintaining, original, pristine, self-reliant, independent, far-out, outrageous, free, spontaneous, ecstatic (*The Practice of the Wild* 8–10).

We know *wild* from both the admiring and the disapproving perspective. So Coyote, that defiantly undomesticated canid, is wonderfully wild when he howls but destructively wild when he kills the chickens or sheep. Coyote's "willfulness" is his unpredictability, his membership in the evolutionary ad-libbing of the world, whereby place and creature converge and mutually change. Humor likewise may be considered wild because it is often marked by surprise or sudden enlightenment, and in its spontaneous upwelling in the body, it is uncontrolled. To have a sense of humor carries few of the negative connotations that *wild* does, for we esteem humor in a person's character and offer serious criticism if we say that one "has no sense of humor." Humor can compel indiscreet behavior, however, such as laughing out of place at a formal gathering. So humor in its inappropriate gusts resembles the naughtiness of Coyote, say, when he raids livestock.

Others have approached the word *wild* more cautiously, as if to give it a buffer, left unfettered even by language. Indeed, John P. O'Grady has written that the wild exists as erotic territory, at basis ineffable, eluding our attempts to describe it (xi). To stalk the *wild* at this respectful distance acknowledges that our meaning-making activities—our stories, myths, definitions, languages—never prove conclusive, being only the discipline we use in maintaining our membership in the household but never a replacement for the house itself. Coyote paradoxically retains his wild, ineffable aura by virtue of being talked about so much. The plethora of myth, the contradictions, the celebration and condemnation of the creature, all serve to make the Old Man more than anyone can say about him. In brilliant trickster fashion, he wears the mantle of our language and disappears under it.

Similarly elusive, humor is often transmitted through language but is fundamentally nonlinguistic when we experience it. Although stories and jokes may jolt us into laughter, we carry humor beyond language, rocking in our bodies. Even the scholarly critics of humor recognize this, usually apologizing at the outset of their books, submitting to their fate as despoilers of the comic spirit. Sensitive to their failure to replicate in intellectual terms anything as pleasurable as a fine laugh, scholars implicitly aver that humor is a mystery, wildness encoded in us all.

Health and Humor

The word *healthy* has often been used to describe wildness. The wild is healthy because it is complete—hale, whole, wholesome, hallow, as the etymology attests. When Aldo Leopold spoke of land health, he called wilderness its "perfect norm" (274), where the membership of organisms is complete, an ecological full house. Such a full house is never static or finished, as the word *complete* might imply, but instead perpetually completed as the member organisms interact. This balance of energies is healthy, and, buoyed by this balance, the wild is self-perpetuating and self-regulating. It is "irreducible essence," as Stephanie Mills says (49), or, more simply, what we call life. No name for life is good enough to account for its spontaneous initiative, but *wildness* conveys the mystery of it, and Alan Watts, Dolores LaChapelle, Gary Snyder, and others tell us, by way of personalizing the mystery, "Our bodies are wild" (Snyder, *Practice of the Wild* 16).

Indian activist Janet McCloud agrees: "Your heart is always beating and your breath is always moving in and out, isn't it? The laws of nature are with you wherever you are. It's marvelous when you see this—when you see that we live in a symbiotic relationship to everything around us. Your body *is* nature. You have a river, a sun, and a moon inside, too. Everything that's out there is also in here" (White 253).

Certainly Coyote's body is healthy despite all the bashing he absorbs in myth and out on the range. Humor is also healthy. Speakers use humor to initiate themselves to their audience—deflate tension, win favor in anticipation of their argument, appeal to a common sensibility that they share with the crowd. Davy Crockett's backwoods humor helped him in Congress, and Ronald Reagan's helped him in the White House.[5] Although the use of humor is not recent, the humor-use movement is.[6] Scores of books attest to humor's power to resolve conflicts, succeed in business, make friends, and cope with stress, offering to educate us to tell jokes well and thus communicate effectively. Such books capitalize on the way humor makes us feel, but they rarely analyze *how* it affects our feelings.

Humor physiologically makes us feel good—it is healthy exercise. Studies of the stimulation that accompanies laughter have led William Fry to contend that "perceiving and enjoying humor involves total body participation." "We laugh," he says, "with our whole physical being" ("The Biology of Humor" 114). The following passage outlines the effects of mirth on the muscular, the respiratory, the immune and endocrine, the cardiovascular, and the central and autonomic nervous systems:

Heart rate goes up; blood pressure rises; blood circulation increases; pulmonary ventilation increases; skeletal muscles are exercised; the brain experiences electrochemical activity which is typically found with greater degrees of alertness; pain perception is decreased; skin temperature rises; hormone production is stimulated; circulating immune substance effectiveness is enhanced (chemical and cellular components) ("The Biology of Humor" 114).

No mere intellectual play, humor happens in our bodies. Fry points out that the aerobic-exercise effect that accompanies laughter is overwhelmingly safe for those who are prone to strokes or cardiac arrest from equivalent aerobic stimulation of a different kind, as from shoveling snow. In contrast to the documented high risk of heart attacks induced by shoveling snow, the mirth-provoked heart attack does not exist—there is no medical literature on such a phenomenon (115–16). In addition to the healthy stimulation humor inspires, the period following laughter also exhibits marks

5. Reagan's humor sometimes had a triumphant clarity that his intellect lacked, winning occasional partial favor even from those who opposed his policies. For example, at a ceremony for a highway project in New York, Reagan apologized that his Interior Secretary, James Watt, could not be present—Reagan explained that Watt was "on assignment strip-mining the Rose Garden" (quoted in Jones and Wheeler 15). Since Watt was known by environmentalists as a political butcherer of wild lands, the absurd prospect of his strip-mining the White House grounds was perfectly apt. So Reagan partly deflated people's anger over Watt by acknowledging Watt's reputation.
6. Norman Cousins' 1979 *Anatomy of an Illness* is a classic of humor popularization.

of health. During it, the body relaxes: blood pressure, heart rate, breathing rate, and muscle activity drop, while for several subsequent hours the immune system can remain charged. Furthermore, the social conviviality that laughter incites (115) leads us back to the word *health* as an expression of wholeness; people who laugh together animate their household, enlivening and uniting it.

Humor and Evolution

The inclusive and stimulating action of laughter—that boon to a body's health—can be seen in the macrocosm as evolution, where each member in an ecological full-house is changing and adapting to other members. Evolution has the form of literary comedy, the unbalancing and restoration of equilibrium[7]; wildness, then, is the comic art of evolution, a healthy drama.[8] So David Brower, discussing the information compiled by genes, identifies wildness as the source of life: "It's wildness, the trial and error, the symbiosis, the successes, the failures, throughout all these years that has shaped everything there is" (White 40). Thus Snyder revises Henry David Thoreau: "Wildness is not just the 'preservation of the world,' it *is* the world" (*Practice* 6).[9]

It is easy to see that coyotes have evolutionary skills: nothing else can explain their success in twentieth-century North America. A host of myths, too, associate the creature with evolution—how Bobcat ended up with a short nose and tail because Coyote played a trick on him, how Coyote came to have a mottled coat or a long nose.

That humor has evolutionary value is a more complex proposition, dependent first on the idea that humor is biological and inherited. Fry gives credence to this supposition by calling attention to a genetic heritage for laughter that includes the higher primates—the chimpanzees, gorillas, and orangutans—thus giving humor "a respectable lineage of about 6.5 million years" ("The Biology of Humor" 112–13). Fry contends that humor's contribution to health aids human survival and evolution (121). The pleasure associated with humor is itself a powerful incentive to profess the value of

---

7. Northrop Frye emphasizes that comedy involves the changes made in a society to accommodate the central character, resulting in a new social order (*Anatomy of Criticism* 43–44). Comedy as a plot (the loss and recovery of equilibrium) and attitude (the acceptance of change and mystery) is important to this book.

8. In the *The Comedy of Survival*, Joseph Meeker writes, "Evolution itself is a gigantic comic drama" (33).

9. To study humor in nineteenth-century nature writers, one would have to focus on Thoreau, for his work is replete with surprise, humor, and wit.

humor to evolution, for what better way to ensure the persistence of an innately useful phenomenon than to wed it to pleasure? In addition to the health ramifications of humor, it has value as play (the continuation of creativity from childhood) and the practice of flexibility.[10]

Fundamental to the perception of humor is our ability to shift perspective and see our world differently, as if to arrive in a new reality. Our bemusement and surprise often arise from the overlapping of perceived worlds—the sudden check of location, attitude, and identity that the contrast provides. Humor jogs us to step partly away from ourselves in order to see our situation clearly; it enables us to escape habits of perception that condition our responses and reduce our flexibility. In using humor, we practice the creative perception essential to quick adaptation, employing a humor test of the world that augments our chances of flourishing. Perhaps because of this style of shifting perspective, humor has often been thought of as a survival skill. To laugh at hardship demonstrates our resilience, since with little resource but attitude, we can endure and even flourish. Loyal Jones, scholar of Appalachian humor, remarks, "if we are to survive, we must laugh whenever we can" (Jones and Wheeler 27). Alice Walker's Sofia says, after returning from eleven and a half years in jail and servitude, "I already had my bad luck . . . enough to keep me laughing the rest of my life" (*The Color Purple* 208). The perspective mechanism that gives us enough distance from ourselves to be interested in rather than despairing over our condition recommends humor as a survival skill. The distance buffers us psychologically so that we do not mistake a dire situation for the state of our character.

Humor, Culture, and Perspective
The wild, finally, besides being willful, self-perpetuating, self-regulating, inscrutable, healthful, and evolutionary, is also, paradoxically, cultural. Robert Pogue Harrison has written that the wilderness, the forests in particular, is inseparable from the history of civilization—forests the essential foil, contrast, and "shadow" of civilization. His story of this juxtaposition coincides with Neil Evernden's argument in *The Social Creation of Nature* that the Pre-Socratics nominally created nature when they held up to it what it was not (20–21). Their books trace the shift that occurred when the wild or nature changed from being our home—the one big household maintained by sweeps of evolutionary housekeeping—to places we con-

10. As play, humor's lineage would go back fifty million years or more, at least to early mammals.

sidered apart from us, defined by difference. Hence the dictionary's negatively styled definition of *wild*. The wild is cultural not because it needs
human culture to exist but because we have come to know it through this
tradition. Although civilization's history of usurping wild lands may in-
cline us to consider the cultural aspect of the wild to be its antithesis, many
read in it the possibility, even the necessity, of reconciliation. As Wendell
Berry in *The Unsettling of America* writes, "our culture must be our response
to our place, our culture and our place are images of each other and inseparable from each other and so neither can be better than the other" (22).
From this conjunction we have Coyote, who is wild partly because he has
passed through human culture, acquiring the names and stories people
gave him and leaving them trailing in his wake as he goes out the door.
With thousands of years' experience with humankind, coyotes have had
their wildness conditioned by civilization—their wildness is street-wise.

Humor too is a half-breed of the wild and cultural. It rises unbidden
from our bodies, and it acquires the vocabulary, tone, and style of our social experiences and place. Europe has as a trickster Reynard the Fox rather
than Coyote because coyotes do not live in Europe. Jokes too are often culturally specific, dependent on knowledge that an outsider might not be
privy to; the pertinent cultural information can initiate the outsider to the
group or be withheld to exclude the outsider. As ethologist Konrad Lorenz
says, laughter "forms a bond and simultaneously draws a line" (293).
Humor is attended by social utility, conviviality, and meaning. The definition of humor via analogy to Coyote includes both the mechanics of humor
and its community significance.

Since the perception of humor requires the flexibility in us to see a situation differently than we previously saw it, humor exercises our perspective, keeping it limber. Such perspective-taking can put us into the
proverbial shoes of another person or into the tracks of a creature like
Coyote; for in the humorous moment, we internalize the view of the outsider while not losing sight of our own customary view. This pairing can
not only unsettle our previously held perspective but also clarify it, helping us form a fuller picture of it by stepping back into the outsider's place
to see it. Humor allows us to become an outsider to ourselves. As the
perennial outsider, Coyote can be useful in illuminating the thrill of this
dramatic nexus of persona-playing. Coyote is awful and sacred and
thrilling all at once because he performs multiple roles—cohort, guide,
gambler, and renegade amalgamated into beloved trickster. We take pleasure in Coyote because he does not abide by the conventions that seem

necessary to a certain populace and place—and he gets away with it, if not always succeeding in his schemes then at least never dying for good. Coyote is the outsider who considers himself free of the norms that condition the denizens' behavior. What Coyote reveals is that ambiguity underlies the norms. He opens the possibility that the rules are inadequate and we need not abide by them. Kenneth Lincoln says, "He gambles with values in the breach; he stirs up original considerations, fringed with moral and epistemological concerns" (123). Through Coyote, we become outsiders too, moving with freedom unaccountable to the mores that bind us. Coyote's indiscretions in myth teach us correct behavior and attitude, but Coyote is not merely a negative example, not entirely the fall guy, not completely wrong even when he does something bad. Though he is an "ancient bungler," he is a "culture hero" too (Lincoln 50)—doing some good for humans and giving us his lead to follow back to myth-time where the action that helped concoct our beliefs and behavior is still under way, and we can participate in the drama. Our visitation to the sources is liberating, so it is with pleasure we accompany Coyote into myth. Humor provides us with a journey of much the same structure and importance. Using its modus operandi—perspective—we adopt an outsider's eye and ability to see free of our ordinary concerns. Humor liberates us.

Surprise is bedfellow to humor because it imbues the provoking shift in perspective with the quality of action or encounter or the discovery, say, of a stranger in your intimate space. All theories of humor involve a notion of altered perspective—the stranger cropping up everywhere. The elements that D. H. Monro identifies as fundamental to humor—the suddenly unexpected, newly freed, and loftily perceived (59)—all depend on the action of perspective. So the major theories fall in line under this rubric: The superiority theory articulated by Thomas Hobbes to explain eminency of a particular point of view, the incongruity theory that Schopenhauer used to account for the contrast between the expected and the perceived, the release theory Freud said demonstrates the purging of the subconscious, and the instinct theory (recent enough not to have formally acquired this title) advanced by scholars such as William Fry and Arthur Koestler (Konrad Lorenz in the wings) to acknowledge the biological nature of humor and the flexibility—boon to survival—that it affords.

The perspective-taking structure of humor can contribute to our understanding of humor's function. The fact that people laugh together more often than alone demonstrates that humor has community significance. The historical burden of evidence in folklore shows that humor is essentially a community experience because of its tendency to bond (and to exclude) and because of its mechanics in amalgamating points of view. Humor has always been at the nexus of community opinion as an arbiter of social morality: it has been touted as a reinforcer of social standards (classical writers were first to call it a social corrective) and an underminer of mores, a revolutionary value identified during the Romantic period. With humor we can have access through the liminal territory that abounds with taboos to the world beyond where all social value is negotiable. In most cases, this transport is a circular journey, returning us to our familiar world reacquainted with the purpose of its norms. But as a social corrective, humor is a volatile tool, able to be misread or to serve an unintended purpose. In *Coyote Stories*, an illustrated volume prepared in 1968 by Robert Roessel, Jr., and Dillon Platero for the Rough Rock Demonstration School in Rough Rock, Arizona, the introduction is careful to connect Coyote tales explicitly with social values.

> These tales are part of the enormous mythological treasures of the Navaho people. They are not meaningless folklore or merely colorful cartoons, as the uninformed observer might think. They have great significance to the Navahos because they express, enhance, and enforce the morals and norms of Navaho society. They are considered actual occurrences and not the result of artistic imaginations.

The fact that the value of the tales might escape an "uninformed observer" reveals the crucial service of the community in defining humor. In this case, to be blind to the morality in Coyote stories is largely to fail their humor, and to see only the morality is likewise a failure, for the morality in these tales is inextricable from humor. Since the function of humor is the concern and result of the community, a definition is best achieved for humor by knowing its source and use in a community, its household significance. A contextualized reading thus precludes the hopelessly inclusive acknowledgment that individuals can all find different things funny in different ways. It establishes a common ground where definition is possible.

Humor is a perspective-taking tool engendered by evolution and sophisticated in human culture. Humor helps keep people wild—alert, flexible, responsive—and so it combats the routine-induced habits of perception that are deadly to creativity and survival. Humor is useful in a community's self-awareness, bonding, and sustainability. The physiological joy that it sparks in the body gives it intoxicating appeal: if we share laughter with people, we agree with them at some fundamental level of common experience. Humor conveys morality by treading on the taboo line so that a message emerges not from pat moralism but from our lively response to an ethical landscape where the view is open in every direction. Through humor, we can issue opinion in which there is not merely favor given or denied but a shifting grounds for judgment. Shared humor can establish community and value while embedding in them the potential for change.

Two Stories of American Humor: A History

Native American Humor
It is possible to read our character and our relationship with nature in this country in the history of our humor. The primary story (for this history is bifurcated) involves the humor of Native Americans, a humor largely unrecognized by scholars—not even, ironically, the subject of Walter Blair's influential *Native American Humor*. Indigenous humor carried in stories is located in the mythic household—the wilderness—where people share space with creatures. The imagination that creates this humor is animistic and intimate; it assumes that the household is permeable, articulate, and full of meaning. Keith Basso's 1977 interview with Mrs. Annie Peaches, a seventy–seven-year-old Apache, elicited this characterization of the household. Peaches said, "The land is always stalking people. The land makes people live right. The land looks after us. The land looks after people" (*Western Apache Language and Culture* 100). Peaches puts people in ecological context by creatively assuming the land's perspective and giving the land agency. As Basso points out, the landscape acts as a mnemonic peg (stories becoming associated with particular places) and so people who live in that landscape are continually reminded of the stories and their teachings. Peaches' statement more directly identifies the land as the ethical source. That the land conveys morality, that its stories stalk people, is not just an idea for Peaches as it is for Basso. She believes that her world functions this way.

Richard Erdoes and Alfonso Ortiz, editors of *American Indian Myths and Legends*, corroborate this quality of faith in the Native American imagination, explaining that the myths in their collection do not just teach and entertain, they are *believed* by people (xv). Thus a grace that escapes postmodern skepticism of language permeates the animistic interpenetration of stories and reality in Native American experience. These people, Kenneth Lincoln writes,

> believed in the bonding and animating powers of words—to invoke and actualize the world through a language of experience. Words were not notational labels or signs, visually affixed to a blank page for material transaction: words were beings in themselves, incantatory, with spirits and bodies. Stories, songs, visions, and names lived empirically in the world, and people could seek them for power, identity, beauty, peace, and survival (18).

Native Americans as characterized by Lincoln would not merely tell a story of Coyote: they *join* Coyote, participating in the drama of other creatures' lives, touring dens, burrows, and outcroppings to stay abreast of community news. Household intimacy and identification animate Native American myth; its humor is bawdy, outrageous, moral, and witty.[11] We can generalize, then, about the character of the people who created this humor and myth. They are not anxious about their place on earth—they belong to it, they have standing among the animals, and they believe the world has meaning that includes them.

With confidence in these matters, the person enjoying this character can acquire the comic spirit that Conrad Hyers says informs Zen Buddhism. One with such a spirit is able to celebrate errant whim, irrationality, and chaos in the world because he or she does not presume to control its machinations, whereas the person who strives to order the world will experience absurdity as tragic (94–95). Unthreatened by ambiguity or nature's seeming chaos,[12] the Native American character can focus on the work of cohabitation, implicitly concerning a land ethic, which can be called a household etiquette. Since the land is literally home—nature the teacher, partner, and elder of people—Native Americans have powerful cultural and personal incentives to live well there. It is not surprising that when Europeans arrived in North America, they found the land fresh, bountiful, and wild—in the tip-top condition of a creature well-loved. To conclude by

11. Just as Erdoes, Ortiz, and Lincoln generalize about Native American imagination, I examine the common characteristics of Native American humor rather than the differences in the humor of different tribes.

12. In *Nature and Madness*, Paul Shepard says that to accept and cope with ambiguity and plurality is the mark of maturity (29).

way of Coyote, we find that despite his shameful Old-Man antics, he also is well-loved; and when we joke about him and dig in with him, we participate in the style of consciousness that gives agency and respect to the land. The humor routes us into a nondualistic animist spirituality.

New World Humor

The other route, the secondary history of humor in this country, accompanies the Europeans who settled here and reveals a different character than the Native American, one less inclined to adopt a land ethic. The debt that American humor owes to frontier experience is often noted, but Constance Rourke's *American Humor: A Study of the National Character* is especially important for the way it links three variables—humor, character, and the land. She asserts that humor is integral to American character because of the North American wilderness. Equating comic spirit with resilience, she deems it essential to survival in the wilderness; furthermore, she claims that humor unified scattered, diverse people, creating bonds that helped establish American identity. According to Rourke, then, humor here was a new thing, unique—call it American—because of the unprecedented wild lands that settlers encountered. Her work establishes fertile ground for further analysis.

Frontier humor was rowdy with exaggeration and well-known in its tall-tale form. That form features a backwoods, vernacular character and his heroic violence against wilderness.[13] Rourke's characterization of the tall tale prepares for the incipience of humorous exaggeration: "Many of the tales and much of the talk verged toward that median between terror and laughter which is the grotesque" (49). "Terror" overstates the case but conveys the mood that might have been created by settlers who felt embattled on their own homesteads. Their homes were not necessarily in places they trusted. Against the wilderness they harbored distrust, antipathy, and fear, as Nash has demonstrated in *Wilderness and the American Mind*. Theirs was a fighting humor, channeled between "terror" of wilderness and nervous delight in their success at surviving in seemingly hostile places. Kenneth Lynn writes that the tall tale "was a way of beating the wilderness

13. Walter Blair and Hamlin Hill remark on the narrative frame that often accompanied the tall-tale hero (especially in Southwestern humor): "Usually when a hell-raiser appeared in literary humor, there was an almost predictable snob lurking somewhere to describe him" (188). Kenneth Lynn writes extensively about the decorous gentleman whose voice and morality control the frame (64). That incongruity between the vernacular and the elitist is a central motif in American humor, according to Louis Rubin (5).

at its own game, of converting terror into *joie de vivre* and helplessness into an exhilarating sense of power. With gargantuan boasts, the frontiersman outfaced an overwhelming universe" (*Mark Twain & Southwestern Humor* 27–28). Lynn recounts the fighting words reportedly exchanged by two drunken boatmen in 1808: " 'I am a man; I am a horse; I am a team. I can whip any man *in all Kentucky*, by G-d.' The other replied, 'I am an alligator, half man, half horse; can whip any man on the *Mississippi*, by G-d' " (27).

Tall tales were a particular, stylized way of screwing up courage. In fact, Kenneth Rexroth believes that humor (which at its best, he says, "has a savagery about it") "is the most effective mode of courage" ("The Decline of American Humor" 374–76). The "masculine" or "savage" quality that has been used specifically to describe the frontier humor of the Old Southwest (Inge 5), the humor touted by Blair and others as the truly "native" style[14]—that style smacks of a house divided. Settlers had little sense of the ecological household they had entered. Flailing with fighting energy into what had been the wide-open, wild home of Native Americans, white settlers built self-contained homes and distilled their fighting energy into humor. Frontier humor was useful to spread settlements but not to settle people into being native to the country.[15]

But the story of the tall tale is not complete. If the impulse to exaggerate was generated partly by the immensity of physical wilderness that settlers faced, why did the first arrivals, who were farthest from the settlements they knew and had the best reason to speak in hyperbole, why did they not talk "tall"? American colonists were not known for their humor, much less for the tall tale. Excavations of their prose today yield the highly refined wit of a gentleman's literary style, imitative of Addison and Steele. Yet there was humor, and it shares the rudimentary purpose of the tall tale to bolster people's courage. Ian Marshall looks to William Bradford's *Of Plymouth Plantation* for humor that rides out hardship and shores up the Puritan community against outsiders. In a study of early American humor, W. Howland Kenney agrees that the reputedly (and deservedly so) dour Puritans nevertheless did laugh, a "stylized" laughter, an instrument of

---

14. See Inge's *The Frontier Humorists*, Blair's *Native American Humor*, and Meine's "Tall Tales of the Southwest."

15. The tall tales were also useful as a form of caricature, amusing the audience with the frontiersman's ironic self-portrait. As such, their appeal went beyond the settlers' relief in their anxious control of nature and arose also from self-analysis, pleasing because it suggested that American identity did exist as something unique, a home-product of experience in North America.

social control that "helped them order their world and protect their identity" (9–12). When eventually colonists came to manipulate the exigencies of wilderness life in humorous contrast with European livelihood, they demonstrated, Kenney notes, "progressive mastery over themselves and their environment" (25).

The tall tale has roots not so much in Puritan laughter as in the Puritan tendency to discover in daily life signs of Divine Providence. Such a tendency, Richard Dorson says, incited sensationalism and corresponded with traditional Old World interest in the supernatural (*American Folklore* 25). If the milk cow that went dry or the butter that spoiled could be emblematic of God's judgment, the possibilities that the vast, unknown wild lands represented were mind-boggling. Ever curious to interpret the emblematic world, people poured their energies and skills into folklore, which at least seemed helpful because it had satisfying details in contrast to religion's stark dictum to have faith. Not surprisingly, New World folklore did not perpetuate the creatures of Old World legend such as fairies and werewolves, for the wilderness already afforded fine populations of potentially threatening animals. Ghost and devil stories from the Old World, however, were sustained here. Apparitions and witches were "popular" in colonial times, according to Dorson (33–37). John Burrison, speaking of ghost stories that have endured in the South, calls them "a type of subtle instructive tale, pages from a survival manual for a time when supernatural beings were a palpable part of the environment" (8). Colonists needed ways to negotiate territory replete with supernatural potential, and they evidently found it in humor. In a comparison of English and American folk narratives, the *Type and Motif-Index of the Folktales of England and North America*, Ernest Baughman found that the American tradition has much more humorous material and hyperbole than the English, so much, in fact, that he concludes that the tall tale is "an overwhelmingly American form" (Mintz 217). Humor was well-suited to bear ambiguity; it became a successful secular response to a problem of religious dimensions—how to manage ideals while beset by the real world.

By using the tension hovering between the ideal and real, humor made incongruity bearable, even valuable, for it became a source of pleasure rather than an inconsistency to fear. In defusing this potential threat, humor was powerful. For example, to survive in the New World was not easy, especially in the winter; yet there were incredible populations of wildlife, and so the wonderful hunt stories put luck and skill on the settlers' side to win them fantastic selections of game. Such stories were bragging to bolster confidence through hard times and to celebrate the good times. Essential to American humor, writes Louis Rubin, is the incongruity between the "cultural ideal" and "everyday fact" (12). The tall tale runs this gauntlet. It plays, no less, what Rubin calls the "Great American Joke" of unmasking both positions (12–14), picturing the ideal as impossible fantasy and uncovering fact as fabrication after all. Tall tales begin with fact (or at least realistic context reputed to be fact) and work through realistic detail toward fantasy but never depart into it, never, Henry Wonham emphasizes, surpass the "exaggerated limit of credulity" of its listeners (287).[16] Again, Wonham: "Put another way, a tall narrative is neither purely true nor purely fantastic but depends for its effect upon the listeners' ability to perceive its relation to both fact and fantasy" (288). Here was pleasure for the cultural insider. The tall tale built confidence by affording one who had appropriate skills and knowledge the chance to move unerringly through a world ambiguous in fact and fiction—to practice discerning truth in a confusingly emblematic world. Thus tall tale humor provided a folkloric entry into problems of metaphysical and spiritual importance—it was powerful because it made answers accessible.

Nature acquired a mythic stature in tall talk optimism: its resources were boundless, and it could absorb the inflated energies of frontier heroes whose prowess centered upon violence against wilderness. Richard Slotkin reads the genesis of the violent "frontier psychology" in this way:

> The first colonists saw in America an opportunity to regenerate their fortunes, their spirits, and the power of their church and nation; but the means to that regeneration ultimately became the means of violence, and the myth of regeneration through violence became the structuring metaphor of the American experience (5).

The "masculine" and "savage" tall tale is part of this frontier myth that glorifies violence. One danger of such glorification, Slotkin recognizes, is that it can persist beyond its origins, continuing out of context to impact people's behavior (4–5).[17] The spirit of the tall tale outlasted the wisdom of its

16. See also Carolyn Brown's *The Tall Tale in American Folklore and Literature*, pages 9 and 58.
17. Slotkin defines America's frontier myth—"the conception of America as a wide-open land of unlimited opportunity for the strong, ambitious, self-reliant individual to thrust his way to the top"—and links it with the manner in which the country blasted into the urban, industrial age without addressing its social problems, and, as a result, suffered the social and civil rights unrest in the sixties and seventies (5).

audience as they grew further away from experience on the frontier. Although exaggerations about the land's incredible fecundity and wealth should have reminded people just how fruitful the country realistically was, instead the tales lost their ironic stature, and their promise of abundance became affixed in the American psyche. Vaguely expecting natural resources to be limitless, people built an economy based on that delusion, which devastated wilderness, polluted air and water, and alienated people themselves from contact with nature. People played and continue to play rough in a way that tall tale heroes and raconteurs only talked tough.

The tall tale itself, whose heyday lasted from 1830 to 1860, lost much of its appeal as it lost complexity. Since it was tied to knowledge of the frontier and the natural world (Wonham 289) and that knowledge dissipated as the country became increasingly settled, the tall tale suffered from simplification. Reduced to mere inflation, it was relatively uninteresting. With the Civil War, the country's attention turned away from the frontier and would never return to nature with quite the same concern—or the same humor—again.

Women's humor, not much recognized until the past few decades despite two early anthologies of women's humor,[18] was traditionally quieter than men's humor, not partaking of its violent excesses. In "Nineteenth-Century Women's Humor," Nancy Walker writes that women "were far more likely to make humor out of the chaos of trying to maintain households in primitive surroundings" than to tell tall tales (87). Women's experience was centered on the home, and so the domestic emphasis of their humor, as Walker and Zita Dresner point out, was natural—as well as subversive and rebellious.[19] Skilled in their perceptions of domesticity, women have focused largely on improving their social status; as their efforts succeed and their energy to reform turns elsewhere, their humor could have an enormous impact on the direction of our attitude toward nature. The household metaphor—women's traditional specialty—will be indispensable in conceiving of our place on earth.

Review: The Two Stories of American Humor

The quintessential New World humor—the tall tale—involved nature, place, and a homely, vernacular speaker, a character at odds with his new

18. These were Kate Sanborn's *The Wit of Women* (1885) and Martha Bensley Bruere and Mary Ritter Beard's *Laughing Their Way: Women's Humor in America* (1934).
19. See Dresner's "Domestic Comic Writers" in June Sochen's *Women's Comic Visions* (1991) and Walker's *A Very Serious Thing: Women's Humor and American Culture* (1988).

home and eager to show mastery over it, particularly if he could prove that he were more knowledgeable (more "native") to the place than someone else. Although the tall tale helped the speaker find meaning in his world, it did so at the expense of the natural world, about which it came to foster misconceptions. The tall tale arranged for nature to be a backdrop, stunning but secondary, a setting for the human agent to strut or ride in. There is only one sense in which nature got to "speak" via tall talk: the voice of the tall tale is thoroughly associated with the vernacular, abundant with earthy figures of speech. But if nature were emblematic for early Americans, they read in it their own image. Women's humor may have domesticity closer at hand, but because it focuses on contesting a male-dominated society its valuable energies may not come to center on nature.

In contrast, Native American humor in myth opens a household more far-ranging than the hermetic Euro-American one at the end of the nineteenth century. Comfortable in a country they considered already settled, indigenous peoples did not suffer the same anxieties as the immigrants who arrived in the same country and considered it wilderness. Native American humor is "at home" in the broadest possible sense: animals participate in it, and places are essential to shaping the action. It is humor aimed at getting along in the ecological household where nature is not solely emblematic but also self-willed and animate. Instead of looking at the natural world for a human reflection, the Native American character discovers how people internalize wild nature and how animals in their own right might be partly like humans. From this imaginative, mixed bloodline, Coyote emerges.

Healthy Limits in the Ecological Household

"HUMANS, AND ALL THE OTHER ORGANISMS, HAVE THEIR OWN SPEcialness—but it is the world that gives meaning to each of us," Snyder writes (*A Place in Space* 210). If we were only to hunker inward toward members of our own kind, we would accumulate such "specialness" as to lose intelligence and even compassion. Given that life in the wild constituted the several-thousand-year process of our evolution, we have a biologically inured appetite for interaction with nonhuman nature. To condition ourselves increasingly to experience and expect only the satisfactions of the human world is the psychic and evolutionary equivalent of inbreeding. Our "specialness" is dangerous if we mistake it for the wider world which ought to be its context. In calling for renewed recognition of the world, Snyder wants to reestablish in our consciousness the traditional full membership of nature that has always driven our development. We must, he asserts, draw ethical lineaments beyond the human: "Such an extension of human intellect and sympathy into the nonhuman realms is a charming and mind-bending undertaking. It is also an essential step if we are to have a future worth living" (210). This is the genius of the North American trickster Coyote.[20]

Coyote creates the circumstances for people to practice their ethical impulses across a wildly and disparately inhabited terrain. Imagining ethical life for other creatures and portraying it in myth, people expand their sympathies and heighten their ethical aptitude. And so humor appropriately dogs Coyote because it implies a style of awareness—flexible, imaginative, "charming and mind-bending"—necessary to the creative work of extending ethics to nonhuman nature.

The ethical and imaginative scope that lets humans see beyond themselves creates an ecological household. Scope here implies not limitlessness but connection with the world, connection to something larger than ourselves, a connection that Snyder says gives meaning to us. This world is often localized: it is the particular place in east-central Arizona around Cibecue where Mrs. Annie Peaches says the world stalks people; it is marginal hill country where farmers know that in spite of their labors the land is most productive in rocks; it is the river flood plain where people settle and get washed out and resettle despite the memory of the high-water mark that never completely recedes. An ecological household can be achieved in specific locales—places people know and remember and deal with in myriad daily ways, for these places enter the community consciousness as powerful characters bringing a nonhuman context intimately to bear within the human household. Such households are often the long-settled communities—what Dorson calls a folk region—that tend to have rich folklore and humor.

> In the folk region, people are wedded to the land, and the land holds memories. The people themselves possess identity and ancestry, through continuous occupation of the same soil. Local events can flower into legend and ballad and proverb, and village ways can harden into custom (*American Folklore* 75).

---

20. Coyote himself may be amoral, but he has moral relevance because he is always testing and clarifying his world's moral limits.

Recognizing the importance of place to culture, Dorson's description of the folk region is romantically patriotic, and he proffers it in contrast to the increasingly rootless contemporary society—with the implication that contemporary society has less culture. The folk region has abundant lore because its people have come to creative terms with living in a place; its limits fashion the context for their livelihood and identity. The folk region has a certain confidence about itself that itinerant mainstream America lacks. And confidence may be essential to humor because confidence allows people to play freely with perspective without the fear of losing their identity.[21] Kenney writes that creative humor is possible only by one "who possesses a clear and firm comprehension of what is going on around him" (26)—a comprehension facilitated by a long-standing relationship to place. We might also say that creative humor is possible only by one who knows him or herself well, since the ability—indeed the willingness—to shift perspective requires one to have secure standing in the first place. Snyder offers this bioregional teaser:

knowing who we are and knowing where we are are intimately linked. There are no limits to the possibilities of the study of *who* and *where*, if you want to go "beyond limits"—and so, even in a world of biological limits, there is plenty of open mind-space to go out into (*A Place in Space* 189).

Limited in place, the folk region has infinite imaginative scope, as the folklore that bountifully arises from it demonstrates. The region's practices do not so much "harden into custom," as Dorson says, as acquire the maverick stamp of originality and the custom fit to a locale.[22] Those grounded in place belong to an ecological household and have access to the "meaning" that that world affords them. They know its capabilities, its resources, its limits. Such knowledge grants people confidence, for it assures them that reality independent of human experience does exist.

It is little wonder, then, that limits inspire humor. Whether supplied by a folk region or another context, they are the necessary foundation against which the play of surprise, incongruity, and absurdity can generate humor. Humans and their humor are saved from self-absorbed "specialness"

21. According to Jesse Bier in *The Rise and Fall of American Humor*, "Objectivity and confidence are the major psychic conditions for a sense of humor" (28–29).
22. The bioregion may be a contemporary version of the folk region except that bioregionalists would be known for their ecological awareness.

when they are wise enough to look for context beyond themselves—to see themselves in relation to the wider world.[23] The limits imposed by nonhuman nature are a source of both meaning and humor for humans—in much the same way that the transgressions of Coyote convey morality.

Lacking Healthy Limits

Although humor is a useful orienting tool, well-suited to contextualize human experience, it is not always granted the healthy limits that can prevent people from being mired in their "specialness." Humor becomes self-centered and myopic when it is used merely as a verbal weapon—when it has no limit or partner. Accused of being shallow in this way—sustained on the shock of invective and other cheap thrills—a strain of contemporary American humor has acquired derogatory epithets like "sick" and "black" as the register of our reluctance to call it humor at all. Our discomfort with sick humor indicates that community context—particularly the meaning that context provides—is an essential foundation for humor.[24] In recognizing no taboo or limit, sick humor is not more free but rather less funny. Three characteristics of sick humor that render it distinctly antisocial include its lack of sympathies, its failure to suggest healthy behavior, and its disavowal of any form of meaning in the world. One example is a joke Drew Carey tells in his *Dirty Jokes and Beer* about the man and woman whose tastes for kinky sex are mismatched and revolting—an incongruity that generates punch-line surprise only because one is more revolting than the other. Earl Rovit calls such humor immature: "the adolescent comic spirit seems curiously unanchored in any practical conception of society or selfhood, unfocused on any goal beyond its immediate *yuk*" (246). Or, as Bier would have it: "The final comic antithesis of all is having no thesis whatsoever, a direction in which the majority of our nethermost humorists are leading" (476).

Such humorists mistakenly seek freedom in escape, disregarding the world, although the greatest freedom attends us when we have a clear conception of the limits placed on us, the household we participate in. This freedom is the "clear and firm comprehension of what is going on" that Kenney says makes creative humor possible (26). Sick humorists have mistaken for

---

23. In *Environmental Ethics*, Holmes Rolston III writes, "the moral life is not complete without a sensitive approach to one's place" (341).

24. Robert Corrigan writes that standards and limits are necessary as a framework for comic subversion but that the modern problem of relativism has destroyed this framework (5–9).

nihilism the ambiguity in humor's taboo-testing play with limits. They have replaced context with themselves, an ersatz ploy. Regarding the authors of sick humor after World War II, Cohen writes, "all created more preposterous fiction to assert the supremacy of their imagination" (5). The problem, of course, is that the imagination most interested in itself, with no external grounding, results in little more than self-absorption. So humor, without a territory of meaning to play across, can spiral into increasingly narrow revolutions until it reaches the self-reflective nadir of being flip side to itself.

The development in canonized American humor from the boasts of the tall tale to the anxieties of the modern man and finally to the violence of sick humor is in part a product of urbanization and specialization—the breakdown of ecological context.[25] It is also a male tradition. Norris Yates' accounting of the humor from the late nineteenth century into the twentieth charts a progression toward sick humor. He identifies three middle-class character types who were the main "carriers" of value for the period (12–13): they embodied the "fixed standards" that Yates says are the necessary grounding of humor (138). These characters stand in poor contrast to the backwoods hero of the tall tale, who optimistically used exaggeration to win confidence for himself and be boosted above the nation's anxieties. Yates' characters personify the erosion of confidence that afflicts those without a secure community or place in the world. From the late nineteenth-century "crackerbox philosopher" and "solid citizen," the comic American character who arrives in the twentieth century has dwindled into the "Little Man," whose fears, anxieties, and insecurities are his main feature. The reasons that Yates posits for the chronological humbling of these American characters all pertain to the breakdown of context: the frontier had closed; modern industry specialized formerly productive people into mere consumers; people were less sure of their identity and values; their status in the universe was unclear (38–39).

His reading is useful for what it accomplishes—historicizing the darkening and increasingly individualistic focus in American humor—and for what it does not accomplish. Loyal to the traditional canon, Yates does not include an analysis of women's humor, which has a different trajectory than mainstream humor. Rather than becoming bleak, women's humor has

25. Sanford Pinsker makes this claim about urbanization in "The Urban Tall Tale: Frontier Humor in a Contemporary Key" (pages 249–62 in Sarah Blacher Cohen's *Comic Relief*). He says that the "urban tall tale" perpetuates the anxious exaggerations of the frontier humorists but amplifies them with the paranoia and pessimism peculiar to urbanized modern America.

become more positive, for women have acquired more social and economic power in the country and have exercised it in their humor to celebrate their experience and debunk stereotypes about women. Lawrence Mintz writes that women's humor has not participated in the sick and black humor that is largely a contemporary male response to feelings of alienation and lack of importance; unlike men, women have had a history of coping with powerlessness, which helps explain how their humor has kept steady (153). Gloria Kaufman's introduction to *Pulling Our Own Strings: Feminist Humor & Satire* affirms that women are increasingly positive in their humor because they are simply not accepting oppression any longer (13–16). Historically conditioned to be the keepers of the home, women who are made newly adventurous with social power may find it easier than men to take the household metaphor into an ecological dimension and find in nature the most inclusive home of all.

Furthermore, Yates does not identify the playing field widely enough, in remaining fully on the human court, to pick out "fixed standards" critical to humor. In fact, by choosing middle-class values as the appropriate standard for humor, he is inadvertently guilty of the isolating of human concerns that has driven much humor toward narcissism. More provocative standards are those that emerge from a context in which human and nonhuman nature intersect, and the limits are fixed by biology but kept open by evolution and culture—always elusive enough to be complex but certain enough to be secure.

Nature Creates New Foundation for Humor

"The human touches us more closely than the nonhuman," J.Y.T. Greig writes in *The Psychology of Laughter and Comedy*, professing that most of our humor involves humans (73–74).[26] While it is true that intimacy is essential to humor, the notion that intimacy is circumscribed by a human world is corollary to the specious belief that meaning and value are also limited to a human world. This particular anthropocentric blindness has occurred within a Western spiritual and intellectual tradition that deviates from thousands of years of *Homo sapien* intimacy with an animated, mysterious, meaningful world. Furthermore, that blindness is currently being challenged by an emerging biocentric belief that nature has its own value and intrinsic worth. "We do not simply bestow value on nature," Holmes Rolston III writes, "nature also conveys value to us" (208). Or to repeat

26. Writing in 1900 about laughter, Henri Bergson more unequivocally stated that the comic is entirely human (472).

Snyder: "it is the world that gives meaning to each of us." With this kind of moral standing, nature is partner to human, and so the intimacy between us can be mutual. Not only can we know the world and have a relationship with it but it also has a relationship with us. In fact, humor might not always issue from us, as Greig or Bergson would imagine. Our humor need not be launched from a perspective of human superiority or derision; it can be more playful and inquisitive than that, assaying a moral landscape that extends beyond human expertise. This is Coyote's role, and it may also be the role of nature writing.

Important to this issue is the fact that the anxieties of contemporary writers are different from those of earlier Americans. Whereas the plenitude of the natural world and its resources was once assumed, now we wonder about the capacity of the world to absorb our population, pollution, and consumption. Instead of fearing wilderness, we worry that we soon might not have any left.[27] Rather than being driven by wilderness, pioneer experience, and parochial anxieties to construct our identity in opposition and relation to the nonhuman world, we find that our relationships more and more involve the urban and technological world of our own making. So our efforts for self-identification are confused by homogeneity, a reduced gene pool, as it were—inbreeding.[28] We increasingly value nature, but we are painfully beset by the knowledge that our lifestyles share complicity in its destruction and that we have less contact with nature since our livelihoods are caught up in the continued manufacture of the modernized world. That we are less confident, more individualistic, and less community-oriented shows in the current dark strain of our humor.[29]

The writers who might afford a different direction for humor in the twenty-first century are writers interested in nature. Concern for a wider context than the human, Krutch notes, distinguishes nature writing from other disciplines (164).[30] According to Tom Lyon, the "moving spirit" of

27. Roderick Nash's *Wilderness and the American Mind* traces this revolutionary change in Americans' attitude toward wilderness.

28. In *The Best of Two Worlds*, Joseph Wood Krutch writes that our human self-absorption has led us to be confused about who we are (163).

29. Although women's humor is currently more up-beat than bleak, it will inevitably register the fact that many feminists—like Susan Griffin and Carolyn Merchant—have already recognized: that the oppression of women and nature has been concomitant, and so to overturn patriarchal values but still participate in a cultural and economic system that destroys nature does not conclusively or fully improve our condition.

30. Stephen Trimble defines nature writing similarly, saying that its broad focus on the world balances the human ego and contributes to moral writing.

nature writing is the practice of perceiving inclusive patterns, that is, context beyond the human (xv). In expanding our perspective, we come into ethical territory; for when we see ourselves within an ecological household governed by its etiquette, how we should behave is critical to survival. Deserving of respect, nature has standing, according to American nature writers. In *The Rights of Nature: A History of Environmental Ethics*, Nash says that the idea that nature has rights is revolutionary, "the most dramatic expansion of morality in the course of human thought" (7). Nature writing carries with it the assumption that our ideas belong in the world, that they ought to affect the way we act. Such nature writing—or, as Snyder would have it, nature's writing itself—has "the potential of becoming the most vital, radical, fluid, transgressive, pansexual, subductive, and morally challenging kind of writing on the scene" (*A Place in Space* 170). He claims that, as such, it may help stop environmental destruction. The activist energy and outward focus of nature writing result from a new sense in America that limits exist: there are limits to the natural world and limits to our behavior.[31] Nature writers' interest in limits does not consign them to a narrow, self-centered world; instead, their concern seems to be an ecological cosmopolitanism in which the exploration of limits takes them into new territory—nonhuman—where previously the intimate legislation of ethics and morality had not seemed to apply. In this newly expanded ethical world, nature writers have the capacity to create a new foundation for humor.

Reading the signs of cultural and natural limits, nature writers replicate out of ecological parameters the folk region, where intimacy with place and nonhuman nature re-institutes the community on a new scale and prepares the way for humor appropriate to it. Besides their role in providing a new moral foundation for humor, nature writers are also often funny. They have good reason to use humor: since they are trying to encourage us to see our place in the natural world from a new perspective, humor can be a perfect persuasive technique; since they are often coping with the loss or potential loss of wild places and place-based cultures, humor provides

---

31. This conviction deviates from historical precedent. As Leo Marx has demonstrated, ecological limits in America have been open to constant negotiation. In *The Machine in the Garden* (1964), he reads the American experience as a pastoral experiment and finds that its plot—the dialectic between city and country—has had no limits; and that, furthermore, proponents of industrial and technological progress have continually reinterpreted the pastoral ideal to include (and even necessitate) the "machine," instrument of the city.

them with a creative means for dealing with anxiety or fear; and since they need to find a way to oppose the attitudes, ideas, and forces they find destructive without themselves becoming bitter or sacrificing the values that give them joy, humor can be a means of both resistance and celebration.

The four writers who are the focus of this book all look beyond human affairs to the natural world and back again to understand people in greater context. Each wants to show that home exists in nature. Each believes that our survival depends on the skill and humor to relate to the natural world, including other people. Each has a unique approach. Edward Abbey flourishes his humor, goading and amusing us in order to expose us to the wild world he loves. Louise Erdrich relies on humor to transform hardship and create a surprising vision of survival. Wendell Berry wields humor to combat threats to independent country people and to celebrate the spirit and life of such people. Rachel Carson subsumes the spirit of humor in her vivid scientific exposition of nature, which demonstrates the comedy of the ever-changing world. Convinced that we must pay attention to the limits of our world, each of these writers works, plays, and teaches with humor.

Nature writing focuses on the nonhuman world, as Tom Lyon and Lawrence Buell define it,[32] but humor sparks a physiological reaction that itself transports us close to nature. Even when it does not turn our attention to nature, humor charges us with a wild state of mind: it stimulates us to be alert, responsive, and spontaneous, and it involves us in its peculiar leap of faith of forging from one perspective to another, bridging the two with a wide-open mind. In leaping, humor conditions us to be creative and perceive other connections in the world. Humor appeals to the wildest paradoxes of our existence—how we can simultaneously participate in our world and yet have a perspective of it that seems to place us outside of it and ourselves. To construct humor literarily or to enjoy it is to accept and celebrate that paradox, indulging in the freedom that comes when we embrace an apparent lack of logic and find that our world still, unaccountably, makes sense.

---

32. See Lyon's preface in *This Incomperable Lande: A Book of American Nature Writing* and Buell's *The Environmental Imagination: Thoreau, Nature Writing, and the Formation of American Culture*, pages 6–8.

In the spirit of that comic adventure, Coyote in contemporary American literature keeps us conditioned for surprise. At its best, the use of Coyote by non-Native Americans is more than a Western cultural tag or the stock-character shorthand for a rebel; when best put to use, Coyote inspires boldness, innovation, and complex-thinking in its authors. The Coyote who was present at Creation in Native American tradition is also present today, in equally challenging and mind-bending capacities as he was in myth.

A return to Coyote between each of the forthcoming chapters is a way of side-stepping the direct discussion of humor so that we may instead practice the state of mind that cultivates humor. Such a mind is alert and willing to be surprised—and it accommodates Coyote as both a trickster and a hero. In addition, stepping to the sidelines puts us in Coyote's position with regard to humankind. Coyote knows people well because he has stayed apart from them and joined them, always maintaining his wild ways; his acumen, bolstered by curiosity and gregariousness, is based on experimenting with many perspectives. Coyote knows a lot because he tries everything out and keeps from getting attached to any certain experience: his intimacies are cosmopolitan because he is always traveling. We, too, can gain something of Coyote's comic skills by dropping out, from time to time, of our established course in order to travel with him for a while. Having taken an excursion, we return to our concerns with a fresh outlook.

Coyote Storyteller, Simon Ortiz

Coyote keeps cropping up in Simon Ortiz' *A Good Journey*[33] as if showing himself to be the avatar of the journeyer, the most practiced lifelong traveler of all time, and probably the best storyteller too. And Ortiz is gracious, giving him ample room. The author's dedication of the volume to his children acknowledges the kind of subordinate position he assumes as a

33. This volume and two other poetry collections by Ortiz were republished in *Woven Stone* (1992) by the University of Arizona Press.

writer. He says, "The stories and poems come forth / and I am only the voice telling them. / They are the true source themselves" (3). Ortiz chooses for himself the quiet role of being receptacle for his subjects, allowing them to collect in and pass through him and claiming no ownership apart from the shape that his voice puts on them. That leaves enough unclaimed space for Coyote to bluster into, making sure he gets talked about.

Bad as he is, disobeying, gambling, tricking fellow creatures, butting his way into other people's business, Coyote cannot fail to give Ortiz something to talk about. Then, too, there is another factor in Ortiz' welcoming attitude, for Coyote is more than a pushy and conspicuous member of the household: he symbolizes much of its continuity and survival. When asked why he writes, Ortiz replied,

> Because Indians always tell a story. The only way to continue is to tell a story and that's what Coyote says. The only way to continue is to tell a story and there is no other way. Your children will not survive unless you tell something about them—how they were born, how they came to this certain place, how they continued (11).

Ortiz is an Acoma Pueblo Indian with an ear for the power of stories in sustaining cultures and people in their traditional way. Part of the reason Coyote stories are helpful is that in them the drama of mythical times is prolonged and revivified. For example, in the poem "Telling About Coyote," Crow is resplendently white, Coyote is jealous, and all the animals are around the campfire to decide when the seasons will be. The dramatic possibilities are exciting. When Coyote begins to throw pitch-heavy pine logs on the fire to make it sooty so that the soot blows over Crow all night long, we feel privy to the dirty deed as if we were contemporaneous to mythical times. The voice of the storyteller enforces that continuity as does the wayward career of Coyote, who keeps on the run out of myth and into the present. So the poem ends with the storyteller giving the latest news on Coyote:

> O yes, last time . . .
> when was it,
> I saw him somewhere
> between Muskogee and Tulsa,
> heading for Tulsy Town I guess,

just trucking along.
He was heading into some oakbrush thicket,
just over the hill was a creek.
Probably get to Tulsa in a couple days . . . (17–18)

The stories about Coyote are not finished, and much of their power lies in this indeterminacy. As Ortiz shows, what really happened with Coyote is hard to know, and because we do not know exactly, we continue to look for Coyote: the lure is that what really happened might yet be what is going to happen. "Two Coyote Ones" has this suspense. Ortiz begins,

I remember that one about Coyote
coming back from Laguna Fiesta
where he had just bought a silver belt buckle.
He was showing off to everyone.
That Coyote, he's always doing that,
showing off his stuff (100).

The traditional story is full of conjecture. Coyote is not to be trusted, of course, and so the value of the fancy buckle is suspect despite all the talk about it. The talk brings that buckle tantalizingly close to first-hand experience, close enough for the speaker to confess, "I never saw it myself, just heard about it / from one of his cousins" (100). It is not even certain if Coyote has kept the buckle; if you ask about it, he might give you a cock and bull story. Something like this:

"Well, let me tell you.
I was at Isleta and I was offered
a good deal by this compadre who had
some nice ristras of red chili. He had
a pretty sister . . ." and so on.
And you can never tell (100).

You cannot know if Coyote is telling it straight or not, if the silver buckle was pricey or not, and if he made a hot deal to get the red chili and pretty sister. The story simply is not over, which moves much of its momentum into our camp; so we are involved in making tradition, and Coyote stories come to have contemporary features. "And you can never tell," Ortiz writes, taking the implicit clue about the personalization of Coyote stories

and proceeding directly into first-person narrative. The speaker says he was
at his campfire with his dog in southern Colorado

> And this
>
> blonde girl came along. I mean that.
> She just came along, driving a truck,
> and she brought a cake.
> *That* was real Coyote luck, a blonde girl
> and a ginger cake (101).

Because he knows Coyote, the speaker has a history to help him understand this crazy and fortuitous situation. Coyote stories are a touchstone; with them he can track his own experience.

The girl says she and her family raise goats and make good money that way—and goats can even be well-behaved. The speaker, whose family has also raised goats, disagrees, though his two-sentence response is so mild it hardly contests her assertion.

> . . . Well
> I don't know about that. We used to raise
> goats too.

In contrast, the three-stanza digression about Coyote and goats is fully candid:

> Coyote doesn't like goats too much.
> He thinks they're smartass and showoff.
> Gets on his nerves he says.
> Goats think pretty much the same of him (101).

For their part, the goats have details of Coyote's mendacity, especially his peddling of a wheelbarrow "that was missing only one wheel" (101). Certainly the digression does not stay right on course about whether goats are lucrative and well-behaved or not, but it gives the speaker a lot of company in handling the remark of a girl he might not be willing to rebuff under the circumstances. The traditional stories can go unspoken and nevertheless accompany him, rounding out the conversation and helping him judge the whole truth.

Thus Coyote is helpful despite his loose touch on veracity. Coyote represents the raconteur spirit: he will tell stories of wild times, and we can also tell stories on him. We can come close to Coyote without taking the risks that he does. We can figuratively be Coyote—with an easy escape and perhaps with a clearer vision as we return to ourselves. The separation between us and him, particularly stretched across the thrilling territory that Coyote roams, is reorienting. In this poem, it helps the speaker cope with his visitor. The style that Coyote as raconteur projects—rambling, extemporaneous, inclusive—is one that Ortiz finds attractive and useful in other poems as well.

For example, in his recipe for how to make chili stew, everything has a place. He begins, "It's better to do it outside / or at sheepcamp / or during a two or three day campout" (36). The ingredients are ordinary, but the directions are unabashedly extraordinary. He mentions the onion when he says to begin with the water and bouíllon and chili and garlic in a saucepan, and he bewails it, for it is onion "which I don't have and won't mention anymore because I miss it and you shouldn't ever be anyplace without it, I don't care where" (36). So then Ortiz recommends a light boil and a good attitude: "cover and smell it once in a while with good thoughts in your mind, and don't worry too much about it except, of course, keep water in it so it doesn't burn, okay" (37). Attitude and awareness are obviously part of the ingredients. He recommends thinking of a song to fit the cooking chili and relaxing when the meat sizzles in the pan with butter and garlic.

> Smelling and watching are important things, and you really shouldn't worry too much about it—I don't care what Julia Childs says—but you should pay the utmost attention to everything, and that means the earth, clouds, sounds, the wind. All these go into the cooking (37).

Ortiz' chili stew is something else. In fact, it is the everything else that goes into it (including the five hours of cooking) that makes the stew so special. The outdoors, the dog (who got the beef scraps), the thoughts, and talk (to Magpies in order to keep them honest) all augment the stew: context is everything. The connections are nourishing. Not only does the recipe for the stew foment a story but it also distills the essence of a good journey—the process of doing practical work with ceremonial bearing.

The stories that Coyote sparks in "Two Coyote Ones" similarly enfold and elevate the present-day experience, particularly the speaker's visit from the girl who has a "nice soft voice" and hair that shines in the light of his campfire (101). There is sexual tension in the encounter. He confesses,

> I had to tell Rex the dog
> to cool it a couple of times. He and I
> were alone a lot that summer, and we were
> anxious but we kept our cool (102).

He does not try anything. After they have a good talk about goats and the speaker's writing, the girl makes a cordial departure. That unexpected and innocent rendezvous has a conclusive ending, for she is set to leave the next day for Denver and ultimately headed to Boston for med school; there will never be a chance by that campfire to get to know her better.

But Coyote has been a constant companion in this experience, and he continues to be. He becomes a way to keep the story open, revisit the experience, and endow the speaker with the opportunity to initiate a new story into the tradition. This is what happens after the goodbyes of the writer and the girl—the concluding two stanzas of the poem:

> There's this story that Coyote was telling
> about the time he was sitting at his campfire
> and a pretty blonde girl came driving along
> in a pickup truck and she . . . And so on.

> And you can tell afterall (102).

In the poem's first Coyote adventure—about his silver belt buckle—the leading phrase "and so on" had also served as an ambiguous ending. But in that case Ortiz had remarked, "And you can never tell," meaning that we will not ever know conclusively what happened to Coyote—will not know what was true. We might be able to route the parts of the tradition we know into pertinent relation to our lives but nonetheless we could not "tell," neither to understand fully nor to adopt that Coyote voice. Here, however, at the poem's end, Ortiz asserts that it is possible to "tell afterall." The difference? This is the speaker not seeking the relevance of the Coyote tradition to his experience but choosing to make tradition himself. Graciously, Ortiz lets the speaker's triumph be our own, for although it is his narrator's campfire experience transformed into a Coyote story, we too gain the enlightenment from that bold move—"you," Ortiz now tells us, "can tell." The power of participating in a Coyote story—imagining and shaping it—puts us in charge of its ambiguities because we can determine which way it leads. So if he wanted (if we wanted), the speaker could pursue via his story a course of behavior with the girl that he did not attempt in person. The story can free him to fantasize (for certainly lusty Coyote would have had plans for a pretty blonde girl) and embellish on his first-hand experience. That could mean that the story goes way beyond the pale, performing indelicacies or transgressions and presenting Coyote in ways we ourselves prefer not to be, which is the fine advantage of role-playing in an oral tradition. Through it, we can test out and know the limits of personal behavior and social interaction. Rather than do something he regrets in his chat with the girl, the speaker can go wild with it in his imagination and then (because it is a story) have the distance to be able to judge it: before he makes a mistake in real life, he can first tell Coyote stories. Cushioned in this manner by the Coyote tales that precede and follow her in the poem, the girl enjoys immunity from potential dangers.

The speaker and his dog do not lose their "cool," nor does Ortiz; though he showcases the Coyote's flamboyant and risky style, it never overtakes the poem. Ortiz has confidence in the gift that the tradition of Coyote stories gives him: that there is a place for aberrant behavior. It fits in. Coyote belongs in the world as much as anyone's good behavior belongs also. The growing tradition of Coyote stories is testimony to the fact that we find relief in being able to acknowledge and, closer yet, take the outlaw position—particularly when we have the route back into our regular lives surely delineated.

What Ortiz' "Two Coyote Ones" demonstrates is how the clear passage between tradition and contemporaneity is maintained. He shows that they are not held temporally apart as artifact versus present reality, for the old stories are awakened in us every time they are told, nor are they estranged by location because Coyote gets around everywhere. The stories about him happen where you live and I live, and they always have. Instead, the connection to tradition is kept alive by stories that both maintain distance and move effortlessly across. In telling and using Coyote stories, Ortiz points to the good journey that gives us transport between our world and our mythical and imagined worlds. The journey is propelled by the words, which, he says, "are the vision / by which we see out and in and around" (3). Within the round of that verbal communion, Ortiz can afford to let stories have their own end, still unarticulated, ever powerful as they go "and so on," toward no final end at all.

Coyote as storyteller and outlaw in Ortiz' work plays the same role that Edward Abbey takes on for himself—that of a literary outlaw. Coyote initiates us to that pose so that we can read the transformative power in it and understand Abbey as both provoker and reformer.

TWO

▼▼▼

Edward Abbey

Laughing Out of Place

IF EVER A WRITER WERE AN OUTLAW, EDWARD ABBEY FITS THAT DE-scription. Born in the Allegheny hill town of Indiana, Pennsylvania, and transplanted by his adult predilections to the Southwest, he came to identify his home with a passion and humor that catapulted it—and its vulnerability—into the national consciousness.[34] He settled in the Tucson area, yet he claimed larger territory, writing in *The Journey Home*, "My home is the American West. All of it" (xiii-xiv). Abbey took to the tall-tale expansiveness of the West without a hitch, as if it satisfied a longing that he had harbored since the beginning. "Like so many others in this century, I found myself a displaced person shortly after birth and have been looking half my life for a place to take my stand," he explains (*The Journey Home* xiii). Claiming the whole ecological household of the arid, mountainous West as his home, he swears to protect it accordingly.

Abbey is a romantic in following his heart, an outlaw in choosing to defend his ideals. He speaks candidly, comically, and often outrageously in favor of a world beyond conventional written laws, one placed entirely within natural moral law. That world and that moral law get Abbey into trouble, where, incidentally, he seems to take pleasure in being.[35] For one

---

34. Abbey claimed that he was born in Home, Pennsylvania; however, the record proves otherwise. As James Cahalan explains, Abbey "always loved a good name" (233).
35. Abbey seems to thrive on feedback from his detractors, publishing excerpts from their letters, as he does in the preface to *Down the River*. Included there, the missive from

▶ 37

thing, his home is a huge place, and his claim on it strikes many as outlandish. Second, his regard for the wilderness presumes that ethical conduct reaches beyond the parameters of human life. The world in question is nonhuman as much as it is human.

Abbey minces no words in proselytizing for this world. His "Forward!" to Dave Foreman and Bill Haywood's *Ecodefense: A Field Guide to Monkeywrenching* pronounces that the ecological household deserves our protection, first arguing that our homes and families ought to be safe against intruders and, second, that our right to self-preservation is a matter of natural law. "Self-defense against attack is one of the basic laws not only of human society but of life itself, not only of human life but of all life" (7). Abbey, whose Masters thesis in the philosophy program at the University of New Mexico was about the morality of violence, and whose political description of himself was as an anarchist, wants to redefine the moral imperative of self-defense so that it also accounts for actions carried out on behalf of the wilderness.

That desire means that he has aligned himself with risky undertakings. The book *Ecodefense* is a manual for how to spike trees, down billboards, disable bulldozers, close roads, and cut fences without getting caught. Its very format hints of danger: a "Standard Disclaimer" follows the title page and states that the book is for "entertainment purposes only" and, moreover, "No one involved with the production of this book—the editors, contributors, artists, printers, or anyone—encourages anyone to do any of the stupid, illegal things contained herein." Edward Abbey is credited by Dave Foreman in the introduction as being the inspiration for the book.[36] From a lawmaker or property owner's perspective, Abbey is tantamount to an outlaw; Abbey, however, has anticipated such suspicions and argues in the "Forward!" that the standards have changed.

> Representative democracy in the United States has broken down. Our legislators do not represent those who elected them but rather the mi-

Daryl S. Allen reads as follows: "If Mr. Abbey is so in love with wilderness, he should take his beer cans and his warped head and go far back in the hills and stay there. The world would be glad to see the last of him and it is obvious he has no place in civilized society" (6). And in the introduction to *Abbey's Road*, this letter comes from a lady in Illinois: "Do you realize how funny you are? Funny in a sick way, I mean . . ." (xiii). 36. In 1980, Dave Foreman and Bill Haywood founded the radical environmental group—more accurately described as a movement because it has no official membership—known as Earth First!. Its most characteristic slogan is "No Compromise in Defense of Mother Earth." And its unofficial guru is Ed Abbey.

nority who finance their political campaigns and who control the organs of communication—the Tee Vee, the newspapers, the billboards, the radio—that have made politics a game for the rich only. Representative government in the USA represents money not people and therefore has forfeited our allegiance and moral support. We owe it nothing but the taxation it extorts from us under threats of seizure of property, or prison, or, in some cases already, when resisted, a sudden and violent death by gunfire (8).

His rhetoric is exaggerated. Nevertheless, it registers the extent of his outrage as well as his willingness to take risks (here rhetorical ones) in order to save his beloved wild land. By persuading his readers that the wilderness is home, he can complete his argument that ecodefense—as outlined in the book—is justified as self-defense. He writes, "And if the wilderness is our true home, and if it is threatened with invasion, pillage and destruction—as it certainly is—then we have the right to defend that home, as we would our private rooms, by whatever means are necessary" (8). Hence Abbey happily endorses the publication of *Ecodefense*.

Abbey is boldly outspoken and bold with his thought. Apart from his expansive notion of morality, which partakes of Deep Ecology, he secures his aura of an outlaw by the way he says things. In his book of aphorisms, *A Voice Crying in the Wilderness (Vox Clamantis in Deserto)*, he paraphrases Robinson Jeffers and quips, "I'd rather kill a man than a snake. Not because I love snakes or hate men. It is a question, rather, of proportion" (87).[37] If there are too many people and too few snakes, as there are, in Abbey's estimation of ecological balance, then fairness—again, this is the fairness of a biocentric reading—justifies Abbey's inclination to dispatch the person rather than the snake. He is persistent in contesting the assumptions of anthropocentrism—again an aphorism: "Are people more important than the grizzly bear? Only from the point of view of some people" (85). From a position of philosophical equanimity, we can believe that bears and people are no more or no less important than each other. The predator-prey implications in additional sayings clarify Abbey's position. "If people persist in trespassing upon the grizzlies' territory, we must accept the fact that the grizzlies, from time to time, will harvest a few trespassers" (86). Here his magnanimous interpretation of place confers on the

---

37. Abbey's literary and philosophical debt to Jeffers and other writers is given superb treatment by David J. Rothman in " 'I'm a humanist': The Poetic Past in *Desert Solitaire*."

bears their territory as property and reduces their human visitors to inter-lopers, personally responsible for their own life-and-death decision to tres-pass. Abbey implies that the justice meted by the grizzlies would be desultory, nothing strict but certainly irrevocable when it occurs. The light tone with which he acknowledges that they "will harvest a few tres-passers" conveys his pleasure in the fairness of that agreement. In Abbey's ideal world, the ecological household has priority.

Never, however, suspect Abbey of philosophical high-mindedness or self-satisfied pleasure. He is forever writing the subtext to his convictions. The humor that he finds in this undertaking makes him radically different from most writers, for he exposes himself mercilessly and joyfully, as if the discovery of humor in his inconsistencies were necessary to maintaining his convictions.

Abbey's comic style is more persistently radical than any of his many unconventional ideas and attitudes. Thus it is through his humor that we find the most illuminating route to his purposes as a writer. He wryly un-dercuts this pronouncement: "In all of nature, there is no sound more pleasing than that of a hungry animal at its feed. Unless you are the food" (86). Having chosen to insist that the food chain fully includes humans—an important message of these aphorisms—Abbey cringes to imagine the personal implications of his thought. He would not want to be food for a predator, and if he were threatened with that fate, he might be one of those "some people" who believe that they are more important than grizzly bears.

Abbey knows well the disparity between professing one's beliefs and living them out. His praise of Wendell Berry is pertly self-reflective: "Berry has been successful in teaching, in farming, and most difficult of all, in marriage; he actually lives what he preaches. Which seems grossly unfair to the rest of us; how can we forgive him his happiness?" (*Abbey's Road* xxi). Abbey himself, with his five wives and five children and with cantan-kerous eating and drinking habits that contributed to his early death in 1989 at age sixty-two, undoubtedly had his share of personal highlights. In the breach he always had humor.[38] It shapes the presentation of his most serious beliefs and helps him to stand alone as a radical.

38. In "A Few Words in Favor of Edward Abbey," Wendell Berry praises him for his clear and comic introspection, saying that few manage it: "I certainly do find it hard. My own goof-ups seem to me to have received merciless publicity when my wife has found out about them" (*What Are People For?* 43).

Vox clamantis in deserto is a role that few care to play, but I find pleasure in it. The voice crying from the desert, with its righteous assumption of enlightenment, tends to grate on the nerves of the multitude. But it is mine. I've had to learn to live within a constant blizzard of abuse from book reviewers, literary critics, newspaper columnists, letter writers, and fellow authors. But there are some rewards as well. The immense satisfaction, for example, of speaking out in plain blunt language on matters that the majority of American authors are too tired, timid, or temporizing even to allow themselves to think about. To challenge the taboo—that has always been a special delight of mine—and though all respectable and official and institutional voices condemn me, a million others think otherwise and continue to buy my books, paying my bills and financing my primrose path over the hill and down the far side to an early grave (*A Voice Crying in the Wilderness* xi–xii).

As a writer, he is not exactly, as he claims to be, the solitary voice with a "righteous assumption of enlightenment." He is much more playful than that, much more the hellraiser, as Ron Steffens calls him (81); much less the rigid moralist and more the comic philosopher, always ready with a quip to poke fun at himself—"A good philosopher is one who does not take ideas seriously" (*A Voice Crying in the Wilderness* 1)—or to acknowledge life's complexities, which is how he begins *Desert Solitaire*: "This is the most beautiful place on earth. There are many such places" (1).

Abbey's penchant to be comic has many sources. He is a romanticist and idealist endowed with a strong ironic wit. He has the academic training to pursue and analyze ideas and also has a country person's background in being beyond the thrall of modern life and its goals and values. Furthermore, he is a writer who must convert his ideas and attitudes into sellable work in order to make a living. Abbey is an outlaw because he decides continually not to choose between those roles. He plays the whole multifarious field, being simultaneously the redneck, philosopher, moralist, wage-earner, rebel, intellectual, joker, dreamer, and gambler. Only his comic style unites the wide range of his roles—and unites them without blurring their details or masking their contradictions. Abbey is a humorist because he has a wide enough mind—and a crazy enough heart—to believe in the value and authenticity of all his tendencies. He accepts himself as a person he would not want to classify; and in doing so, with eyes peeled to the ludicrous truth of his character, he makes it funny. He survives his inconsistencies because he is funny, and he sustains his commitment to preserve a diminishing natural world also by being funny. Rather than give up, he laughs and fights back. And so, by virtue of its necessary alliance to his convictions, humor becomes part of his message that the wilderness is our true home and that the wildness in us is part of our claim to that home.

▼ ▼ ▼

ABBEY'S WILDNESS KEEPS READERS ON EDGE, FOR WE NEVER KNOW what he might say, and we never can be sure that we will agree. The introductions to his works of nonfiction—including *Desert Solitaire, The Journey Home, Abbey's Road, Down the River, Beyond the Wall, Slumgullion Stew*[39], *One Life at a Time, Please*, and *A Voice Crying in the Wilderness*—show how unpredictable and consistently provoking Abbey can be. His style teaches us resilience and independence.

He introduces *Desert Solitaire* by explaining that he was a seasonal park ranger at Arches National Monument in southeast Utah and that he lamented the plan to modernize and develop the park. The plan went through (the place is now Arches National Park), but his lament is neither over nor entirely passive—he concludes with a cautionary note that he drops like a fireball in our laps.

> Do not jump into your automobile next June and rush out to the Canyon country hoping to see some of that which I have attempted to evoke in these pages. In the first place you can't see *anything* from a car; you've got to get out of the goddamned contraption and walk, better yet crawl, on hands and knees, over the sandstone and through the thornbush and cactus. When traces of blood begin to mark your trail you'll see something, maybe. Probably not. In the second place most of what I write about in this book is already gone or going under fast. This is not a travel guide but an elegy. A memorial. You're holding a tombstone in your hands. A bloody rock. Don't drop it on your foot—throw it at something big and glassy. What do you have to lose? (xii)

The book we have in our hands we expect to tell of the desert, but Abbey lays it into us with eucharistic energy, transforming tome into symbol of

39. Reprinted in 1987 as *The Best of Edward Abbey*.

loss and weapon for resistance. The paragraph is not so much a word of caution as it is a challenge and provocation. Volatile from its opening rant against the automobile and its suggestion for a hands-on introduction to the desert, it acquires an increasingly abbreviated, chant-like rhythm, augmenting Abbey's energy and horror until we are gathered by it into alliance with him against the ignorant tourists dependent on motorization and the "big and glassy" world they represent. His final question, "What do you have to lose?" is a painful concession that what is most precious already has been lost, or nearly so. Thus the question emerges from despair, fighting back.

The entire introduction has this same blend of anguish and belligerence, expressing his love for the beautiful and concern over its demise. He beguiles us with an account of his strategy for writing about the place.

> This is not primarily a book about the desert. In recording my impressions of the natural scene I have striven above all for accuracy, since I believe that there is a kind of poetry, even a kind of truth, in simple fact. But the desert is a vast world, an oceanic world, as deep in its way and complex and various as the sea. Language makes a mighty loose net with which to go fishing for simple facts, when facts are infinite (x).

Anomalous as it is to compare the desert and ocean, Abbey succeeds with the metaphor in conflating two largely mysterious realms, aligning their reputations in order to grant the desert the same mythical status as the sea. We may not know the desert at all, and we may only know it less after Abbey's detour into metaphor, but his comparison ensures that we begin to anticipate surprises in the desert and this author. At every step in this brief passage about his methods, he risks contradiction, for he says that facts manifest both truth and poetry but then pursues facts through language. His style is "fishing," not science: "Not imitation but evocation has been the goal" (x). We want to hear what this man has to say, for his style and thought are provocative. He appears tantalized by the promise in the desert: "If a man knew enough he could write a whole book about the juniper tree. Not juniper trees in general but that one particular juniper tree which grows from a ledge of naked sandstone near the old entrance to Arches National Monument" (x). We want to hear what he knows because this is a man in love, whose intimacy with the desert has made him curious, insatiable, and jealous. Richard Shelton characterizes *Desert Solitaire* as being, to a large extent, a love lyric (103). Even in Abbey's "strident and abrasive" tone, he hears "the voice of a lover trying desperately to protect the thing he loves" (116).

Whatever our bond to this writer, we find that he is not the only one who will be taking risks with his affections. He writes,

> Certain faults will be obvious to the general reader, of course, and for these I wish to apologize. I quite agree that much of the book will seem coarse, rude, bad-tempered, violently prejudiced, unconstructive—even frankly antisocial in its point of view. Serious critics, serious librarians, serious associate professors of English will if they read this work dislike it intensely; at least I hope so. To others I can only say that if the book has virtues they cannot be distinguished from the faults; that there is a way of being wrong which is also sometimes necessarily right (x–xi).

However charming his initial concession about his faults may be, Abbey makes clear that we risk being insulted. We might be disposed to like him, to sympathize with his love for the desert, to accept the wide swings in his prose between the lyrical and the angry, but if we continue to read him, we must face perhaps unsavory surprises, ones that keep us from being un-conditionally his followers. Abbey does not want our simplistic agreement. The fact that he apologizes for being rude and bad-tempered does not make him hesitate in the following sentence to point out with a disrespect bordering on loathing that "serious" readers are not ones that he cares to cultivate. He names critics, librarians, and professors in this affront, so we suspect that he is targeting the professionally serious—those who believe they produce important ideas for the rest of us. However, we are still painfully aware that we ourselves are or know folks who are those serious professionals. If we can bear the insult, Abbey gives us ambiguous com-fort; he explains that a thing may be wrong and right at the same time, leaving it to us to understand that his unqualified condemnation of serious readers is wrong insofar as it is comprehensive and is right in that it scorns self-important seriousness.[40]

40. Readers and critics have long grappled with this Edward Abbey, who is as easy to love as he is to hate. There are those who, like Diane Wakoski ("Joining the Visionary 'Inhumanists' "), ignore his rude, inflammatory, and sexist characteristics in order to benefit from what they value in his work. Others express their anger and outrage. Still others, also angry, try to understand how that reaction suits Abbey and stands in rela-tion to their more positive reactions to him. Luis Alberto Urrea is one of these disen-

In the same way that Abbey keeps us from wholly trusting him as a writer, he levels an ironic tongue at his own effort to be graceful as a writer. In the introduction to *The Journey Home*, he tells why he is not a part of nature writing.

> Much as I admire the work of Thoreau, Muir, Leopold, Beston, Krutch, Eiseley and others, I have not tried to write in their tradition. I don't know how. I've done plenty of plain living, out of necessity, but don't know how to maintain a constant level of high thinking. It's beyond me. Some itch in the lower parts is always dragging me back to mundane earth, down to my own level, among all you other common denominators out there in the howling wilderness we call modern American life (xii).

Characteristically, neither his praise nor his self-deprecation stand without their equal and opposite truth. We suspect immediately that "a constant level of high thinking" is probably not a sufficient goal. Those who can do it, whom he lists appreciatively, may be missing a more prosaic reality. Rather than bemoan his failure to uphold the elevated style of nature writers, Abbey enjoys a bawdy escape, choosing to rebel from it by speaking of scratching in public and thus remaining in the material world where most other folks are. He has fun with the whole rarefied issue of classification by claiming not to be a specialist. He opens this introduction on that theme: "I am not a naturalist. I never was and never will be a naturalist. I'm not even sure what a naturalist is except that I'm not one. I'm not even an amateur naturalist. The only Latin I know is *omnia vincit amor*—and *in vino veritas*" (xi).

Far from attempting grace or the serious tone of one who is, in his essays, calling seriously for the preservation of the American West, Abbey takes an almost petulantly naughty tone. And he maintains it, stepping deliberately into as many forbidden spots as possible: He does not wish to be followed, which is why he makes such a fuss over the fact that he is not a naturalist. Describing his "nature books"—*Desert Solitaire* and the texts he wrote for three scenic landscape volumes[41]—he prevaricates,

---

chanted admirers. His "Down the Highway with Edward Abbey" compromises neither his outrage at Abbey's cultural bigotry nor his admiration for the writer's passion and causes. His indictment of writers as "happy hypocrites" (41) includes himself in Abbey's company, which is the way he has found to reconcile himself with Abbey.

41. These include *Appalachian Wilderness*, *Slickrock*, and *Cactus Country*, followed by *The Hidden Canyon* and *Desert Images*.

All the technical information was stolen from reliable sources and I am happy to stand behind it. But as people who may have read them should know, those four books are in the main simple narrative accounts of travel and adventure, with philosophical commentary added here and there to give the prose a high-toned surface gleam. They have little to do with biological science (xiii).

Poking fun at the assumed authority of his voice in those books, Abbey goes on to ruffle more dander.

For I am not a naturalist. Hardly even a sportsman. True, I bagged my first robin at the age of seven, with a BB gun back on the farm in Home, Pennsylvania, but the only birds I can recognize without hesitation are the turkey-vulture, the fried chicken, and the rosy-bottomed skinny-dipper (xiii).

He tries out all the politically incorrect moves he can, bragging about his precocious start in hunting (the beloved robin as his target), flaunting his unsophisticated upbringing ("back on the farm" where he had a BB gun and got a taste for fried chicken), and speaking with sexual glee about his eye for "the rosy-bottomed skinny-dipper." Abbey chooses to be frank so that he can clear us off his trail, for who would—according to his implicit logic—want to be as crude, sexist, and insensitive as this writer? Certainly a reader who suffers Abbey's banal jocularity would neither have the desire to call him a naturalist nor include him among the ranks of esteemed nature writers. Using such a strategy to reinforce his declared claim to be writing mostly "personal history" (xiii), Abbey pulls free of the debate and, with it settled, concludes *The Journey Home* introduction with a celebratory verbal rollick.

Final note. If certain ideas and emotions are expressed in these pages with what seems an extreme intransigence, it is not merely because I love an argument and wish to provoke (though I do), but because I am—really am—an extremist, one who lives and loves by choice far out on the very verge of things, on the edge of the abyss where this world falls off into the depths of another. That's the way I like it (xiv).

Abbey likes the precarious edge where he thrills and offends his audience for the same reason that he is a comic: because from that vantage point he has the contradictory contour of things in front of him. It forces him to stay aware of his dual urges to be both the idealist and the realist, and though he remains in a painfully exposed position there, he can brag about it and play. He is humorous, for example, about his life as a writer, whence most of his opportunity for extremism issues. In the introduction to *Abbey's Road*, "Confessions of a Literary Hobo," he points out that writers hide behind their literary creations: "Writers are shameless liars. In fact, we pride ourselves on the subtlety and grandeur of our lies" (xv). Forever confessional and forever eluding critics, Abbey tells James Hepworth at the start of an interview in 1977, "I'm not responsible for anything I'm about to say" ("The Poetry Center Interview" 50); he goes on to talk about his favorite authors, his books, and his persona as a writer.

> I'm dimly aware of some sort of mythical Edward Abbey, but I don't take him seriously, don't attempt to live up to it. I'm surprised that anyone would ever want to meet me because I don't live up to the characters in my books, don't try to. It sometimes seems to me that the Edward Abbey who writes these articles and books and so on is just another fictional creation, not much resemblance to the real one, to the one I think I know. The real Edward Abbey—whoever the hell that is—is a real shy, timid fellow, but the character I create in my journalism is perhaps a person I would like to be: bold, brash, daring. I created this character, and I gave him my name. I guess some people mistake the creation for the author, but that's their problem (60).

Much of his bravery in standing on "the edge of the abyss" comes from his choice to be there as a writer. As that person, he can face dreadful facts with good humor. He can write that we should have hope for the disappearing wilderness: "That world can still be rescued. That is one reason why I myself am still willing to write about it. That is my main excuse for this book" (*Abbey's Road* xxi). He can make light of how his old girlfriends fail to write him: "Even former wives—women I was legally and solemnly married to—never write directly, keeping in touch with me only through their attorneys and the occasional sheriff's deputy bearing important documents" (xv). As a writer, he can be the brave Edward Abbey whose life is funny and whose ideal world is possible.

However far Abbey distances himself from his persona, he has claimed repeatedly that, in his essays and journalism, he is writing personal history. In *A Voice Crying in the Wilderness*, he asserts, "I am myself the substance of

my book. There is no reason why you should waste your leisure on so friv-
olous and unrewarding a subject" (xiv). In *Pioneer Conservationists of
Western America*, Peter Wild concurs that Abbey makes his life the subject
for his books, dovetailing the Romantic tradition (189). Further discoursing
on Abbey's character, Wild writes, "Frequently, it isn't clear where Abbey
the disgruntled idealist ends and Abbey the leg-pulling mischief begins. It
may be that Abbey himself doesn't know—and doesn't care" (187). It may
be instead that there is no good reason to divide the man by such roles, for
the one is necessary to the other. It is unlikely that he could maintain his
idealism without humor to buoy it, and his humor depends on idealism to
blaze new perspectives on contemporary life. Wild further claims that the
writer is defending what he loves for his own sake, not society's (188). The
literary outlaw is indeed an individualist, first set to shake things up,
changing opinion and saving himself. Abbey's purposes and perversity inspire Wendell Berry to a recognition unparalleled among critics of the
man's personal complexity. In "A Few Words in Favor of Edward Abbey,"
he addresses the "problem" of Ed Abbey.

> The problem, evidently, is that he will not stay in line. No sooner has a
> label been stuck to his back by a somewhat hesitant well-wisher than he
> runs beneath a low limb and scrapes it off. To the consternation of the
> "committed" reviewer, he is not a conservationist or an environmental-
> ist or a boxable ist of any other kind; he keeps on showing up as Edward
> Abbey, a horse of another color, and one that requires some care to ap-
> preciate (*What Are People For?* 36).

Not to be deterred by Abbey's unpredictability, Berry honors him with the
attention and care that he says are required to get the full benefit of his fellow writer's work. He demonstrates the manner of that care by doing a
reading of "problem" passages. For one he chooses this statement of
Abbey's in the introduction to *Down the River*: "None of the essays in this
book requires elucidation, other than to say, as in everything I write, they
are meant to serve as antidotes to despair. Despair leads to boredom, elec-
tronic games, computer hacking, poetry, and other bad habits" (3). Berry, a
poet himself, has some trouble handling the parity of poetry with computer play—and greater trouble with the idea that poetry is a bad habit.
But Berry probes beyond his initial disinclination to the statement, saying—"*Am* I, then, a defender of 'poetry'? The answer, inevitably, is no; I am
a defender of *some poems*. Any human product or activity that humans de-

fend as a category becomes, by that very fact, a sacred cow—in need, by the same fact, of an occasional goosing" (*What Are People For?* 42). Through this analysis, Berry gives us an example of the kind of energy we ought to muster in order to deal with Abbey's often insulting remarks; he also suggests that we keep a sense of humor in digesting what Abbey says, since he, like any other person, "is not always right or always fair," in Berry's words (41).

Berry's understanding of Abbey's position as a literary outlaw is acute and gracious. He explains why Abbey, though "advertised as an environmentalist" (39), is not one.

> If Mr. Abbey is not an environmentalist, what is he? He is, I think, at least in the essays, an autobiographer. He may be writing on one or another of what are now called environmental issues, but he remains Edward Abbey, speaking as and for himself, fighting, literally, for dear life. This is important, for if he is writing as an autobiographer, he *cannot* be writing as an environmentalist—or as a special ist of any other kind. As an autobiographer, his work is self-defense; as a conservationist, it is to conserve himself as a human being. But this is self-defense and self-conservation of the largest and noblest kind, for Mr. Abbey understands that to defend and conserve oneself as a human being in the fullest, truest sense, one must defend and conserve many others and much else (39–40).

Above all, Abbey conserves his sense of humor, which he maintains by dishing it into every topic he pursues. There is humor in his recollections of childhood, when he and his brother lugged their father's cement-mixing wooden box to the creek for their first float trip: "We clung to the gunwales as our scow sank, peacefully and immediately to the bottom of the creek, leaving us sitting in water up to our necks" (*Down the River* 2). There is humor in his acknowledgment, "Environmental journalism is not a cheerful field of work" (6), particularly since he defies that statement, writing a friend, "'Be of good cheer, the military-industrial state will soon collapse'" (4). And, there is humor in his tolerance for the bitter responses he gets to his environmental opinions. He prints a selection of them in *Down the River* and remarks, "I have dozens of such communications in my treasured file of nasty letters, some on heavyweight corporation stationery, many unprintable in a decent book meant for family reading . . ." (7).

Humor is an "antidote to despair," as Abbey claims his writing is: it has helped him cleave his emotion to his intellect and to his convictions and thus be whole as an autobiographer (in Berry's sense of the word) who knows that he belongs to a world greater than himself. What Abbey chooses to defend in conserving the self may be different than what Berry would choose in the same effort. One believes that Berry would be domestic, polite, and rather ceremonious. Abbey the outlaw insists on his opportunity to be wild, whether to insult others or to be risque in forwarding serious opinions, such as the following statement: "The defense of wildlife is a moral issue. All beings are created equal, I say. All are endowed by their Creator (call that God or call it evolution) with certain inalienable rights; among these rights are life, liberty and the pursuit—each in its own way—of reproductive happiness" (*Beyond the Wall* 39). It may be difficult at first to believe that he is defending "many others" until we remember that the nonhuman figures among them. The huge difference in the style and taste of the two writers enhances their common certainty that their homes are larger than the confines of their intellect or their house.

Although humor gives Abbey a way to undermine the rich, pompous, and greedy (and all those parts of techno-industrial culture he abhors), it plays a more meaningful function in his thought than that of a weapon. Humor has influenced his style of perception, making it comic from the outset so that he perceives things with an eye elevated enough to pick up patterns of congruity, dissonance, and absurdity and an eye also on himself, to see where he fits in or disrupts the pattern. Abbey's comic outlook means that he is skilled at seeing connections and bringing the results close to home. Who else but Abbey would quote Heraclitus as saying, "Dat ol' man river, he jus' keeps rollin' along…" (*Down the River* 3)? The Greek philosopher's koan that you cannot step in the same river twice is enlightened, and Abbey appreciates its wisdom, seeing the same wisdom in the Negro spiritual whose words he has dubbed over those of Heraclitus. The anachronistic result is partly a breach of respect because it puts a hallowed Greek philosopher on a plain with anonymous black slaves. But Abbey more importantly is bringing us home to see what philosophical and spiritual profundities can arise from native soil. Besides that, he plays the lip-sync trick with Heraclitus because his book *Down the River* is about rivers, and the point that we cannot go into the same river twice is exactly why he wants to try it. The river is always arriving in the continuing course of water, and as such, it reminds us that we are new people every time we return to a river: we are reborn into it. Hankering for new float trips, Abbey shows he has acquired a taste for this sort of pagan resurrection.

Resurrection is a theme that Abbey appeals to repeatedly. It provides a structure for registering despair and hope, so it is well-suited to the romantic realist—to the lover who might be doomed were it not for a sense of humor that allows him to see his way out of trouble, or, more broadly, to see the wilderness come up from a nose dive and out of its trouble. The resurrection theme can be applied with seriousness or with a flippancy that Abbey finds appropriate, for example, to the story of his most famous book's arrival to the public. With melodramatic emphasis, he writes, "on a dark night in a back alley in the dead of winter, *Solitaire* was released from its cage and turned loose upon an unsuspecting public" (*Beyond the Wall* xiii). Abbey has set the new book up for a quiet sweep down to the nadir of success. "The publisher let the first edition go out of print, and within a year my little book had died a natural death. Not surprised, I found myself a job as a fire lookout on North Rim, Grand Canyon, and continued working for a living" (xiii). But the story of *Desert Solitaire* had only lapsed; the book's "death" was not irrevocable. He continues:

> Three years later, however, *Desert Solitaire* was exhumed and resurrected in paperback, in which form it has enjoyed a modest but persistent life, burrowing along from year to year about two feet underground like a blind and seditious mole. I haven't had to turn my hand to an honest day's work since 1972 (xiii).

Most importantly in this comic biography of the book is Abbey's portrayal of it as a wild thing—a creature.[42] It was uncaged, it died, it returned to life, and now it perseveres in a humble but tenacious existence. The plot offers a template for the course of events in other matters, also described in the introduction to *Beyond the Wall*:

> About 98 per cent of the land surface of the contiguous USA already belongs to heavy metal and heavy equipment. Let us save the 2 per cent— that saving remnant. Or better yet, expand, recover, and reclaim much more of the original American wilderness. About 50 per cent would be a fair and reasonable compromise (xv).

With a casual reclaiming of the word *reasonable* for the cause of conservation (always condemned as "unreasonable" for its quarrel with economic

---

42. Similarly, Abbey speaks of *A Voice Crying in the Wilderness* as having "emerge[d] from its shell" in being published (ix).

growth), Abbey suggests that we resurrect the wilderness. That which has gone under, he implies, may still come back. After all, his appeal is patriotic as well as conservationist: "Open space was the fundamental heritage of America; the freedom of the wilderness may well be the central purpose of our national adventure" (xv).[43] His intention is to resurrect in us a kind of pioneer spirit in relation to the land—this one focused on conserving rather than consuming it. "We need no more words on the matter. What we need now are heroes. And heroines. About a million of them. One brave deed is worth a thousand books. Sentiment without action is the ruin of the soul" (xvi).

If resurrection suggests to Abbey a plot for a last-ditch effort to save the wilderness, it shows his desire for an ecologically comic world, not utopian escapism or longing for other-worldly existence. He insists passionately that we have no more profound reality than the physical world of nature. *Desert Solitaire*:

> A weird, lovely, fantastic object out of nature like Delicate Arch has the curious ability to remind us—like rock and sunlight and wind and wilderness—that *out there* is a different world, older and greater and deeper by far than ours, a world which surrounds and sustains the little world of men as sea and sky surround and sustain a ship. The shock of the real (41–2).

Even in an intellectual pursuit like writing, his commitments remain with that material world and our reactions to it. In fact, in the introduction to *The Best of Edward Abbey*, he accounts for his career as the outcome of his emotions:

> [W]hich is not and never was a career anyway, but rather a passion. A *passion!* Fueled in equal parts by anger and love. How can you feel one without the other? Each implies the other. A writer without passion is like a body without a soul. Or even more grotesque, like a soul without a body (xiii).

Abbey is not one to love an idea or an abstraction. He prioritizes body above soul, for he distrusts spirituality not embodied, philosophy not grounded, convictions not acted upon. His opinion of writers turns harsh

43. James Hepworth lauds him as "a great patriot" ("*Canis Lupus Amorus Lunaticum*" 134).

when he suspects they are contriving subjects rather than writing with the kind of heart that has faced "the shock of the real": "you do not have to write endless disquisitions about suburban hanky panky, Toyota dealers, self-hating intellectuals, male mutilation, lesbians in bearskins, to live and live happily as a writer in America, God bless her" (xiii). He has no patience for the gawking of civilization at itself, that big-screen reproduction of the narcissistic, self-interested individual. To be real, in Abbey's estimation (and to be a decent writer), we must be in relation to a larger, preferably nonhuman world. The ticket to that ecological household lies in each of our bodies, for he counsels "to have faith in the evidence of your senses" (xiv). He has further hope for the writer in America.

> You do not even need to be psychoanalyzed, Rolfed, estered, altered, gelded, neutered, spayed, fixed, Mooned, acupunctured, meditated, Zenned, massaged, Cayced, yogied, New Aged, astrocharted, holisticized, computerized, megatrended, therapized, androgynized, evangelized, converted, or even, last and least, to be reborn. One life at a time, please (xiii-xiv).

Abbey strives for a resurrection of our consciousness that will put us back down into our ordinary, sexual bodies, where we can be alert to the physical world around us. He realizes that not everyone will want to take the jolt that characterizes his delivery, but since that jolt is very much a part of changing our habits of perception, he does not hold back. And he is not above making a parting verbal shot, which is how the introduction to *One Life at a Time, Please* ends: "Very well. If there's anyone still present whom I've failed to insult, I apologize. Cheers!" (5).

ABBEY IS CONSISTENTLY THE PURVEYOR OF LIMITS, A RESTLESS SOUL, A questioner, an extremist, and a romantic committed to practical and material reality. Although it is far from fatuous to call him a trickster, it is almost too easy. As a writer, he lives up to that description in countless ways, executing, among other things, a kind of verbal feint intended to surprise and shock us. Take this example from *The Journey Home*:

> For example, I enjoy climbing the local mountains, scaling the most hideous bare rock pitches step by step, hand by hand, without aids, without rope or partners, clinging to fragments of loose shale, a clump

of bear grass, the edge of an overhanging snow cornice, above a night-marish abyss, picking a route toward even higher and more precarious perches—through these U.S. Navy 7x50 lenses. The effortless, angelic, and supine approach to danger (33–4).

Abbey is lightly mocking himself for not being the daring mountaineer that he has the opportunity to be, employed as a fire lookout in Glacier National Park on Numa Ridge. Instead of such exploring, he verbally dreams of heroism and then pops that bubble for both himself and us. His trickery is unique because he flaunts it, foregrounding the feint: he has explained that his wife and he keep busy with chores, reading, and "just gazing at the world through binoculars" (33). With that he plunges into the previous passage, absorbing us in details of his various (imagined) ascents and so pulling off the sleight of hand in front of us. We are surprised back into knowing what he had told us in the first place. This may be a cocky move on his part, but it carries with it the understanding that we can be tricked or shocked even by what we know and see. Nature is often the supreme trickster, in Abbey's estimation. He notes that he and his wife see a golden eagle flying "*below us*, pursued by—a sparrow hawk?" (33). He cannot believe his eyes, and, though he wants us to trust our senses, he makes that difficult, repeatedly leading us out by one series of observations to a point where he reverses direction and leaves us gaping. It is faulty predication transmogrified as adventure thriller and performed with perfect grammar. Further discussing their occupations at the fire lookout, he writes, "Striving to uphold the natural superiority of the male, I have beaten my wife—at chess—five games straight. Now she refuses to play with me. You can't win" (33). And you cannot easily get away with talk like that in the supposedly liberated end of the twentieth century. Abbey does not intend to. He means to get in trouble—and get out of it, or at least to dangle himself on that edge where he might fall either way.

We suspect that he will land on the run regardless of where he falls. In her eulogy for Edward Abbey, Terry Tempest Williams romanticizes the writer directly into the Coyote tradition: "The canyons of southern Utah are giving birth to the Coyote Clan—hundreds, maybe even thousands of individuals who are quietly subversive on behalf of the land" (202). She calls this clan passionate, "raucous," and "serene" (203), and she expects us to see that these are Abbey's progeny, Abbey the quintessential Coyote. The correlation makes good sense. His writing has the lusty, outrageous, foolish, heroic, and rebellious characteristics that generate Coyote's fine infamy. Abbey seems to enjoy making the kind of trouble that gives people a chance to see their own limits and the nature of their opinions. By blasting aside punctilious (or even just careful) behavior and speech, Abbey shows that there is a different and wilder—though not always right—way to be. Also from Williams' eulogy: "Members of the Clan court risk and will dance on slickrock as flashfloods erode the ground beneath their feet. It doesn't matter. They understand the earth re-creates itself day after day . . ." (203). Why Abbey plays the fool and skillful trickster is partly linked to that faith in the capacity of the earth to get itself in trouble and then come out okay. Not only does Abbey want to show that we can be more free than we usually are—less confined by the strictures of a society that has proven itself to be destructive, wasteful, and greedy—but he also wants to recreate the survival plot of the ecological household. He wants to reassure himself that it is possible for earth that has been mined, logged, polluted, developed, and disrespected to persevere, recover, and flourish—possible also for a writer to be outrageous and crude, reviled and ignored by critics, and still manage to enjoy a happy and successful life as a writer. In all his dangling from the edge (which he does imaginatively, we have learned, at a distance provided either by binoculars or by his pen), he is practicing the nerve it takes to face the horrific facts of the destruction of the earth. His humor is essential to his nerve.[44]

Not always in the same essay does Abbey's outlandish humor appear with his courage. Nevertheless, humor cleaves to him, reinforcing him whether or not he is outwardly funny. In an essay with a modicum of humor, like "The Damnation of a Canyon" in *Beyond the Wall*, we can discern the comic moves that he makes in arguing rationally and, indeed, solemnly that the Colorado River ought to run free. His sense of humor is strong enough to support his idealistic hopes even in the face of environmental tragedy—the damming of the Colorado. The fate of the Glen Canyon Dam in particular is not an issue that Abbey takes lightly: it reveals the anger he feels over the destruction of wild land and the faith he

---

44. Abbey's character Jack Burns displays that nerve in the novel *Good News* when on horseback he approaches the heavily guarded inner-sanctum of a military state. Burns responds smilingly to the malicious scrutiny of the guards, who want to know what his business is with the high-ranking officer (his son) he has requested to see—Burns says, " 'Well—social. This is a social visit' " (146). Such incongruity! The old man has come visiting in the most hostile and inhospitable of places. He knows that a polite call is not appropriate and, in fact, ludicrous, but he tries it in case he can surprise the guards into better behavior. Humor gives him the nerve and the means to search for his wayward son.

has that nature will prevail regardless of human machinations. He starts with a nostalgic and lyrical appeal: "There was a time, when, in my search for essences, I concluded that the canyonland country has no heart. I was wrong. The canyonlands did have a heart, a living heart, and that heart was Glen Canyon and the golden, flowing Colorado River" (95). Abbey our speaker has introduced himself as a fallible, inquisitive, and sensitive person, one who has a particular passion for the canyonlands, and one who could be trusted to speak honestly. In that brief introductory paragraph, he uses the word *heart* four times, first in denial that the canyons could have a heart, then in discovery and celebration that they do, and finally in sorrow that that heart has been lost. In effect, he summarizes the issue with astounding concision and emotional force that orient us sympathetically in agreement with him. And if we thought we could trust this earnest, candid speaker from the start, he immediately gives us further reason to, pointing out the experiences he has had rafting down the Colorado (before the dam) and working as a park ranger in Glen Canyon National Recreation Area (after the dam). He sums up that experience with a piquant and reasonable tone: "Having thus seen Glen Canyon both before and after what we may fairly call its damnation, I feel that I am in a position to evaluate the transformation of the region caused by construction of the dam" (96). Damnation. At play with words, Abbey is set to lambaste as a sacrilege the destruction of this beautiful and wild place. The implication is that this canyon and river are more than the heart of that area—they are holy.

Abbey next provides a humorous accounting of himself, which is meant to accept and dismiss criticism of his politics and focus this argument on the material evidence.

> One should admit at the outset to a certain bias. Indeed I am a "butterfly chaser, googly eyed bleeding heart and wild conservative." I take a dim view of dams; I find it hard to learn to love cement; I am poorly impressed by concrete aggregates and statistics in the cubic tons (96).

Abbey advances our initial trust in him again by making a confession, this time about his "certain bias." Note that his colorful march into the phrase "bleeding heart liberal" (embellished by "googly eyed" and "butterfly chaser") is reversed suddenly by the exchange of "wild conservative" for the expected "liberal." This comic twist expresses Abbey's opinion that it is fundamentally conservative to love the earth, respect it, and oppose the developments that waste it. Abbey claims that a great many Americans share his bias, though he has seemed to apologize for that boldness, calling his opinion a "weakness."

> But in this weakness I am not alone, for I belong to that ever-growing number of Americans, probably a good majority now, who have become aware that a fully industrialized, thoroughly urbanized, elegantly computerized social system is not suitable for human habitation. Great for machines, yes. But unfit for people (96).

Abbey undoubtedly is flouting popular opinion to assert that twentieth-century progress is actually a disgrace, but he makes that claim as if he trusts his rhetoric to wake up and change even the staunchest supporter of industrial and technological development. This is a fine trick! He calls his bias a weakness to appear harmlessly deferential; simultaneously, he conscripts us to rebel with him and be among those unable to "love cement" or the industrial world it supports. His full persuasive powers include the marshaling of facts to convince us that we do agree with him—that the Glen Canyon Dam is a travesty.[45]

To oppose a dam that has already been built may seem like a useless gesture; but Abbey retains the humor to imagine otherwise, to think of the massive dam as just a big Army Corps of Engineers mistake—and reversible—and to regale us with descriptions of the canyon before its damnation. He has not given up the hope that the canyonland can return to a state of wild grace. Abbey's idealism is founded on the ecological potential of the place. Being hopeful that we too might acquire his comic spirit, he shows us the situation as he sees it, saying that Glen Canyon was as different from Lake Powell, the impoundment caused by the dam, as life is from death. From the "bathtub ring" left by fluctuating water levels to the lack of plant and animal life at the shoreline, all the signs show that Lake Powell is no lake, just a "man-made impoundment," a "graveyard" (98). He expects we shall side with life, though that means choosing a canyon

---

45. In *The Hidden Canyon*, Abbey gives this subject his full emotional energy: "Thinking about the dam, I feel a renewal of the wholesome murderous rage that has enlivened my river thoughts for the last sixteen years. Those bloody swine, I'm thinking. Those servile technicians, those corrupt and evil Utah-Arizona politicians, those greed-crazed hogs from the construction companies, those goons and gangsters who boss the unions. We're going to get their stinking dam. We've got secret plans. . . ." (31). Abbey centered his novel *The Monkey-Wrench Gang* around a scheme to blow up the dam.

that is, in large part, gone. This is an irrational step, maybe, but Abbey is persuasive with his descriptions and we end up with his nerve, imagining away the massive Glen Canyon Dam in order to return to the canyon.

> Within a generation—thirty years—I predict the river and canyons will bear a decent resemblance to their former selves. Within the lifetime of our children Glen Canyon and the living river, heart of the canyonlands, will be restored to us. The wilderness will again belong to God, the people and the wild things that call it home (103).

Abbey also claims that democracy is better served without the dam, an argument that butts up directly against the dam's proponents, who say that more people can enjoy Lake Powell than could ever make a float trip through Glen Canyon. They say that recreation is now more accessible, as are sights like Rainbow Bridge, previously reached by a six-mile hike and now within range of a motorboat. Abbey is incensed by such logic: "This argument appeals to the wheelchair ethos of the wealthy, upper-middle-class American slob" (99). As vicious as his rebuttal may be, the accuracy in describing reliance on mechanization as a "wheelchair ethos" is witty: it redefines privilege as debility. And he makes the "privilege" of easy access seem ugly—"if Pikes Peak is worth getting to, then why not build a highway to the top of it so that anyone can get there? Anytime? Without effort?" (99). His delivery suggests that it would be appalling; in truth, we need places that require us to expend ourselves—using bodily and spiritual energy—not just the money from our pockets. Accomplishments entail effort, Abbey's logic goes, and, using that logic, we can see that a trip to Rainbow Bridge via motorboat bypasses the personal effort that makes it a fantastic event rather than a purchased visual souvenir. Furthermore, privilege requires a lot of money—a motorized tour of the reservoir is much more costly than a walk or a float trip. Thus the wealthy are served, Abbey argues, and the ordinary people are shut out. He insists that Glen Canyon is less accessible now.

> Because of the dam the river is gone, the inner canyon is gone, the best parts of the numerous side canyons are gone—all hidden beneath hundreds of feet of polluted water, accumulating silt, and mounting tons of trash. This portion of Glen Canyon—and who can estimate how many cubic miles were lost?—*is no longer accessible to anybody.* (Except scuba

divers.) And this, do not forget, was the most valuable part of Glen Canyon, richest in scenery, archaeology, history, flora and fauna (100).

The "defenders of the dam" (99) might say you can get to more places because of the reservoir, but Abbey counters that now there are *fewer places to visit*. He emphasizes this twist with the comic aside that scuba divers can still access the flooded canyon; Abbey marginalizes the population to whom the canyon is more accessible, for scuba divers were not whom the advocates of the dam had in mind. His final dose of wry humor serves to highlight a most repulsive result of privileging houseboats with access to the lake: the worst of the wastes collecting in the stagnant waters is human sewage. Abbey ironically uses the lake's official sobriquet in describing how ugly the scene could become:

> It will take a while, but long before it becomes a solid mass of mud, Lake Powell ("Jewel of the Colorado") will enjoy a passing fame as the biggest sewage lagoon in the American Southwest. Most tourists will never be able to afford a boat trip on this reservoir, but everybody within fifty miles will be able to smell it (102).

With its "accessibility" inflated to horrific olfactory proportions, no one would want to visit the Glen Canyon Dam. The fetid result of our quest for "clean" electricity is comic justice, and Abbey advertises it as such, for he wants us to realize fully how we have dammed and damned Glen Canyon. Should we, as he proposes to do, drain the reservoir, the extent of the damnation would be clear.

> This will no doubt expose a drear and hideous scene: immense mud flats and whole plateaus of sodden garbage strewn with dead trees, sunken boats, the skeletons of long-forgotten, decomposing water-skiers. But to those who find the prospect too appalling, I say give nature a little time (103).

He, at least, is hopeful.[46] He can imagine the resurrection of the wild canyon and its river. He had the faith to assume our fraternity with him in

46. Currently, there is evidence to believe that his hope has spread. Thirty-five years after the construction of Glen Canyon Dam, the Sierra Club, the National Audubon Society, and other environmental groups are backing a proposal by the Glen Canyon

choosing life over Lake Powell. He had the good humor to risk making serious social criticism, to be funny despite tragic circumstances, and to use
comic skill to ground his idealism.

At the same time that humor helps Abbey escape despair, it keeps his
readers alert, showing us a way to enjoy wildness, despite anguishing over
the loss of wild country. In "Floating" in *Down the River*, Abbey relies on
humor more extensively than he does in "The Damnation of a Canyon" in
Beyond the Wall; he torques up the level of despair along with the humor,
and his philosophical tone is equaled by slapstick comedy. He begins,
"Each precious moment entails every other. Each sacred place suggests the
immanent presence of all places. Each man, each woman, exemplifies all
humans" (*Down the River* 230). Feeling expansive and fraternal, Abbey is
inclined to universalize—projecting from his trip down Rio Dolores in
Colorado to everything else, which is the nebulous point from where he
starts back, questioning his route.

> What am I trying to say? The same as before—everything. Nothing
> more than that. Everything implied by water, motion, rivers, boats. By
> the flowing . . .
>
> What the hell. Here we go again, down one more condemned river.
> Our foolish rubber rafts nose into the channel . . .(230)

The questions he cannot answer he abandons in favor of returning to the
present reality, in this case the river; in the introduction to *Desert Solitaire*,
that reality is the physical presence of the book itself, which he says can be
used as a weapon. Abbey's capacity for extremes is enabled by his humor,
for it seeks out concrete realities when he cannot fathom the conclusion of
his own meandering thought.

If everything in the universe is hitched to everything else, to paraphrase
John Muir, Abbey bears that load consciously.

> Every river I touch turns to heartbreak. Floating down a portion of Rio
> Colorado in Utah on a rare month in spring, twenty-two years ago, a
> friend and I found ourselves passing through a world so beautiful it
> seemed and had to be—eternal. Such perfection of being, we thought—
> these glens of sandstone, these winding corridors of mystery, leading

---

Institute to dismantle the dam and drain Lake Powell, which has gained notoriety as a
huge mistake. This issue is part of a world-wide reevaluation of big dam projects, according to a recent article in the *Utne Reader* (McNamee 20–21).

each to its solitary revelation—could not possibly be changed. The philosophers and the theologians have agreed, for three thousand years, that the perfect is immutable—that which cannot alter and cannot be altered. They were wrong. We were wrong. Glen Canyon was destroyed. Everything changes, and nothing is more vulnerable than the beautiful (231).

Abbey wants the real and romantic beauty of a world he cannot have, a world where he finds the promise of meaning bound to mystery. He wants that world because it is satisfying and complete and unending. Instead he is forced onto grim facts, the destruction of a canyon and the collapse of his faith in the power of perfection. The world that is all hitched together includes facts we might rather ignore. Abbey will not ignore them, but to have the courage still to embrace the immensely complicated world, he must make a comic recovery. The passage continues:

> Why yes, the Dolores, too, is scheduled for damnation. Only a little dam, say the politicians, one little earth-fill dam to irrigate the sorghum and alfalfa plantations, and then, most likely, to supply the industrial parks and syn-fuel factories of Cortez, Shithead Capital of Dipstick County, Colorado. True, only a little dam. But dammit, it's only a little river (231).

This news about the proposed dam stays his philosophizing and swings him into the rhetorical gear—humor—that helps him cope with trouble and ultimately return to an ideal world. This time the humor is bitter, deriding the intended use of the dam and the population it is meant to serve. In *The New West of Edward Abbey*, Ann Ronald says that all Abbey's work falls out in pursuit of an ideal world, since Abbey is a romancer. In her words, the romancer is one who "calls into question the ethical, social, and moral assumptions of his age. The resulting exorcism of values, conceived in idealism but processed as revolt, fulfills for him his need to re-hammer the unmalleable world in which he lives" (18). Abbey revolts against the "plantations" of sorghum and alfalfa that are the undertaking of agribusiness, out of scale, entirely inappropriate to arid land; as for industrial development, he gives it a crude assessment, his vulgarity itself suggesting the failure of such progress to improve us or our world. The revolt that Ronald says is the romancer's "exorcism of values" is for Abbey typically embedded in humor, for humor allows him to express anger without being seduced by his rage. Humor can be both quickly employed and abandoned.

Abbey wants to return to the better—wilder and freer—world rather than spend all his effort attacking or counterattacking the techno-industrial world: Humor is the trademark of his skill to be that revolutionary homebody. The passage about the damming of the Rio Dolores breaks off with Abbey's call to himself to return to his place on the river, momentarily beyond politics or bitterness: "Forget it. Write it off. Fix your mind on the feel of the oars in your hands . . ." (231).

The meanderings on this river have just begun, and in recounting them Abbey conflates the ride and his politics:

> Women and rivers. Rivers and men. Boys and girls against United Power & Gas. Concentrating too hard, I miss the snag but pivot off the submerged rock beyond, turning my boat backward into the rapids. My two passengers look anxious—
> "For godsake, Ed, didn't you see that rock?"
> "What rock?" (232)

That dreamy boatman, Ed Abbey, has been thinking again. It is sure to get him in trouble, we see, as he repeatedly careens off rocks in that river. His mind is launched toward other dangers, like the impossible fight represented by "Boys and girls against United Power & Gas." Surely, corporate industrial power could be opposed, Abbey hopes dimly, descending from that dismal prospect and that dangerous rock to pure foolishness—and the next rock.

> —but I have no fear. Hardly know the meaning of the word. God will carry us through. God loves fools, finds a need for us, how otherwise could we survive? Through all the perilous millennia? Fools, little children, drunks, and concupiscent scriveners play a useful function, its precise nature not yet determined, in the intricate operations of evolution. Furthermore, I reflect—
> "Watch out!" (232)

Abbey the writer is having fun here, showing that his thinking, seen in his persona Ed, is not always aimed at useful ends. Occasionally, it is joyful creative blather. Besides his self-critique, Abbey is using this foolishness for comic relief from his dark thoughts about the futility of fighting power companies (the kind that want to make dams on free-flowing rivers). He knows he may be a fool for opposing the industrial economy—as much as for being an oblivious oarsman—and so he chooses gleefully to accept and whimsically defend that reputation, claiming justification under God and evolution. His affectionate list of the folks included with him as apparently useless people is quixotic, defying consistency. He puts little children together with fools and drunks and then adds "concupiscent scriveners" to confound the logic further: he pretends to defend them essentially by offering no defense at all, instead bandying about obfuscating language concerning the "precise nature" of their function.[47] Distracted in this manner by his own wayward thought, Abbey the boatman cruises down the Dolores to the punctuating cries of his passengers. This comedy is driven primarily by pleasure, Abbey playing the float trip and the pondering off of each other in counterpoint plots united by their unpredictability and wildness.

Abbey raises the stakes by moving beyond rivers in his disquisition about the places of our recreation. He asks, "But where is home?"

Surely not the walled-in prison of the cities, under that low ceiling of carbon monoxide and nitrogen oxides and acid rain—the leaky malaise of an overdeveloped, overcrowded, self-destroying civilization—where most people are compelled to serve their time and please the wardens if they can. For many, for more and more of us, the out-of-doors is our true ancestral estate. For a mere five thousand years we have grubbed in the soil and laid brick upon brick to build the cities; but for a million years before that we lived the leisurely, free, and adventurous life of hunters and gatherers, warriors and tamers of horses. How can we pluck that deep root of feeling from the racial consciousness? Impossible. When in doubt, jump out (237).

Jump out of the civilized bandwagon, he means, and reestablish our primal connections to nature—go to the rivers, the wilderness, and discover there what those connections mean. (Underwriting his message is an appeal for self-preservation: save the wilderness and the rivers in order to save our chance to know ourselves and belong somewhere.) Abbey appears to play both sides of the debate, continuing:

47. In fact, his grouping of children, fools, drunks, and writers does make sense. Psychologist Lev Vygotsky has noted that young children's thinking is "primitive," employing images and symbols rather than logic. He asserts that primitive peoples and schizophrenics share this style of thought with children (113; 128–29). He neglects to add writers to the group, although his definition of primitive thought can serve as well to define poetic thought.

Ah yes, you say, but what about Mozart? Punk rock? Astrophysics? Flush toilets? Potato chips? Silicon chips? Oral surgery? The Super Bowl and the World Series? Our coming journey to the stars? Vital projects, I agree, and I support them all. (On a voluntary basis only.) But why not a compromise? Why not—both? Why can't we have a moderate number of small cities, bright islands of electricity and kultur and industry surrounded by shoals of farmland, cow range, and timberland, set in the midst of a great unbounded sea of primitive forest, unbroken mountains, virgin desert? The human reason can conceive of such a free and spacious world; why can't we allow it to become—again—our home? (237)

Abbey would perhaps never get us to listen to his scheme for reorganizing the infrastructure and life in the United States were he not amusing in doing it. Although he is deadly serious about the idea, he mitigates the riskiness of his efforts by continuing to be the showman and the comic. Our culture can be characterized differently from Abbey's flippant portrayal of it as "kultur," but he is comprehensive in covering the fine, useful, and the trivial aspects of contemporary life. We see in it things that we would be willing to give up—and so Abbey teases us into hearing his plan for compromise, which would entail, at the very least, our giving up land in order to receive it back as wilderness.

Both "The Damnation of a Canyon" and "Floating" propose radical changes in the status quo. "Damnation," however, in relying less on humor dares less in terms of a full-scale critique of civilization than does "Floating," whose slapstick adventure style keeps it entertaining while Abbey bitterly decries dams and modern industrial life. With humor, he pushes to the precipitous edge and proves himself again to be an unaccountable trickster.

▼ ▼ ▼

WE MUST HAVE GOOD HUMOR TO READ ABBEY BECAUSE MUCH OF READing him involves withstanding him. At the same time that he speaks inclusively of the plenitude who believe that wilderness is "our true ancestral home," he seems to require a space where he can throw verbal fits and assert his individuality. He clears that space like a stage around him and performs there with the immunity of a comedian. On one hand, he wants to be persuasive about the necessity of wildness in our lives, and on the other hand he would rather play than preach. He gets caught up in "verbal exu-berance," as he once described his writing (*Confessions of a Barbarian* 38); that leads him into dicey situations. Abbey is occasionally bigoted and sex-ist. He does not try to be nice because he has a higher goal, which he con-siders to be speaking the truth. In "A Writer's Credo," he says that a writer "should be and must be a critic of the society in which he lives" (*One Life at a Time, Please* 161)—and to do that, he must speak the truth as he knows it, the subjective truth. Abbey's biggest concern about the truth is this: "The task of the honest writer—the writer as potential hero—is to seek out, write down, and publish forth those truths which are *not* self-evident, not uni-versally agreed upon, not allowed to determine public feeling and official policy" (166). Although Abbey's opinions may diverge so far from popular ones that most people would reject his, he is not chary of challenging his audience. More important to him in his pursuit of the truth as a writer is to be honest and forthright about his ideas, perceptions, and feelings. He pri-oritizes candidness over politeness or nicety. But Abbey's truth was itself initially difficult for him to identify. At age twenty-six, in 1953, he wrote in his journal that he must be honest, as difficult as that is.

> Why should the truth be painful? Because I lead a double life. Because there is a part of me that wants to be good, to be kind and generous and gentle with others, to be tolerant and forbearing, not to hurt, not to alarm. Because there is that other part or faculty or demon, my cynic self sitting on my left shoulder, seeing into myself and others, or merely ob-serving unpleasant externalities, and reporting harshly and directly what is under observation (*Confessions* 113).

Abbey has long recognized the split in his character, writing a year earlier in his journal, "I'm not a good man. Nor am I, much as I would like to be, an evil and wicked man. Damn it, no; I belong to the great mass of the in-betweens, hapless and impotent, slow and dull and awkward, sentimental, easily moved to tears, full of big hopes, bigger doubts, gigantic fantasies" (33). Abbey himself has had to have a sense of humor to make sense of the truth, filtered, as it were, through the bifurcated scope of his "double life."

As much as Abbey wants us to share his passion for the wilderness, he is happy simply to unsettle us so that we will be responsive, looking around, alert, interested, and alive. If he can accomplish that, making us sensitive to our responses, we have begun a step into the world around us.

A journal entry in 1979 asks, "Me, a 'conservation writer'? Read my books and you'll discover that only about ten percent of my words are concerned with conservation issues. The rest is play. Entertainment" (*Confessions* 264). But play is Abbey's essential literary practice for influencing his audience. In 1982, his journal records "Why I Write":

> Not so much to please, soothe or console, as to challenge, provoke, stimulate, even to anger if necessary—whatever's required to force the reader to think, feel, react, make choices. Such is my aim. (What's yours?) And, of course, to entertain. To generate tears and laughter.
>
> Or, I write to amuse my friends, and to aggravate—exasperate—ulcerate—our enemies (*Confessions* 284).

Given that he writes to amuse his friends, consider his friends to be conservationists, as they often are. According to his own figuring, he is only ten percent the conservation-oriented writer. These particular friends will not be predisposed to agree with the majority of his work. They might easily disapprove of Abbey's tastes or choices—they might be offended. Fully aware of the incendiary potential of his writing, Abbey stalwartly asserts that he writes to amuse his friends. We who feel some kinship with the writer and consider ourselves numbered among his friends must take stock of his comic intentions, understanding that he hopes for us a humor that will help us cope with him and mitigate, perhaps, our purist notions— our seriousness about ourselves.

To stimulate readers in this way is tricky—it is provocation infused with humor, both compelling our passions and encouraging us to step back from them. Knowing what we feel is just as important as thinking twice about why we feel that way. He wants us to be flexible, and he intends to further us along that path by being the fool himself and making us laugh at his nerve. A selection of his aphorisms from *A Voice Crying in the Wilderness* challenges us to appreciate his bawdy energy. About his work, he writes: "There is a fine art to making enemies and it requires diligent cultivation. It's not as easy as it looks" (60); "I am happy to be a regional writer. My region is the American West, old Mexico, West Virginia, New York, Europe, Australia, the human heart, and the male groin" (51). Indeed, Abbey effects the off-color and the rude quite easily, making virtually no topic he pursues safe for polite reading. He does not expect us to like his persona—he counts on us to be interested. He strikes a blustery pose: "I hate intellectual discussion. When I hear the words *phenomenology* or *structuralism*, I reach for my buck knife" (3); "I always write with my .357 magnum handy. Why? Well, you never know when God may try to interfere" (10).

If Abbey fails to offend us in one respect, he scores in another, for we cannot ever be sure which way he is about to turn or prepare ourselves for the next move. He has, as Peter Wild says, confusing politics, supporting conservation (considered a liberal cause) and also conservative individual rights (187)—such as the right to own guns. But for Abbey (never the right-winger), firearms support anarchic politics—they have everything to do with revolution and liberation: "The tragedy of modern war is not so much that the young men die but that they die fighting each other—instead of their real enemies back home in the capitals" (23); "War? The one war I'd be happy to join is the war against officers" (25). He assumes his role as a critic with a positive spirit: "In social affairs, I'm an optimist. I really do believe that our military-industrial civilization will soon collapse" (25). This humor cloaks Abbey's outrage in the more acceptable guise of outrageousness. If we are appalled or offended, we are also amused by his daring, a positive reaction that prepares us to be swayed by Abbey's beliefs. Wendell Berry writes, "Humor, in Mr. Abbey's work, is a function of his outrage, and is therefore always answering to necessity. Without his humor, his outrage would be intolerable—as, without his outrage, his humor would often be shallow or self-exploitive" (*What Are People For?* 44).

Abbey's humor does not always seem to be driven by its anchor, outrage. He sometimes merely flaunts it as he does his verbiage. That is what transpires in an *Abbey's Road* essay about traveling on the Central Australian Railway, for he writes that his train "crept on" and then leaps to defend the description.

> The train crept on. Wheels roll, you say, they do not and cannot creep. What do you know, insolent reader? Eh, what do you know, you crass whelp of a dingo bitch, you foal of a hunch-back camel, you sore-eyed, scab-covered noseless dropping of a syphilitic two-dollar Baton Rouge, Louisiana whore? I ask you. The train *crept* on, I say.
>
> (The purpose of the literary device illustrated above is to suggest to the reader a state of extreme boredom without at the same time lulling the reader asleep. Henry James used it often in the middle to middling pages of his later novels.) (50–51)

This verbal excursion does little to further the tale of his journey through Australia but much to display the author's own persona, one who is vigorously independent, experimental, and nervy. He jumps on the "insolent reader" by first being an insolent writer and volunteers a curse much in excess of the reader's supposed crime (to contest his diction). Furthermore, when he withdraws to the polite distance of parenthetical explanation, he equivocates in saying that his outburst was a "literary device"; he fails to justify his modification on the "gentle Reader" appellation, interested instead in throwing a slight to Henry James about the prolonged length and tedium of his works. There is little in this imagined tiff to warrant outrage; indeed, Abbey is at play—not feeling outrage at all. His fun is self-indulgent. Even so, for its surprise value, it has a place in Abbey's repertoire as a literary outlaw, for it demonstrates his freedom to speak candidly and dispense with formalities that could obscure the truth. Abbey's truth. Abbey's road. The staged display of wildness is Abbey's forte.

Sexuality is part of that repertoire, part of his wildness, and part of almost everything in his *oeuvre*. Abbey is nearly as fascinated with women as he is with the wilderness, and he writes about them with equal interest and intensity. Even his language about both is similar. This query in *Cactus Country*, "Which desert did I love the most?" he answers: "Which lady did I love the most? I loved them all. But one was lovelier than any other. One was richer, more complicated, most various. For all its harshness, loneliness, cruelty and cunning, one desert haunted me like a vision of paradise" (20). The Sonoran Desert here appears to be the tawny woman who wins out; however, this is only a rhetorical competition, and Abbey does not have to choose between them. More often than not, in his experience, they coincide. From *Abbey's Road*: "Landscape and women. Whenever I discover a natural scene that pleases me, that I find beautiful, my first thought is: what a place to bring a girl! And our world is so rich in both—beautiful places, lovely women" (181). His parallel sensual appreciation of them— his desire to have both at once—is occasionally shaken by the woman's contrary desires. In such a case, Abbey has to choose. *The Journey Home* recounts the cross-country, car-wrecking, desert journey that he took with his fiancée—in her car, a Ford convertible. Although he is sensitive to her desire to preserve her car and her control of the situation ("a sort of premature, premarital honeymoon, a week in the wilderness to cement, as it were, our permanent relationship" (23), he has other wishes and overrides her concern. At each vehicular tragedy with sand, rock, or cactus, Abbey the lover feels compelled to see what lies "beyond the next ridge" (26) more than he is driven to mollify his sweetheart. She is stricken. When they finally flap out of the wilderness, their relationship is over, and the car is largely ruined, but he appears cavalier about the whole affair, succoring himself with the couplet, "A woman is only a woman / But a good Ford is a car" (29).

Abbey appears to love the desert with more respect than he loves women. It is clear from his journals and essays of personal history that he fell in love countless times and had sexual relationships with many women. For all that experience, he may not have known women well, though he became an expert on the scope of his own desires. In 1977, Garth McCann wrote, "Abbey has long been obsessed by a love-hate relationship with women" (9); by the time of his death in 1989, Abbey was married to his fifth wife and had, in sum, five children. He never appeared satisfied by monogamy or convinced that it is the right cultural course. These remarks in *A Voice Crying in the Wilderness* attest to that: "I, too, believe in fidelity. But how can I be true to one woman without being false to all the others?" (78); "Women: We cannot love them all. But we must try" (78); "I've wrecked and ravaged half my life in the pursuit of women, and I suffer the pangs of about seventeen regrets—the seventeen who got away" (78). Abbey glorifies his passions with a biological explanation for promiscuous desire: "every good-looking girl instantly appeals to my reproductive instinct" (*Confessions* 23). Sexual attractiveness—his definition of femininity—determines his response to women; if a woman is feminine, he is immediately attentive to her, whereas if a woman is not, "my head may be willing to pay her polite attention, but the vital spark of erotic electricity is absent, seeking elsewhere for its magnetic polarity" (*One Life at a Time, Please* 200). Whether his erotic interest will be polite or not does not concern Abbey, for he is ultimately more intrigued with his reaction and with his love of women than he is committed to any particular woman. Although he does recognize that a critique of his reactions could be raised, he does not produce it. His only afterthought is mild: "Now this is a hell of a way to react to my fellow man. But there it is, an involuntary reaction no more under my direct control than the beating of my heart or the breathing of my lungs. . . . Such is the nature of the male primate" (200). If Abbey sometimes lacks respect for women, it is because he judges them first in relation to himself and neglects their importance as independent people, not beholden to his character or his interests.

Abbey also romanticizes women, which further inhibits him from knowing them well. He quips, "A pretty girl can do no wrong" (*A Voice*

Crying in the Wilderness 77), and repeatedly in his journals he praises the woman he is involved with in such strings of superlatives that we are left stunned that he has found the "perfect" woman, since no other kind would merit that praise. But the praise issues from his idealization of women, which survives the waning of each of his particular romantic passions. Despite all his romantic idealism, his wry comic side graces him with the savvy to know that pretty women are not perfect or necessarily good. His romanticism creates the opportunity for a humorous backlash against women, and that humor corrects his delusions. The woman he finds in an Australian pub prompts this program of responses:

> The barmaid who served me had the heartbreaking face of an angel: skin of a rosy perfection, violet eyes with charcoal lashes, cherry lips, a glorious crown of fair, glossy, long and flowing hair. Her fragrance, as she leaned toward me, revealing a pink swell of bosom, was sweet as wild strawberries in fresh cream. And then that delectable mouth opened, the perfect pearls of her teeth parted, and out from the angelic face came the seraphic voice, addressing not me but something beneath the bar: "Wot yer doin' 'ere, ye bloody little shit?" (*Abbey's Road* 53)

She is addressing her child as she kicks him away. This woman is like other women in that she does not and cannot live up to Abbey's idealistic expectations. If, as McCann states, Abbey has an ambiguous relationship with women, it is because he adores them too generally and is therefore vulnerable to being disappointed by their specific characteristics. He hates the failure of women to be as perfect as he desires them.

His frustration with women manifests itself in humor at their expense, particularly about feminism. He remarks, "In everything but brains and brawn, women are vastly superior to men. A different race" (*A Voice Crying in the Wilderness* 77). Were women a different race, Abbey would have far less difficulty with them; as it is, they are his kind, which puts him under pressure to know them realistically. He is not particularly good even at knowing their politics: "The feminist notion that the whole of human history has been nothing but a vast intricate conspiracy by men to enslave their wives, mothers, daughters, and sisters presents us with an intellectual neurosis for which we do not yet have a name" (*A Voice* 81). Abbey is outraged by this charge because he has misunderstood and exaggerated it; he does not seem to know that most feminists recognize that men, too, suffer in patriarchal cultures. Abbey's outrage translates into humorous attacks.

To the editors of "Mizz Magazine," he writes, "Dear Sirs . . . Are old wim-min is trouble enuf to manage as is without you goldam New Yorkers sneaking a lot of downright *sub-versive* ideas into their hard heads. Out here a womin's place is in the kitchen, the barnyard and the bedroom in that exackt order and we don't need no changes" (*Abbey's Road* xvi). Crude and distasteful humor such as this registers the extent of Abbey's frustra-tion and disillusionment.[48]

His real and literary dealings with women inform us about his relation-ship with the desert, which he also has the tendency to romanticize. Ann Ronald has asserted that Abbey's genre—the romance—is aimed at creat-ing a mythical world; she says that Abbey mythologizes the desert in order to "know, possess, embrace the real one" (65). In fact, that route into ideal-ism was counterproductive for him to know women, and Abbey seems de-termined not to mythologize or romanticize the desert. Ronald is right in classifying Abbey's style as she does, but she misreads his intentions. *In spite of* his desire to see the desert with utmost clarity, he romanticizes it, or, as Richard Shelton remarks, "*Desert Solitaire* was written by an arch-romantic trying desperately not to be romantic" (102). In *Desert Solitaire*, we see this struggle in full light: he forswears the imposition of meaning onto the desert (for he wants to preserve it from being abstracted into any-thing but what it is), yet he is endlessly in pursuit of its meaning. Abbey endeavors to glean from an old juniper tree some larger significance: "The essence of the juniper continues to elude me unless, as I presently suspect, its surface is also the essence" (30). Failing to be enlightened, he resorts to what he can see, identify and react to—the surface or appearance of the ju-niper. When Abbey contemplates the appeal of the desert in *Beyond the Wall*, he focuses on appearances and their implications, saying that in the desert there is "always the promise of something unforeseeable, unknown but desirable" (154). Ineffable, the mystery of it attracts Abbey and leaves him to focus on his reactions, which he can articulate. So we have in *Desert Solitaire* his explanation about the appeal and power of Delicate Arch.

> If Delicate Arch has any significance it lies, I will venture, in the power
> of the odd and unexpected to startle the senses and surprise the mind

---

48. A similar pattern is at work in Abbey's fiction. With his ironic and humorous eye op-posing his romantic vision, the style that results is romance exaggerated to its limit, not debunked but engorged by melodrama, hyperactive adventure, and vulgarity. The grotesque romance that characterizes his fiction is thus a result of both his tendency to and caution not to romanticize.

out of their ruts of habit, to compel us into reawakened awareness of the wonderful—that which is full of wonder (41).

Abbey attaches the essence or significance of things to his reaction to them. He does the same with women, offering up the biological imperative of re-production to account for his own cupidinous urges and to explain the mysterious appeal women hold for him. He can self-reflectively romanti-cize women, but the desert eludes him. At the end of *Desert Solitaire*, he writes, "The finest quality of this stone, these plants and animals, this desert landscape is the indifference manifest to our presence, our absence, our coming, our staying or our going. Whether we live or die is a matter of absolutely no concern whatsoever to the desert" (301). The desert is im-placable enough to resist all overtures to it. Women are not so implacable; women's desires can match Abbey's; and women's attractiveness partly substantiates his idealization of them. Women can also fail Abbey's ideals, so they are easy targets for his humor, and they bear much of the rudest ex-tremes of it. In contrast, the desert does not match Abbey. When he roman-ticizes it, he is clearly facing himself—being creatively autobiographical. So his comic backlash, when it emerges to rebut his idealism, does not strike out at nature (as it does at women) but at the author himself. In de-fying explanation, the ecological world is spared the outrage that Abbey feels for other tantalizing—but more comprehensible—subjects.

When Abbey's sexist humor seems to exclude women from the ecologi-cal world that he adores, we can remember that he is the most celebrated fool in his work. Women are beloved by him; the attention they receive from him is merely as flawed as he is. He constructs intentional literary blunders to implant in his writing the pattern for the rest of his blunders, to allow himself to be crude and outrageous, for he knows that he has way-ward opinions and a contradictory character. And he loves to make a scene, whether it is describing someplace—"My lone juniper stands half-alive, half-dead, the silvery wind-rubbed claw of wood projected stiffly at the sun" (*Desert Solitaire* 155)—or being subversive:

Teamwork, that's what made America what it is today. Teamwork and initiative. The survey crew had done their job; I would do mine. For about five miles I followed the course of their survey back toward head-quarters, and as I went I pulled up each little wooden stake and threw it away, and cut all the bright ribbons from the bushes and hid them under a rock. A futile effort, in the long run, but it made me feel good" (*Desert Solitaire* 67).[49]

He loves the wildness in nature and in himself, becoming an impassioned advocate of the first and a showman of the second. Being wild, for Abbey, has meant personal defiance of civilized ways and polite manners while at the same time cultivating a civilized audience to share his concerns. Such fine, slick, and courageous talking he pulls off primarily because of his sense of humor, humor that has been essential to his survival as a romantic and maverick writer. The outlaw Abbey may offend us with the same alacrity that he amuses or energizes us. But if we can sufficiently retain our equanimity to give his work the attention it deserves, we will have learned much from him, precisely this: that we need humor to acquire patience, cope with paradox, be independent in the modern world, and have faith that the wilderness will have a comic fate, resurrected at last. Abbey comes to us boldly passionate. It is lucky for us that he was not more careful or consistent, for then we would invariably lose that force in his writing that inspires it, and we would lose the thrill of facing a trickster, challenging and provoking his audience into glimpsing the world as he sees it. His humor encourages us not to follow him but to step out ourselves into the wild world, free and alive.

49. In *Desert Solitaire*, Abbey called for a ban on vehicles and new roads in national parks. In November 1997, the Clinton administration announced a virtual ban on cars in the three busiest national parks; instead, a transit system will bring visitors into the parks.

SHORT CUT

▼▼▼

Coyote Magician, Ursula Le Guin

Ursula Le Guin's short story "Buffalo Gals, Won't You Come Out Tonight" complements the effect of Abbey's work to stimulate our attention and cleave us to wild nature. The twists in her modern-day Coyote tale begin with the surprise that this Coyote is female.

The story tells of a girl's journey into the animal world after a plane crash strands her half-blinded in the desert and Coyote shows up.

"You fell out of the sky," the coyote said (17).

Without Coyote to prod the girl, she would not have gone anywhere, certainly not as far as she does, all the way to the town where the Chipmunks take her into their home and she sleeps for days.

"Did you lose an eye?" the coyote asked, interested (18).

The girl is cold and bewildered. Conversing with a coyote! She thinks she might still be on the plane to Canyonville. Coyote will have none of that, starting up amicably to look for the lost eye. The sagebrush stretches around them, endless.

"Aren't you going to look?'" it said, suddenly sitting down on its haunches and abandoning the search. "I knew a trick once where I could throw my eyes way up into a tree and see everything from up there, and then whistle, and they'd come back into my head. But that goddam bluejay stole them, and when I whistled nothing came. I had to stick lumps of pine pitch into my head so I could see anything. You could try that. But you've got one eye that's OK, what do you need two for? Are you coming, or are you dying there?" (18)

Until the child follows and they finally stop around noon to rest at a creek where the coyote cleans her wounded eye, she does not know that Coyote is female. The child embraces her.

After that, the eye relieved and comforted, she sees differently. The next time she catches up with Coyote, who is eating crow carrion, she sees a "tawny-skinned woman" (21) with bare feet, blue jeans and an old white shirt, cooking in a pot over a campfire, inviting her to eat crow and starting to dip into the pot herself.

> "Ow! Shit! Why don't I ever have any spoons?" She broke off a dead twig of sagebrush, dipped it into the pot, and licked it. "Oh, boy," she said. "Come on!" (21–22)

Now Coyote will never be anything but human to the girl, and always a woman. We learn the girl's name too—Myra, or Gal, as Coyote calls her. After this, all the creatures Gal meets she sees as if they were human. Chipmunk, for example, who gives her a bed, is a "fat-cheeked woman" (26) in a striped shirt. Likewise, they all see her as their own kind—a pup, chipmunk, owlet. She is part of them. She sleeps. When Blue Jay proposes a dance so that he can perform in public to fix her eye, they all gather— Coyote close on hand to keep Jay honest.

> "What is it, Jay?" she was asking, peering at the new eye. "One of mine you stole that time?"
> "It's pine pitch," Jay shouted furiously. "You think I'd use some stupid secondhand coyote eye? I'm a doctor!"
> "Ooooh, ooooh, a doctor," Coyote said. "Boy, that is one ugly eye. Why didn't you ask Rabbit for a rabbit-dropping? That eye looks like shit" (32).

Again she licks the eye, and this time Gal can see fine. Healed and independent enough to live in Coyote's rough household, Gal adopts her, calls her mom, and learns a lot about the facts of life, coyote-style. The boyfriends are sometimes hard to take—Coyote has a lot of them and none are shy; they have sex anywhere in the house or even in the yard or in the bed with Gal there too. Gal gets embarrassed about the way Coyote pees in public too.

> The thing that worried the child most, maybe, was when Coyote did number two anywhere and then turned around and talked to it. That seemed so awful. As if Coyote was—the way she often seemed, but really wasn't—crazy (38).

Gal rakes up the turds in the yard one day and buries them where the other animals in town deposit their waste. But her mom will not abide the house-cleaning—she calls out to the defecated litter, digs them out, and talks with them a long time.

> "It's just easier when they're all around close by," Coyote said, washing her hands (38).

> "I kept stepping on them," the child said, trying to justify her deed. "Poor little shits," said Coyote, practicing dance-steps (38).

Coyote is crazy only because she is not afraid of crossing over and coming at the world from a different vantage point—the turds', for instance, or Gal's. She knows that the rabbits see Gal as a rabbit and the hawk has her to be a fledgling. She knows Gal is a human but looks like a pup to her. So it is no surprise that she was the creature who could cross over into the girl's human world and rouse her after the plane crashed. She was crazy and skilled enough to do this. When she jokes to Gal that people come in two kinds—those who say there are two kinds of people and those who do not—she laughs her way beyond either niche into the in-between. Her claim to both the self-conscious, separatist side (mostly the human) and the inclusive side (mostly the animal) make her a comic in a deadly serious game against the "new people." Humans.

> "We were always here. We are always here. Where we are is here. But it's their country now. They're running it . . . Shit, even I did better!" (36)

Still, Gal eventually misses humans and goes with Horse to visit a ranch, though they are frightened there and flee immediately. Coyote is not pleased when she finds out about their attempt to socialize.

> "Horse?" Coyote said. "That prick? Catfood!" (47)

Proprietary but not condemning, she says,

> "If you're going to do damn fool things, next time do 'em with me, at least I'm an expert" (47).

Soon enough, they go traveling, this time to a town that Gal does not want to approach, but Coyote intends to.

> "We won't go all the way in. No way! We'll just get a little closer and look. It's fun" (53).

> Coyote became business-like, responsible. "We're going to be very careful," she announced. "And look out for big dogs, OK? Little dogs I can handle. Make a good lunch. Big dogs, it goes the other way. Right? Let's go, then" (53).

They do go in. Get shot at. Run. Gal is upset; Coyote is fired-up, running at the mouth, excited.

> "But they're your folks," Coyote said. "All yours. Your kith and kin and cousins and kind. Bang! Pow! There's Coyote! Bang! There's my wife's ass! Pow! There's anything—BOOOOM! Blow it away, man! BOOOOOOM!"
> "I want to go home," the child said.
> "Not yet," said Coyote. "I got to take a shit." She did so, then turned to the fresh turd, leaning over it. "It says I have to stay," she reported, smiling (55).

She likes the action and will not leave. Gal stays with her. But Gal does not eat the meat Coyote finds that looks like an offering but smells burnt to the girl. Coyote thinks it is smoked. Once she eats it, she knows better—it is poisoned.

This is how Coyote dies in Gal's arms, and Gal returns, complete with her new eye, to humans she does not trust.

▼▼▼

CRAZY WOMAN, THAT COYOTE! GRANDMOTHER SPIDER TELLS GAL THAT COYOTE "gets killed all the time" (59), but for the child at the time the death is irrevocable.

It is tragedy in a comic world. It is environmental consciousness. Those with this consciousness find small comfort in the faith that evolution will resurrect the wild when particular loved ones or beloved places fall. No philosophy about a comic, always-rebounding world consoles when a part of it we are attached to is destroyed. Our grief is personal and necessary. "I'm not one of them" (59), Gal says to Spider. Unwilling to be identified with cruelty or destruction, we sometimes repudiate our own kind. But then who are we? Gal goes back to the human world a New Person, with a pine-pitch, coyote-polished eye and a bevy of relationships with nonhuman nature. She knows and feels more than she once did. We can practice this awareness, reaching out into the world for new parameters that might identify us. We can look to nature writing for its tentative steps toward defining our life as a facet of other life, ever multifarious.

Coyote herself has reason to be confused about her identity but is not—she has a consciousness that delves into the human world and enough intimacy with the animal world to be able cogently to reveal Blue Jay's pride or Fox's exclusivity. Elsewhere, Le Guin has said,

> Coyote is an anarchist. She can confuse all civilized ideas simply by trotting through. And she always fools the pompous. Just when your ideas begin to get all nicely arranged and squared off, she messes them up. Things are never going to be neat, that's one thing you can count on (White 119–20).

In "Buffalo Gals," Coyote plays this role of anarchist for the animal community. When Fox believes that he can avoid messy interactions with others simply by living apart and putting up a sign, "Fox. Private. No Trespassing!" Coyote steals food from him (52). She purposefully undercuts his complacency. But with such a protean consciousness, with an awareness of the destructive take-over humans have staged in the world, with a commitment to keeping a decent balance among creatures, does Coyote not become anxious, unsure, or confused? How can she know who she is? It is Coyote's style—indeed, the tone of Le Guin's short story—that teaches us most about transcending confusion and handling tragedy. Through all her attachments to place and community, Coyote stays nonattached. In the beginning, Gal asks where they are going and where they are.

> "This is my country," Coyote answered, with dignity, making a long, slow gesture all round the vast horizon. "I made it. Every goddam sage bush" (23).

A fool thing to do, maybe, making so much sagebrush. Coyote's home is a beautiful fool world that she has let go with a grace that seems too wild to be graceful. Coyote takes off her pants and dances around the campfire. She pees on it so the steam can rise between her legs. That Coyote in the twentieth century has shown up in Le Guin's story as a woman emphasizes her independence and nonattachment and comic style. She whelps what she then sets free. She is pointedly bound by no convention—careless about housekeeping, always ready to go out traveling and leave town. Her skill at nonattachment even makes her casual about copulating with her own son—"pick of the litter," she later tells the girl. "Listen, Gal. Have daughters. When you have anything, have daughters. At least they clear out" (39).

In her relations with Gal in particular we see that nonattachment does not mean flippancy or coldness. When the "pick of the litter" son tries to fondle Gal, Coyote kicks him out—"You think I don't got any standards? You think I'd let some coyote rape a kid in my bed?" (37). Though she never directly returns Gal's endearments to her, her generous acceptance of the girl bespeaks affection. None of the other animals, Gal knows, treat her with the same intimacy that Coyote does. Coyote loves her well enough to return her (as best she can, dying in the process) to a human settlement when she senses that Gal desires to go back.

Nonattachment is paradoxically essential to Coyote's commitments to land and community. In order to sustain allegiance for things that change, she must maintain a comic spirit to hold herself apart. Loving people and place without controlling them but drawn always to be involved in their affairs, Coyote lives in ambiguity—and acknowledges it in humor, a style that celebrates her ability to live wildly, to love a world that is morally dynamic, and to stay unattached so that no loss remains a tragedy. The vitality of our environmental consciousness depends on that comic spirit—our ability to cope with tragedy and remain healthy, hopeful, and creative. And if we can be a little crazy, like Coyote, we shall be exercising humor not as a pastime but as a practice of wildness that can help us be a part of the ecological household, which weds conscious creatures like us and Coyote with the world of instinct.

Le Guin's female Coyote prepares us for Louise Erdrich's humorous and passionate vision of survival on earth.

▼▼▼

Louise Erdrich

Seeking the Best Medicine

LOUISE ERDRICH IS PART GERMAN AND PART CHIPPEWA, A WRITER WHO has settled in New Hampshire for her married life but who remains, in her spiritual and creative interests, largely at home in North Dakota. This circumstantial exile has been a boon for her writing. Working collaboratively with her husband, Michael Dorris[50], in a literary partnership of fascinating intensity and in a domestic arrangement that included their adoptive children as well as three biological daughters, Erdrich has written six novels and one memoir on motherhood—all in the span of a decade or so. In her dedication of *The Blue Jay's Dance: A Birth Year*, she writes, "I am not a scientist, not a naturalist, not a chef, not an expert, not the best or worst mother, but a writer only, a woman constantly surprised" (x). Surprise attends all her work. She is attentive to it, ready to grant it the humor it sparks and, in doing so, celebrate its serendipity. Each of her novels is imbued with humor and set in her home territory, as if to counter her growing attachment, through her daughters' lives, to the Northeast. Her homecoming from exile is a dual and simultaneous journey accomplished by her family life in New Hampshire and the families' lives she creates in writing about her native North Dakota.

In some ways Erdrich resembles the blue jay that she describes in her memoir: "The blue jay is an opportunist, and opportunists are survivors in

---

50. Dorris committed suicide in 1997. How Erdrich will cope and what course her literary career will take are, at present, unknown.

every sense. They are adaptable, clever, and unprincipled" (*The Blue Jay's Dance* 159). As such, their prolific population makes sense; much like the coyote, blue jays survive in places altered by humans. Although she claims to have no affinity for blue jays, she too has been a survivor of circumstance, taking advantage of the distance from her original home to write with love, clarity, and humor about it.

Her description of the birds continues: "Blue jays are stubborn. They mob owls, scream convincingly as hawks . . . there is something about blue jays that both delights and irritates. Audacity thrills, even from the most exasperating source" (160). The birds' greedy, voracious stake in where they are enables them to make their home just about anywhere. They put on a fine show in defense of what they consider to be their territory. For one such display, Erdrich was spectator. She saw a gray hawk dive and strike into a cluster of jays, separating one, who tumbled to the snow. She saw the jay right itself and face the hawk, who landed on the snow a foot away. What happened next was a surprise to Erdrich: "The struck jay thrusts out its head, screams, raises its wings, and dances *toward* the gray hawk" (194). The hawk could obviously crush it. There is nowhere to hide, and the jay has nothing but verbal help from its buddies on the sidelines. The hawk screams too, jabbing at the jay. "Yet the jay, ridiculous, continues to dance, hopping forward, hornpiping up and down with tiny leaps, all of its feathers on end to increase its size. Its crest is sharp, its beak open in a continual shriek, its eye-mask fierce. It pedals its feet in the air" (194). Beyond any reasonable odds, the hawk gives ground and goes away, confused and perhaps fascinated, Erdrich thinks, at the smaller bird's performance. The jay is a survivor. No matter what the fright, the chance, the threat, the imminent fate, there it is, "that manic, successful jig—cocky, exuberant, entirely a bluff, a joke." Erdrich considers it seriously, continuing, "That dance makes me clench down hard on life" (195). For her baby and for herself, she vows to take the challenge that the jay's dance has conjured before her—to be the dancer who faces tragedy and survives because she moves toward it with all the faith and humor she can muster.

The blue jay's dance is her practice of a comic attitude, one that embraces surprise with courage and grace. Erdrich's writing features that comic attitude, focusing it on family and wildness, themes expressed in her children's book, *Grandmother's Pigeon*. From the start, the story is entertaining and suspenseful. The narrative heroine is a little girl in a family of four, and her grandmother is the catalyst for adventure—a talented, brave, kind, healing, and unusually canny woman. The grandmother initiates this par-

ticular adventure simply by leaving—or, really, not so simply. The family is
on vacation at a beach on the west coast when, suddenly, "she sailed away
on the back of a congenial porpoise." It is a light-hearted move, a whim:
"'Good-bye!' she called. 'I've always wanted to see Greenland!'" Seemingly magical, she is nevertheless real, not above making mistakes or just
getting disoriented; "Grandmother had always been bad on geography,"
our narrator tells us. Although her shortcomings make her recognizable to
us, this grandmother is not ordinary, not about to lose her way finding her
car in a parking lot or negotiating the streets out of a suburb—she gets
turned around sailing a porpoise to Greenland. She heads west into the
Pacific, a huge error. When the girl's brother shouts out a warning, she
serenely remedies course, turning south, immediately planning to circle
South America, "'I'll go the scenic route!'" With an aplomb that is hilarious
considering her mysterious choice of transportation, the grandmother disappears.

Her room in the family's house remains untouched for a year until they
at last go in to visit her things—for they have had no word from her and
miss her—and there they find one bird's nest in her collection unaccountably harboring three eggs. And the eggs are hatching. The room's windows
are shut tightly. There is no explanation for the presence of the eggs, except, illogically, the stuffed pigeon with the glass eyes. The kids glance at it;
their parents remain mystified. The mother cares for the creatures, and she
has the hunch that leads her to call an ornithologist.

The woman who arrives (for all the key players in this story are female)
is shocked by her examination of the birds. "'Impossible,' she stated.
'Completely impossible. Yet true.'" The pronouncement sounds like the
kind of paradox that will stir things up, which it does, with full drama and
comic flair.

> "It is impossible," said the ornithologist, adjusting her glasses, "that in
> your kitchen you have raised three members of an extinct species.
> *Ectopistes migratorius*. These are passenger pigeons. Once upon a time,
> these birds were so abundant that they traveled in flocks that took three
> days to pass overhead, 300 million birds per hour. Their nesting colo-
> nies sometimes stretched forty miles long. They seemed limitless as
> leaves."

Her lecture, though eminently serious and informative, concluding fairly
that "nature is both tough and fragile," stands as the comic as well as nar-

rative climax in the story. The discovery of the passenger pigeons is a veritable miracle—anachronistic, impossible, unprecedented. Of course it has occurred in a small family's kitchen, the perfect homely place to deflate the public magnificence of the phenomenon and to locate the source of magic within the family's reach. Furthermore, the ornithologist's manner is comic, from her appearance in "looking oddly like the birds she studied" and in having, during her lecture, "the same grim and sadly surprised look that Grandmother's pigeon usually wore" to her reaction to the news she has delivered. She politely plans out her shock: "'Perhaps I shall sit down now, before I fall over.'" She wants tea to revive her. The fact that the long-lost grandmother had made bitter teas as medicine for the kids to revive them when otherwise they felt too bad to go to school means that we know something of the ghastliness of her brews. In his haste to prepare tea, the father inadvertently makes some of that "bitter medicine"—"There was no mistaking the odor of singed moth wings." The ornithologist drinks it without hesitation, an event that is, for the kids, as monumental as the fact that the birds in their house are fluke remnants of an extinct species. According to our narrator, "She drank cup after cup, and we looked at her with new respect." This is a comic underpinning to the main plot—the drinking of that tea rivals the new passenger pigeons. Indeed, miracles do happen in the most mundane events, not merely in startling headline news.

The news of the pigeons brings so much wearying attention upon the family and the birds that the kids hatch a plan to save them all. So the end of the story comes rapidly: the kids write messages for the pigeons to carry to their grandmother and let them go. Soon in the mail they receive a letter from her, explaining that her trip was longer than she had expected ("I had to change porpoises three times and catch a whale") and that she would be coming home soon. The story is a classic Erdrich performance. It features strong female characters; it revolves around a series of surprises; it deals with loss and recovery; and it places the locus of magic, love, and adventure in a human community that is at the center of a wild world. And its most consistent tone is humorous.

Erdrich's humorous tone has a complex foundation. *Grandmother's Pigeon* shows us some ways in which she makes humor happen: the primary joke is built into the story's structure, with a disappearing woman obliquely responsible for a huge mystery—dropping out of her family's world and, after a portentous absence, promising to return. It is hide-and-seek of extraordinary dimensions. Her quirky letter that concludes the story is meant to be a welcome discovery and relief, the conclusion of a game. We are tickled by the unusual hitchhiking she reports to have done between porpoises and a whale. Erdrich makes the letter blithely casual in contrast to the starkly incredible journey to accentuate the humor of the letter's arrival, the long-awaited accounting of the missing person. We laugh in pleasure and relief.

In *The Blue Jay's Dance*, Erdrich further explores humor by looking to its origins in the development of her baby.

> She first laughed at her sister's peekaboo face, popping unexpectedly toward her. It was such a pure sound that we all laughed too. The sound of her laugh gives everybody pleasure, and so we all encourage her to make the sound again. We experiment. What causes her laugh is this: a combination of the new and the expected with a hint of fear thrown in. Just at the moment she is afraid that your face won't appear, her expectation collapses. When you do appear she laughs the loudest (81).

And thus, Erdrich decides, "The source of laughter lies in anxiety from the very first" (81). According to her, *funny* usually rests on unpredictable foundations, and the more dangerous or tragic that position, the more intense the humor that is witness to it. "Laughter is our consolation prize for consciousness," she continues. "The capacity for humor develops alongside the knowledge that familiar faces vanish" (81). Erdrich accepts the dark underpinnings that her world has offered, yet she does not cave in to them as a defeatist might; instead, loss and fear of loss she acknowledges with humor, that gift so often spirited out of hard times. So the grandmother returns, and a few passenger pigeons are magically resurrected from an extinct species. With humor, hope blossoms.

Humor is a survival technique, one that can be taken up like the blue jay's dance to negotiate trouble. For Erdrich, that humor is embedded in her heritage as a Native American. Counting her husband's bloodlines too, she has remarked, "We're a mixture of Chippewa and Modoc and German-American and French and Irish. All of these different backgrounds have aspects that are part of us. If we took ourselves too seriously in any way, we'd be overwhelmed" (Chavkin 144). As her husband (and collaborator) says, the two of them are not spokespeople for Native Americans, for the different tribes are numerous—"Plus we're mixed bloods . . . So it would be presumptuous to pretend to be more than we are. We can only speak for ourselves" (Chavkin 120). Even so, given their complicated ancestry, the practice of speaking for themselves requires creativity. Erdrich continues on that subject, "Probably we don't take ourselves seriously enough even as writers, although that's the deepest thing in our lives. But the most serious things have to be jokes. Humor is the way we make our life worth living" (Chavkin 144). This is a powerful endorsement of humor, and it proceeds from the writers' taste for life: they prefer the quirky edge where there can be humor found in complexity and pleasure made of it.

To better understand Erdrich's appetite for humor, we can look to her cultural explanation of it: "It may be that the one universal thing about Native Americans from tribe to tribe is survival humor—the humor that enables you to live with what you have to live with. You have to be able to poke fun at people who are dominating your life and family—" to which Dorris adds, "—and to poke fun at yourself in being dominated" (Chavkin 144). Erdrich believes that the humor and irony prevalent in Native American tribal life do not get portrayed "often enough" (Chavkin 68), and it appears that her work is partly an effort to rectify that. She asserts, "if there is any ceremony which goes across the board and is practiced by lots and lots of tribal people, it is having a sense of humor about things and laughing" (Chavkin 100). The characters in Erdrich's novels continually play in and out of their misfortunes with humor, and Erdrich herself takes solace in comically turning around her frustrations. She says she has learned to trick herself into defusing her tension and calming her baby's prolonged crying; juxtaposing sound with sense, her sweet exclamations offer comic relief. "I use my most soothing tone of voice to call her names. The tone helps her, the words help me. . . . *You're a crank!* I whisper, holding her tenderly. *A goddamn crank! You're driving me completely nuts!*" (*The Blue Jay's Dance* 66).

Survival is the sustained theme of Erdrich's work, a survival broader than any one character's development or success. The survival that interests Erdrich entails a larger, more inclusive community. Just as the passenger pigeons hatched to a family ready for adventure, ideal survival, in Erdrich's eyes, involves people living in a wild world. That wildness is internal and external. As the children's story implies, the flocks of passenger pigeons still ought to exist, wild in the open skies. The wildness of nature is "both tough and fragile," in the words of the story's ornithologist. The other kind of wildness issues from the human spirit when it opens itself to possibility and chance. That is the kind of wildness that accepts the ineffable and thrives in paradox.

Nature's wildness—in the form of a deadly blizzard—is answered by human wildness at the end of *The Bingo Palace* when precocious young Lipsha is stranded in a vehicle and Fleur, the last of the mysterious Pillager family, walks out into the snow by her home in order to choose death herself and take Lipsha's place, saving him. She is an old woman who has outlived countless others, mystically trading off her death onto others. The night of the blizzard, Fleur disappears across the frozen lake into a death that unites her with the nonhuman wild world and secures her everlasting presence in legend. "In later days, there would be some who claimed they found her tracks and followed to see where they changed, the pad broadened, the claw pressed into the snow" (273). Fleur embodies mystery and wildness.

> She doesn't tap our panes of glass or leave her claw marks on eaves and doors. She only coughs, low, to make her presence known. You have heard the bear laugh—that is the chuffing noise we hear and it is unmistakable. Yet no matter how we strain to decipher the sound it never quite makes sense, never relieves our certainty or our suspicion that there is more to be told, more than we know, more than can be caught in the sieve of our thinking (274).

Fleur's survival as a mysterious presence keeps the community alert and psychically alive.

Mysteries abound in Erdrich's fiction, where survival entails coping with the multiplicity and surprises of the wild world. Regarding her experimentally bold novel *Tracks*, in which Fleur stars as the woman who has drowned three times in Lake Matchimanito and not yet died, the author partly explains her intentions, saying that the book suggests, "There is no quantifiable reality. Points of view change the reality of a situation and there is a reality to madness, imagined events, and perhaps something beyond that" (Chavkin 224).[51] As she has said often about herself, she has a high tolerance for chaos and disorganization. That aptitude has meant that she is open to the vagrancies of reality, quick to shift perspective. In fact, she admits both that she has found no theological or epistemological certainty in the universe and that her work probably reveals this (Chavkin 228). What her work clearly suggests is that we find steps through the uncertain world as one would learn a new dance, by being open to its possibilities. To embrace the stretches of apparent meaninglessness that attend

51. Susan Perez Castillo describes both *Tracks* and *The Beet Queen* to be postmodern in their portrayal of reality as provisional (292).

the dance, to make peace with mystery and chaos, to understand that we exist in relation to a larger, wild world, more than can ever "be caught in the sieve of our thinking" is to experience the thrill of surprise. It helps to have a sense of humor.

How Fleur Pillager casts that thrill around her is prime material for Erdrich's humor. For example, the lake's supposed water monster, Misshepeshu, is greedy for her but desirous to keep her alive, ensuring her survival. "The first time she drowned in the cold and glassy waters of Matchimanito, Fleur Pillager was only a child" (*Tracks* 10). This is a bold statement of impossible fact, and, coming from humorless Pauline, it is funny because she reports it as if she were being subtle. But nothing is subtle about the fact that Fleur drowns and manages to deal her life back to herself by instead trading in the life of the man who finds her. He dies, and she lives—testimony to the power emerging from the wild Pillager family line. Nothing is subtle either about the way she deals cards; she is unabashed, playing with a group of men in the evenings in the Argus butcher shop where she works and winning a dollar each night. Her consistency transcends luck and tantalizes the men—"it wasn't just that she was a Chippewa, or even that she was a woman, it wasn't that she was good-looking or even that she was alone that made their brains hum. It was how she played cards" (18). Fleur plays beyond the reach of their tolerance, succeeding in winning the pot even on the night they decide to throw her off by upping the ante, risking it all. She wins, and their fury moves them. White-skinned, fat Lily leads the pursuit, though his first moves are abortive. He intends to jump on Fleur at the stock-pen, but she manages to dump the pig slops on him and flee into the pen. He follows but trips on a huge sow, sleeping in the muck. In the ensuing tumble, which momentarily protects Fleur, Lily and the pig battle as if they were as obstinately like-minded as they are matched in bulk.

> The sow screamed as his body smacked over hers. She rolled, striking out with her knife-sharp hooves and Lily gathered himself upon her, took her foot-long face by the ears, and scraped her snout and cheeks against the trestles of the pen. He hurled the sow's tight skull against an iron post, but instead of knocking her dead, he woke her from her dream.
>
> She reared, shrieked, and then he squeezed her so hard that they leaned into each other and posed in a standing embrace. They bowed jerkily, as if to begin. Then his arms swung and flailed. She sank her

black fangs into his shoulder, clasping him, dancing him forward and backward through the pen. Their steps picked up pace, went wild. The two dipped as one, box-stepped, tipped one another. She ran her split foot through his hair. He grabbed her kinked tail. They went down and came up, the same shape and then the same color until the men couldn't tell one from the other in that light and Fleur was able to vault the gates, swing down, hit gravel (*Tracks* 25–6).

The dance that Lily and the sow perform together is not so much shared as torn from each other. It is vicious and wretchedly funny, a man formidably opposed by a pig and forced to stoop literally into his bestial nature by wrestling in the pen. The muddy dance is a prelude to gang rape. All the men get to Fleur, not just Lily. The sow, in contrast, seems to be protecting her caretaker when she flings herself into the bellicose, embattled steps with Lily; she does not stoop but symbolically rises up, meeting him with her better nature goaded to answer his aggression. Fleur suffers—and leaves Argus—but she survives because she is wild, a connection that Erdrich codifies by enfolding it in comedy. Not only is Fleur repeatedly resurrected from the lake but she also is attended by circumstances that make funny sense: the sow's dance and the tornado that rips through Argus after she has left. That tornado drives the covey of men who raped her into the meat locker for protection where the boy Russell locks them in to freeze. (Russell and Pauline had witnessed the rape.) Only one man can be thawed out to show any vital signs, and then he has a horrific recovery—as Erdrich writes, "Dutch James rotted in the bedroom sawed away piece by piece" (62). Wildly dark humor such as this not only describes the fate of the rapists, it marks the process by which Fleur again survives.

Wildness, humor, and survival coalesce in Erdrich's choice of setting. She places her novels in the west partly because it is the genesis of her imagination and because the fictional families she creates offer the homecoming that she cannot have there with her young family. To Erdrich, North Dakota is wild (*The Blue Jay's Dance* 90). She thrives psychologically in that territory where wild nature's provoking patterns hint at being meaningful but endlessly defy explication. Wild nature is the avatar of comedy in ecological terms, always doubling back through change to emerge anew, poised to circle and change again: what is wild survives, though it remains vulnerable. To guard against that vulnerability, Erdrich recommends that we learn from Indians, since they have lived here without pushing the land toward ecological disaster (Chavkin 147).[52] The most essential mark of "Indianness" in her work is her sense of humor, if we are to corroborate her statement that humor may be the most common factor among all the tribes—a primary ceremony. How Indians have managed to maintain a long equilibrium with nature is implicitly answered in Erdrich's celebration of wildness through humor. For humor does not merely buoy the oppressed against the oppressor or temporize one's oppression, it is part of an attitude that accepts and embraces mystery and chaos in our lives. It helps us negotiate our relation to the larger wild world beyond our grasp and find creative inspiration from it. If humor is the most serious thing "we do," as Erdrich says of her life with Michael Dorris, that is because it is the practice of an attitude that, in the experience of Native Americans, has proven itself to work on this continent. Humor is a sign of a native and successful worldview in action.

▼ ▼ ▼

ERDRICH IS A BRILLIANT PLAYER WITH NARRATIVE PERSPECTIVE, DE-lighting in the surprises that come of it and the revelations that those surprises fashion, for shifts in perspective lay out different paths to the truth. Such is the multifarious nature of reality that absorbs Erdrich. The surprises in her prose mean that she has looked around at the fictional landscape and its characters, speculating about them. "I don't have omnipotent control over the characters and voices" who appear in her work, she says, happy to portray them as complex and unpredictable (Chavkin 224, 231).

Unpredictable aptly describes June Kashpaw in the opening scene of Erdrich's first novel, *Love Medicine* (1–7). She is waiting for a bus to go home to the reservation. A man motions to her from inside a bar, and she goes in "without hesitation" to accept his invitation, casual about the possibilities, wondering if she knows him or not. Perhaps it is no surprise that an Indian woman who has had a hard life and resorted to making money from men in an oil boomtown will accompany a stranger from bar to bar while they get drunk; or that in the first bar she peels the bright shells of

52. In an article in *The New York Times Book Review*, she also recommends that we learn from fiction that features landscape: "although fiction alone may lack the power to head us off the course of destruction, it affects us as individuals and can spur us to treat the earth, in which we abide and which harbors us, as we would treat our own mothers and fathers. For, once we no longer live beneath our mother's heart, it is the earth with which we form the same dependent relationship, relying completely on its cycles and elements, helpless without its protective embrace" ("Where I Ought to Be: A Writer's Sense of Place" 24).

hard-boiled Easter eggs displayed in cartons and eats voraciously; or that her sweater, a pink shell, has a rip across the stomach that she carefully conceals; or that she carries in her purse the doorknob to her room because when she leaves she cannot lock it any other way. And it is no surprise, only the sad truth, that she finds that this man is "no different," as she had blindly hoped he would be. When they park out on a snowy distant county road and he lapses from his clumsy lovemaking into a drunken stupor, she acts with startling grace, driven by the desire to keep herself intact, un-cracked. She walks off, resolving to go home. This decision makes her more vulnerable to the wild and more powerful a person than she ever has been. June Kashpaw dies in a snowstorm that night, but somehow—cracked shell and all—she has managed to preserve herself.

> Even when it started to snow she did not lose her sense of direction. Her feet grew numb, but she did not worry about the distance. The heavy winds couldn't blow her off course. She continued. Even when her heart clenched and her skin turned crackling cold it didn't matter because the pure and naked part of her went on.
>
> The snow fell deeper that Easter than it had in forty years, but June walked over it like water and came home (7).

In this telling, June's fate is almost not a death at all because she is escaping her dismal struggles and spiritually returning home, although her family mourns her as dead. So Michael Dorris says of *Love Medicine*, "basically this is the story of the reverberation of June's life" (Chavkin 21). Not death but life is the emphasis. Thus in the succeeding chapters, through other characters, we return tangentially to June and learn via them about her part in the Kashpaw and Morrissey families. We move so thoroughly into their lives that we drop our focus on June and find instead that she is res-urrected repeatedly in others. It is Easter, after all, when she heads home in a snowstorm. Her death is accomplished as a return home into family life.

Twelve years later, in the novel *Tales of Burning Love*, Erdrich returns to the scene of June's rendezvous, this time from the perspective of the man who picks her up (3–11). For the reader, the revisitation is suspensefully promising, as if it will clarify the event. We think we might learn better why June died. Instead what happens is a complication of the truth as we know it from her perspective in *Love Medicine*, for we develop sympathy for this narrator. The man is Jack Mauser, also raised on the reservation, and he has a terrible toothache. He is on his way to the dentist when he stops in the bar for "temporary anesthesia" and happens to see June. She knows immediately that something is wrong with him and suggests for his toothache cloves, horseweed, or a hammer. For strangers, they are candid and bold, as this exchange shows, yet also cautious, hiding things from each other for self-preservation. June keeps the tear in her pink top hidden, we know from *Love Medicine*, and now we learn that Jack tells her his name is Andy and tries to conceal his Indian relation to her. They shy away from each other even as the night draws them closer. Talk about unpredictable! They have a bar wedding and "beer-can pop-top wedding rings," which they are almost too drunk to lace onto their fingers. Their fatal encounter cannot be blamed on either one of them, and though we discover that Jack was not unconscious and could have followed June when she left into the snow, the truth is that he was as vulnerable as she was. Neither his rescue nor hers came.

> She'd take him in like a stray, he vaguely felt, protect him the way she thought he was protecting her. Once he entered her he would be safe. He would be whole. He would be easy with who he was, and it would all turn out. His life. By climbing into her body, he would exist (9).

But this fantasy preceded his attempt to make love to her when he cried instead and chose to keep still rather than have her see him so weak. For her part, June decides to prevail by choosing to head home, despite the conditions that prove it to be a fatal mistake. Jack is part of her mistake. That he is guilty for the circumstances of her death is a revelation that serves to enhance June's transcendence. In agony, he waits out the snowstorm in his apartment, swallowing his pop-top wedding ring to get rid of it when the cat refuses to do so. In the search party after the blizzard, Jack finds her.

> She'd gotten tired of walking in those thin shoes, and sat down against a fence, lost. To wait for the bus, he thought. She was looking east, her hair loaded with melting stars. No one had touched her yet. Her face was complex in its expectations. A fist of air punched Jack to earth and he knelt before her with his hands outstretched. But then the officer reached past him, thumbed her eyelids down, took her purse from her lap, knocked off her blanket of snow (11).

This last picture of June as she was when she "walked over [the snow] like water and came home" (*Love Medicine* 7) is presented more than a decade after the publication of *Love Medicine*. Although it makes the fact of her death more literal, the scene preserves that sense of the marvelous with which Erdrich's first novel had endowed it. Death surprises June, coming down like the snow that blankets her, that puts the "melting stars" in her hair, and obviously death never curtails her emotional drive to go home.

Survival is a complex proposition in Erdrich's fiction. June dies surviving, as we see from two different points of view; she prefigures the sometimes fatal struggles endured by five interrelated families on the reservation.[53] The nature of that endurance is manifested in Erdrich's narrative technique, which splits the munificent stories of this place between the characters so that they get told at different times and from different perspectives. What we learn from one character is complemented by another. The narrative power lies in the conjunction of the stories as much as in the individual tales. No single story satisfies Erdrich to tell the fictional truth, for the inconsistencies and variation among the stories best celebrate her notion that the world is wild, as we are wild within it. June's symbolic survival begins *Tales of Burning Love* in a long plot of how Jack survives June—and his four other wives—and how they survive him as well as each other. The resulting web of voices produces a kind of family ecology that is characteristic of Erdrich's fiction and, according to Paula Gunn Allen, of Native American literature.

> Traditional American Indian stories work dynamically among clusters of loosely interconnected circles. The focus of action shifts from one character to another as the story unfolds. There is no "point of view" as the term is generally understood, unless the action itself, the story's purpose, can be termed "point of view" (*The Sacred Hoop* 241–42).

Erdrich's technique purposefully encourages unpredictability, for the juxtaposition of tales creates surprises that the individual accounts do not. She sees that the survival of these families lies in their ability to cope with the surprises they face in the crazy world and in each other; thus the format of her novels—that polyphony of voices—suggests the kind of strength to be found in relationships, often the very relationships that foment surprise. Each voice contributes to the context where all voices are linked in a powerful family ecology that endures change and loss. Her refracted narration radiates with that endurance.

53. These families are Nanapush, Lamartine, Lazarre, Morrissey, and Kashpaw.

To practice surprise—which is one measure of a survivor—means making humor and seeking it out. As a writer, Erdrich has serious aims, and these infuse her humor. She says, "Contemporary Native American writers have . . . a task quite different from that of other writers. . . . In the light of enormous loss, they must tell the stories of contemporary survivors while protecting and celebrating the cores of cultures left in the wake of the catastrophe" ("Where I Ought To Be: A Writer's Sense of Place" 23). Erdrich's work makes it clear that she does not have a particular belief that answers the problems of Native Americans (or Americans in general), but she does have recourse in the practice of humor, which is infinitely accommodating and flexible, not a formula but a skill. Rather than tell us how contemporary Native Americans survive, Erdrich calls on her skill to be funny in order to show us how life can feel, how uplifting and powerful. That celebration comes via her fiction in joking or twisting plots.

Her humor is verbal and circumstantial—and happens in the most serious moments. In *The Bingo Palace*, for instance, when Lipsha Morrissey and his half-uncle/half-brother Lyman Lamartine are both in love with the same woman, Shawnee Ray, they make an uneasy partnership, thrown comically together by their similarly miserable situation. The complications are immense. They like each other, they respect each other, they help each other—and they fight. Lipsha fraternally asks Lyman to arrange for him a spiritual quest, and since Lyman already has a fast planned for himself, he agrees to include Lipsha. They both need guidance, but inevitably they will be pitting their spirituality against each other in competition for their beloved. As Lipsha reflects, "I go looking for a god I cannot resist, try to get to heaven through the ozone hole, land on any old star. I look for peace, I look for love. I end up in a religious war" (158). Lipsha is Fleur Pillager's great grandson, and though he has her touch, he does not yet command the same patience or experience that she has.[54] The competition that the two young men wage with their vision fasts is ridiculous, almost making mockery of the tradition they hope to attach themselves to. Prelude to their spiritual effort is their meal at the Dairy Queen—it is a nice gesture, their eating together, Lipsha paying the bill though Lyman is the wealthy one. But it turns out to be subject to the same wild, jealous energy that skews their ceremonial fasting. Just like a little boy, Lipsha provokes a fight.

54. Lipsha's dad is Gerry Nanapush, whose name, Erdrich has acknowledged, echoes the traditional Chippewa trickster hero Nanabozho (Chavkin 252). James McKenzie contends that Lipsha is "a contemporary transformation" of Nanabozho (60). William Gleason calls Lipsha a "modern pinball medicine man" (59).

I get so upset looking at the strong arms and winning bone structure of Lyman Lamartine that my teeth clench on the plastic straw. I raise the straw up, and then I spray pop onto our reservation's biggest tamale (167).

It is a childish way of losing control. The slapstick, ice-cream-smashing fight that follows proves to be an exuberant release for both men, and it includes everyone in the melee, from the woman whose shirt front is "sluice[d]" with chocolate and pineapple and begins "an immediate and deadly argument about who will pay the bill for the dry cleaning" (167) to the man "who is massaging a banana split" (167) into Lyman's hair. The fight makes them friends as much as it reinforces the depth of their frustration and pain. William Gleason notes that "humor mirrors hurt" in *Love Medicine* (52), and the same may be said of *The Bingo Palace* and Erdrich's other novels.[55]

In the sweat lodge preceding the fast, Lipsha is worried that his prayer will not be as good as Lyman's, which "sounds like it could be used to open up a conference" (193). But Lipsha is succored by the fact that, as he says, "heat adds to my praying ability." "I try to cool off by talking faster, praying louder, as if my tongue is a little fan, but then I give up and fall quiet" (193). With humor, Erdrich gleefully curtails the superficial climb of traditions onto a sacred plane beyond the grasp of ordinary people. She revels in showing that Lipsha is understandably cranky. It is hot in the sweat lodge, and he goes through a spectrum of emotions, including anxiety, oblivion, anger, panic, and serenity. He is not noble and does not feel remarkable after the experience—he is ordinary, and he is an Indian. In showing us a clumsy and unskilled practice of one Native American tradition, Erdrich deflates the assumption that Indians are privy to communion with the world more than other folks are. The idealization of tradition makes it intimidating, untenable, and impossible to practice; Erdrich instead wants it down where the rest of us muddle along, where it is part of our humor and aspirations for enlightenment. She represents tradition humorously so that it may be accessible and exoteric. In fact, her conviction is that the sacred cannot be contained exclusively in solemn ritual. Upon explaining that writing and reproduction address our need to "partake of the eternal," she counters, "and once we realize that nothing really does, anything can—pulling weeds, picking apples, putting children to bed" (*The*

55. According to Gleason, Erdrich's "expert and caring use of humor" makes the pain and trouble portrayed in *Love Medicine* not tragic but transformative and hopeful (51).

Blue Jay's Dance 79). Ordinary activities—especially the repetitive ones that we do out of necessity—are the rudiments of spiritual practice, according to Erdrich. Gary Snyder's *The Practice of the Wild* further elucidates that power in the mundane.

> Repetition and ritual and their good results come in many forms. Changing the filter, wiping noses, going to meetings, picking up around the house, washing dishes, checking the dipstick—don't let yourself think these are distracting you from your more serious pursuits. Such a round of chores is not a set of difficulties we hope to escape from so that we may do our "practice" which will put us on a "path"—it *is* our path (153).

For Erdrich, humor democratizes the sacred, displacing it from lofty status so that it may enter the quotidian world. Humor may be the most common ceremony practiced by tribal people because it insistently puts the sacred within daily life. So Lipsha is peevish and inadvertently funny during the sweat, feeling outraged when his rival sprinkles more water to make things hotter: "I could kill Lyman. I'm a cooked steak" (*The Bingo Palace* 194). His fast goes no more smoothly, especially the first night when he wakes up in the darkness, afraid and panicked, clearly not at home in nature. "Deer could step on me down here on the ground. I think of their pointed hooves. Then I think of teeth. Fangs, tusks, rabbit incisors. Jaws for tearing. Sharks. Forget sharks. Bears. Raccoons" (196). Lipsha's stream-of-consciousness descent into fear takes him far beyond the dangers that the place—the midwest—could offer. Yet the young man hears "jaws" in his rattled interior monologue and thinks *sharks* since he is a modern kid, after all, and probably saw the movie *Jaws*. To readers, the joke reveals the extent to which Lipsha is inattentive to his native place, though it could empower him as it has empowered Fleur. Lipsha is contemporary to a fault—and beloved for that very reason.

The woman both men are pursuing is a contemporary survivor. She is talented, ambitious, and traditional; she intends to market her original designs for ceremonial dance costumes to finance her way to college. Lipsha daydreams about her this way:

> You can see Shawnee Ray deep in the past, running down a buffalo on a little paint war-horse, or maybe on her own limber legs. You can see her felling the animal with one punch to the brain. Or standing bent-elbowed with a lance. You can see her throwing that spear without hes-

itation right through a cavalry man or a mastodon. Shawnee Ray, she is the best of our past, our present, our hope of a future (12–13).

In this woman, Erdrich has made the mix of traditional culture with modern times appear graceful. Lipsha's attraction to her is symbolic of his desire to be an Indian who retains his ancient connections to the world and the ability to flourish in the present, where the skill to take down a mastodon will not help him buy condoms at an all-night gas station in preparation for a motel date with Shawnee Ray. She has insisted he purchase them. When he suggests romantically, "'Let's not think about tomorrow,'" she retorts with maternal savvy: "'That's how I got Redford'" (70). Lipsha conversationally jousts with the attendant on the late shift but manages to make the purchase anyway, puzzling, "It's strange how a bashful kind of person like me gets talkative in some of our less pleasant border-town situations" (71). He does not have the same graceful composure as the woman he adores, but his discomfort in being caught between two worlds is at least mediated by humor. The vision he finally gets when fasting is an embarrassment. He has higher aspirations than to be psychically accosted by a skunk and then sprayed by it. But that is what happens—and it shocks everyone out of respectful composure. When he walks out of the woods and first meets his spiritual guide, Xavier Toose, Lipsha is mystified by his behavior.

> I think at first he's been shot, had a heart attack, that he's finally bought it, for he collapses on the ground and begins to roll this way, that, over and over so quick it looks like he's in agony. But now, as I run to him, as I try to help, his arms flap helplessly, his face is screwed up but not with suffering. He's laughing, and laughing so hard there is no use talking to him, no use at all (201).

Lipsha retires to the spread of picnic food and gets to eat alone, while everyone gathers at a safe distance to call out and laugh. Lyman, of course, has a serious and profound vision, which he retells with drama and passion.

Despite Lyman's proficiency during the vision fast and his success in general, he does not win Shawnee Ray's love. The differences between him and Lipsha clarify Erdrich's preferences for the kind of Indian who will endure best, maintaining cultural skills in a spirit worthy of the ancestors. Lipsha is this Indian in large part because he is not perfect as Lyman seems to be. In Lipsha's vision, the skunk speaks with a voice that Lipsha hears inside his head, *"This ain't real estate"* (200); those words and that skunk come back to him, nagging him, once he is in his bed at home. He is peeved to have such a persistent and pitiful vision, and talks back to the skunk.

> "Excuse me," I say, "I got the wrong vision. Could you change the channel?"
>
> To *what?*
>
> "I don't know. Maybe to some horses who split the sky with their hooves. Or a bear, an eagle with a bald head and long brown wings to carry me a saying to mess with Lyman's mind" (220).

Lipsha would prefer a vision of stereotypical repute, complete with traditional noble animals. The skunk wrecks all that, laying waste to idealized pictures of enlightenment and in the process baffling Lipsha, who resorts to humor to cope with the wild surprise. On the other hand, Lyman manages to have an experience that does not call upon humor to be understood.

The opposing opinions that the two have about money also differentiate them and indicate the kind of economic philosophy that suits Erdrich. Lipsha does not trust money to be predictable; to him it is dead. His rival, however, maintains that it is alive and acts upon understandable principles: you cultivate it, it grows. Lyman is rich. Lipsha is lucky (he won big at bingo, which is what occasions the lecture about money that Lyman gives him), and Lipsha stays lucky as long as he does not try to profit from it. This is one of the remarks that the skunk makes, *"Luck don't stick when you sell it"* (220). At first, Lipsha is jocular about his new wealth, jazzing up Lyman's steadfast explanation of money's increase by calling it "'The facts of life'"—but Lyman takes the joke seriously, using "'The sex of money'" as a metaphor that will get Lipsha's attention. When it does, Erdrich notes that the younger man's humor about money ends (101). Keeping his humor, Lipsha kept his luck. But considered for economic potential rather than a gift, his luck dissipates. Thus Lipsha learns that it may be lost along with his healing touch, legacy from the Pillager line, for both are gifts, impossible to increase by management but beneficent if given up freely and given away. In the end, Lipsha's attitude toward Lyman's "bingo palace"—slotted for construction right by Lake Matchimanito where the skunk lives—is clearly approved of by the author. Lyman is too deeply enamored of his money-making skill to have the philosophy that Lipsha develops. Lipsha figures this:

It's not completely one way or another, traditional against the bingo. You have to stay alive to keep your tradition alive and working. Everybody knows bingo money is not based on solid ground. . . . The money life has got no substance, there's nothing left when the day is done but a pack of receipts. Money gets money, but little else, nothing sensible to look at or touch or feel in yourself down to your bones. . . . Our reservation is not real estate, luck fades when sold (221).

The skunk of his absurd and embarrassing vision was on the money after all, in terms of speaking for the right of the land to be exempt from economic assessment and remain a wild, scruffy place where the Pillagers once lived, where troubled, love-sick Indians can go to fast and feel as if they are out in the wilderness—to remain a gift. Fundamental to Erdrich's portrayal of Lipsha is her approval of his humor, humor that makes him receptive to a skunk's advice and capable of imagining that the worth of things may be beyond their quantifiable or even human value. Wildness eludes property rights, cannot be bought or sold or retained in any way but as a gift since it is not something we can know completely or control. And humor, a gift in itself, gives us a taste of wildness, good preparation for whetting the palate and welcoming wildness as it comes via the unpredictable skunk and the woods on the banks of the mysterious Matchimanito. Shawnee Ray falls in love with Lipsha, not Lyman, making the younger man with the quicker humor and the wild, powerful Pillager touch her match—and in Erdrich's eyes, the match necessary to contemporary successful Indian life as represented by Shawnee Ray. The fact that humor gives Lipsha access to new perspectives about old traditions means that Erdrich's play with perspectives among her characters practices the humor that she sees healthy to Native American survival. Updated by humor, old ways remain contemporary.

▼ ▼ ▼

ERDRICH IS NOT DIDACTIC. UNLIKE ABBEY, BERRY, AND CARSON, SHE does not explicitly advocate conservation or wilderness preservation or community life; unlike them, fiction is her primary medium. When an interviewer once asked her, "Is part of your intention…to instruct and reform," she exclaimed, "God, no!" (Chavkin 235). Strong and swift, her reaction indicates how she conceives of the effect of her work. Since she does not pretend to have answers to profess, she does not appeal for us to agree with her. Instead she wants to transport us via her writing to emotional and imaginative participation in the fictional world centered on an Indian reservation and nearby Argus, North Dakota. What she teaches is embodied in what she celebrates and how she makes us feel. Her greatest thrill is to surprise us with the wild things that go on in this human community; her most direct acknowledgment of wildness in the wider ecological community comes in her exploration of the mysteries that abound here, tantalizing us with the suggestion but never the assurance of meaning.[56]

In her fictional world, setting is a trickster. It suggests that there may be a comprehensive design in the universe but never confirms that. In regard to intuiting that design, we readers are not so different from most of her characters. We may be informed by stories about their relatives or townspeople, but we do not surpass any of them in anticipating the surprises that nature harbors. So the snowstorm comes up from what June expects is a Chinook wind, and the lake has a spirit man who lives in it and lusts after bold young women but gives back ones like Fleur so she can come to him again, be drowned and resurrected. That lake man saves Lipsha as a baby when his mother, June Kashpaw, sinks him in it to drown. His survival is something he remembers only when waking from dreams that follow his fast, for it is too deep and too far in the past for him to know with his ordinary mind (*The Bingo Palace* 216–18). The mysteries leave our rational understanding behind, which is something Lulu Nanapush, Fleur's daughter, knows.

> All through my life I never did believe in human measurements. Numbers, time, inches, feet. All are just ploys for cutting nature down to size. I know the grand scheme of the world is beyond our brains to fathom, so I don't try, just let it in. I don't believe in numbering God's creatures. I never let the United States census in my door, even though they say it's good for Indians. Well, quote me. I say that every time they counted us they know the precise number to get rid of (*Love Medicine* 281–2).

Lulu ought to know that some things are too wild to quantify. She is the one whose passions were lit as a teenager when she traveled across Lake Matchimanito to seduce the crazy, island-dwelling hermit Moses Pillager,

---

56. Also unlike Abbey, Berry, and Carson, Erdrich is not typically considered a nature writer. The inclusion of her here demonstrates how flexible the nature writing canon could be and how much it would benefit in terms of diversity and originality were it to include writers like Erdrich.

and whose lover of five years, Nector Kashpaw, decides to leave his wife, Marie, but in waiting at Lulu's house drops a cigarette and accidentally burns the whole place down—which forces him back to his wife (*Love Medicine* 76–82; 139–45). Both situations go out of human control, though the passions of Lulu and Moses and Nector all spark the events. As Lulu said of her sexual quickening with Moses, "I was not immune, and I would not leave undamaged. To this day, I still hurt. I must have rolled in the beds of wild rose, for the tiny thorns—small, yellow—pierced my skin. Their poison is desire and it dissolved in my blood. The cats made me one of them—sleek and without mercy, avid, falling hungry upon the defenseless body" (82). Lulu's desire for men, which she describes here as an animalistic urge, came straight from the wildness of the man Moses, who Lulu realizes is himself a conduit: "He was his island, he was me, he was his cats, he did not exist from the inside out but from the outside in" (83). Wound out of that place and the lake her mother had drowned in so often, the wildness has marched right into Lulu. How it spreads around her the rest of her life is comic, resulting, in one instance, in Nector's impatient passion and the foolish, coincidental torching of her house that he accomplishes with a crumpled love letter, his discarded cigarette, and his moral inertia.

Some folks in Erdrich's fiction are closer to intuiting the ineffable natural patterns that enfold us all. While they too may be surprised, they are quicker to participate in and guess at the significance of fateful events. When Gerry Nanapush, Lulu's son and radical Indian activist, knows he is to be transferred from a prison in Florida to one in Minnesota, he is glad and acutely sensitive. The plane ride promises much purely in terms of sensory experience, which affects Gerry powerfully after his long incarceration. Attuned to his surroundings, he feels lucky and open to anything.

> He knew from sitting in the still eye of chance that fate was not random. Chance was full of runs and soft noise, pardons and betrayals and double-backs. Chance was patterns of a stranger complexity than we could name, but predictable. There was no such thing as a complete lack of order, only a design so vast it seemed unrepetitive up close, that is, until you sat doing nothing for so long that your brain ached and, one day, just maybe, you caught a wider glimpse.
>
> Some people, lightning struck twice. Some people attracted accidents. Fate bunched up and gathered like a blanket. Some people were born on the smooth parts and some got folded into the pucker. When

the engine skipped and chattered and burped back into its drawl, Gerry opened his eyes, alert, and asked if there wasn't some way to remove the bar from his legs while airborne (*The Bingo Palace* 226).

Apart from getting his leg bar removed, which he cannot persuade the federal marshals to do, he could not have planned a better piece of good fortune than what follows—they are blown down by a storm. Gerry gets out through the busted plane and hops off. "And all the while, as he moved, not cold in the least because of the effort, his life kept surging up between his feet, his bound wrists, welling up like black water when you step on thin ice, spreading up through his arms, choking him, practically killing him with the accumulated joy" (227). No explanation can be posited for the timing of the flight, the storm, the crash. Whatever design may have prompted these events to transpire, Gerry does not question. Instead he bounds into brush, around cattails and onward, escaping, his emotion the most eloquent acknowledgment of his reentry into the unaccountable design of the wild world. It is snowing just as it was when his lover, June, walked away from Jack Mauser's pick-up toward home. In this crisscrossing of details from disparate events, Erdrich gestures at oblique correspondences in her characters' lives, as spread through the plots of several books. One truth that arises is that storms are beneficial—they release people, setting them loose and wild again. But Erdrich is as careful not to delineate meanings as Lulu is to obfuscate the truth for the federal agents who come to the nursing home where she lives in order to interview her about the escape of her son Gerry. This is the voice of the other nursing home residents, commenting on what happens:

They were very smart, these federals. No doubt they were wise. They had seen a lot of hard cases, chased a lot of criminals, solved a great many crimes that would stump us ordinary Chippewas. And yet, the fact is, they had never encountered Lulu. For that reason, they spent a long time questioning a fish in the river, they spent a longer time talking to a turtle in its shell, they tried to intimidate a female badger guarding the mouth of its den and then to fool an old lady coyote who trotted wide of the marks her pups had left. They spent hours, in which they should have been tracking down their wary escapee, asking Lulu one question, in many different ways, until she seemed to break down, shaking her hands and fanning herself with feigned distress (*The Bingo Palace* 263).

Lulu has a story for the officials—many stories, much confusing evidence. In this way, she who has wrangled for Gerry's transfer to Minnesota is cannily poised to step in sync with the snowstorm that has extracted him from his captors; she increases his chances of staying free by acting as if her memory is as capricious as fate itself. Lulu shares the knack for being elusive. As she said before, "I know the grand scheme of the world is beyond our brains to fathom, so I don't try, just let it in" (*Love Medicine* 281).

Since the place—its weather, its lake—behaves as a trickster, then some of its people are bound to follow suit, capturing the spirit of their swerving world laden with signs. Instances of characters who manipulate or falsify signs abound in Erdrich's work. In each case, they are seeking meaning and trying to cope with their world; each time, how they cope is imbued with humor, whether Erdrich's or their own. The first false sign issues from the Sacred Heart Convent on the hill at the edge of town. Marie, Nector's future wife, goes there in her early teens to become the holiest Catholic around. She is fierce in her devotions, as fierce as the vicious Sister Leopolda, who takes Marie as her charge.[57] The confrontations between the two escalate until the nun pours scalding water from a kettle onto the girl's back, and Marie tries to jab her into the oven, hot for making bread. Marie's words retell it: "The oven was like the gate of a personal hell. Just big enough and hot enough for one person, and that was her. One kick and Leopolda would fly in headfirst. And that would be one-millionth of the heat she would feel when she finally collapsed in his hellish embrace. Saints know these numbers" (*Love Medicine* 57). Ironically, both women have aspirations to sainthood. Because the nun is holding a poker when Marie pushes her, it hits the back wall of the oven and bounces her back out—then she stabs Marie through the hand. Thus they have a miracle on their hands, so to speak, for there is no other way to cover up their bitter tussle than to announce it as a holy vision, which gave Marie the stigmata—a mark of the crucifixion—in her hand. Leopolda offers the story, and Marie assumes a beatified attitude when she regains consciousness. Although enemies, they are thrown together to construct this fake miracle—their holiness a sham, a painful joke.

The episode that gives *Love Medicine* its title actually involves a fake substitute for real love medicine. Lipsha is too scared, you see, to go ask Fleur Pillager for advice about such a medicine, yet he wants to make his

57. In *Tracks*, we learn that the young Pauline, who failed to help Fleur when she was raped, becomes Sister Leopolda. We learn also that Marie was her illegitimate, abandoned daughter.

Grandpa Nector forget Lulu at last and love only his wife, Marie. Lipsha decides he can get the hearts of two Canada geese, who mate for life, and have his grandparents eat them. But his patience snaps after waiting a long, chilly day in the rushes and missing the geese he shoots at, so he decides to buy frozen turkeys at the store and use their hearts. His rationalizations for this "evil shortcut" (245) are extensive—"I told myself love medicine was simple. I told myself the old superstitions was just that—strange beliefs" (245). He argues with himself about the constancy of faith—"Higher Power makes promises we all know they can't back up, but anybody ever go and slap an old malpractice suit on God? . . . I finally convinced myself that the real actual power to the love medicine was not the goose heart itself but the faith in the cure" (245–46). Lipsha's logical contortions are pitiful and amusing. He can even see the error: "I didn't believe it, I knew it was wrong, but by then I had waded so far into my lie I was stuck there" (246). He decides to wade farther, bringing the package of hearts to the Catholic mission to get an official blessing, but neither priest nor nun will deign to bless it, leaving Lipsha to snatch their sanction as he can—with his fingers quickly dipped in the holy water so that he can sprinkle the unworthy package of turkey hearts. Not only does his ersatz medicine not work but it also prompts a comic battle between Marie and Nector—her trying to get him to eat the heart—that ends tragically with his death. She knocks him on the back to make him swallow the heart, and he chokes on it. It is undoubtedly dangerous medicine, this fooling with faith and false signs. Lipsha underestimates the extent to which his healing touch must be based on the power intrinsic to the wild physical world. Honesty requires acknowledgment of greater powers, Lipsha learns. His misadventures represent many of Erdrich's characters' effort to plumb the crazy world for some meaning, to find a way to know the "Higher Powers."

In *The Beet Queen*, a novel centered on the town of Argus and its German as well as Indian residents, another questionable miracle satisfies scores of people but does not fool its principal witnesses. It happens at St. Catherine's School when Mary Adare, whose mother had abandoned her and her brothers by flying off with a stunt pilot at a fair in Minneapolis, chose to disobey the nuns and go down the slide, slick with black ice. She goes headfirst, figuring she can slide across the yard on her stomach. But she does not—she hits face first, blacking out on impact. From her friend Celestine James' perspective, the miracle is not communicated via the actual imprint of Mary's face in the ice but by everyone's reaction to it. The nun who lifts Mary tells Celestine "frantically" to fetch Leopolda.

> And so I run, so amazed and excited at how she has expressed herself, not like a teacher but just like a farmer, that I do not ring the convent bell but leap straight into the entryway and scream up the echoing stairs. By then I know, because it is in the air of the school yard, that some kind of miracle had resulted from Mary's fall.
>
> So I shout, "A MIRACLE" at the top of my lungs. To do that in a convent is like shouting fire in a crowded movie. They all rush down suddenly, an avalanche of black wool (42).

Sister Leopolda comes with tripod and camera, giving Celestine reason to analyze the fervor. "It is like she has been right behind her door, armed with equipment praying year in and out for this moment to arrive" (42). Both girls are circumspect in relation to the chaos that has broken out on the schoolyard. The face broken into the ice, everyone fancies, is the face of Christ. Celestine goes to the infirmary, bearing that news to Mary.

> "They say it's a miracle," I tell. I expect her to laugh but she grips my hand hard. Her eyes take on a glitter that I start to suspect.
>
> "It was a sign," she says, "but not what they think" (43).

Mary is not amused because she swears the sign portends her brother Karl's return, which she is loathe to imagine. Celestine herself cannot see a thing in the spot but crushed ice. Both girls have complicity in the public frenzy, however, letting people feed spiritually on the fake sign. The hunger for the miracle reveals a common desperation for assurance that divinity exists, that our lives have purpose and meaning. Yet what people see may be only the result of how they are influenced by the collective surge of imaginative faith. Erdrich gives us a comic perspective on all this through the girls' experience, deflating the miracle. Miracles happen mostly because we need them to happen, Erdrich suggests, and even then they are subject to natural forces. This is from Mary's perspective, describing the aftermath of the event.

> And then one day, the sun came out and suddenly warmed the earth. The face of Karl, or Christ, dispersed into little rivulets that ran all through the town. Echoing in gutters, disappearing, swelling through culverts and collecting in basements, he made himself impossibly everywhere and nowhere all at once so that all spring before the town

baked hard, before the drought began, I felt his presence in the whispering and sighing of the streams (40–41).

The way the imprint melts further deflates it as a miracle but simultaneously conflates it with the passage of the seasons. As such, as part of the equinoctial round, it joins a miracle so taken for granted it is nigh invisible. Miracles do happen in Erdrich's fiction. The more unaccountable the event, the more tantalizing it is in terms of revealing some sign about the world—thus the preoccupation of Erdrich's characters with signs. What we see repeatedly is that surprising things happen, and the moment of surprise when things are most wild, least predictable, tells us most about the world. For within that moment, we cease to attempt to control anything—we become reactive, adaptable, and creative. We experience the certainty that we are connected to a greater whole; we feel the freedom of participating in what we are given up to, what moves us. Because it is a skill to enter these moments of abandon and because they are impossible to replicate in explanations, Erdrich surrounds and pervades them with humor. Humor helps her negotiate meaning and meaninglessness in the world. It is not that surprise is always funny, but that humor gives the author an experiential, nondidactic way of communicating to us the thrill of surprise. Surprise satisfies our attraction to miracles by giving us a quick taste of revelation.

▼ ▼ ▼

IN *THE BLUE JAY'S DANCE*, WHEN ERDRICH SPEAKS OF MISSING THE WILDS of North Dakota, she turns to the trees of the Northeast to console herself and satisfy her longings. She revels in their sound and imagines their experience in the wind.

> If there is a vegetative soul, an animating power that all things share, there must be great rejoicing out there on windy days, ecstasy, for trees move so slowly on calm days. At least it seems that way to us. On days of high wind they move so freely it must give them a cellular pleasure close to terror (92).

The wind shapes trees, keeping them flexible and paring them down, toppling them; it is, more or less, a necessary danger. Ecstasy. The wind-whipped twist and grind of trees is ecstasy. That she imagines this experience to be "cellular pleasure close to terror" underscores her acceptance of risk, her wide delight in beauty. Erdrich is particularly interested in the beauty and perfection of our most absurd or horrific moments. Her sense of humor enables her to construct and deal inclusively with the unseemly, showing that it fits and celebrating it by making us gape or laugh. Because humor is one of our most comprehensive reactions, coalescing, as it does, emotional, intellectual, and physiological responses, Erdrich makes us laugh to reinforce through our experience her conviction that things are in harmony. Even the most painful experiences can be beautiful ones; when we laugh, we restore the world's comic order.

Her account of labor and childbirth accords them ecstasy, terror, and comic energy. She wants to amuse us and to position us with her in awe of the experience. Regarding her behavior, her reflections bar no confession.

> On the way into labor with our first natural-born child I was in a fury of cleaning—every spot of dirt made me weep with rage. The cats sliding in and out through the broken foundation of the basement sent me quivering with hatred into the bathroom to stare at myself and ask: *How can a being grow so vast?* Look! There was no part of me unstretched— even my toes were little clubs in my shoes! I was a big, mad, absurd woman stirring food in a pot, writing desperately, trying not to smoke. I whined and roared in the house, alone, after Michael and our older children were gone. I began to scrape at the bathroom sink with a scrubbing pad when calmly, from deep within this great lumbering mound of myself . . . she began to be born.
>
> There was just time to set my hair with electric rollers! (*The Blue Jay's Dance* 40–41).

Pregnant to full term, she is comically compulsive—and more than a little ridiculous, especially when it comes to the curlers. Yet even in this description, she suggests that compulsion is a deeper, calmer force that drives (more inevitably than her idiosyncrasies) the process of childbirth. That compulsion has both outcomes, the tantrums and the work that brings forth the child. Erdrich neglects neither and does not pretend that she entirely approves of the body's forcefulness.

> Birth is dictated to the consciousness by the conscious body. There are certain frustrations in approaching such an event, a drama in which the body stars and not the fiction-making mind. In a certain way, I'm jealous. I want to control the tale. I can't—therein lies the conflict that drives

this plot in the first place. I have to trust this body—a thing inherently bound to betray me, an unreliable conveyance, a passion-driven cab that tries its best to let me off in bad neighborhoods, an adolescent that rebels against my better self, that eats erratically and sleeps too much, that grows another human with my grudging admiration, a sensation grabber, unpenitent, remorseless, amoral (43–44).

Her pointedly realistic estimation of her body is not meant to mitigate the sacred passage of the pregnancy, the plot that climaxes in birth. Rather, Erdrich is candid about her weaknesses because she holds them coeval with the more celebrated functions of her body. All of its characteristics are beloved—just as they are provoking, frustrating, challenging. And all of what the body is contributes to its sweep into labor. Erdrich describes that experience two ways, explication and narration. First the explication:

> Rocking, breathing, groaning, mouthing circles of distress, laughing, whistling, pounding, wavering, digging, pulling, pushing—labor is the most involuntary work we do. My body gallops to these rhythms. I'm along for the ride, at times in some control and at others dragged along as if foot-caught in a stirrup. I don't have much to do at first but breathe, accept ice chips, make jokes—in fear and pain my family makes jokes, that's how we deal with what we can't change, how we show our courage (42).

She might say that humor is involuntary too. At least it attends her even in labor, important enough to write about. Her sense of humor manifests itself in the multifaceted way she tells us about the experience. The narrative account is surfeited in images:

> The contractions move in longer waves, one after another, closer and closer together until a sea of physical sensation washes and then crashes over. In the beginning I breathe in concentration, watching Michael's eyes. I feel myself slip beneath the waves as they roar over, cresting just above my head. I duck every time the contraction peaks. As the hours pass and one wave builds on another there are times the undertow grabs me. I struggle, slammed to the bottom, unable to gather the force of nerve for the next. Thrown down, I rely on animal fierceness, swim back, surface, breathe, and try to stay open, willing. . . . Whether I am standing on the earth or not, whether I am moored to the dock, whether

I remember who I am, whether I am mentally prepared, whether I am going to float beneath or ride above, the waves pound in. At shorter intervals, crazy now, electric, in storms, they wash. Sometimes I'm gone. I've poured myself into some deeper fissure below the sea only to be dragged forth, hair streaming. During transition, as the baby is ready to be pushed out into life, the waves are no longer made of water, but neons so brilliant I gasp in shock and flourish my arms, letting the colors explode from my fingertips in banners, in ribbons, in iridescent trails—of pain, it is true, unendurable sometimes, and yet we do endure (45–46).

To endure impossible pain. Acknowledging that paradox and acknowledging all the others—that her fallible, weak, ordinary body is capable of such glory—Erdrich quietly evinces her comic spirit. It is that attitude that allows her to look in on the painful or the foolish and see in them the beautiful. She may not be able to explain exactly how her vain or fitful sides influence her transcendent moments, but the fact that she documents them all means that her sense of humor about herself rests on faith in a comic order, where all variables shall come to work in harmony.

Erdrich is a trickster that we know how to trust. In all the big surprises she pulls in her fiction, she never abandons us. Instead she leads us with her into full sensory participation in the fictional moment, sharing with us her comic attitude, that genius for adaptation and love. We enjoy her surprises for the beauty that she makes us feel in them and for the humor that keeps the beautiful accessible—on the layman's side of the sacred. The end of *The Beet Queen* is full of such surprises, all centered around the festival of the sugar beet—Argus' great cash crop—and the crowning of the sugar beet queen. There is a parade, of course, and the infirm Indian veteran Russell (the same who had revenged Fleur by locking the men in the freezer) is being propped up in his wheelchair on the American Legion float. It is hot. He is the representative of heroic service, of war, of death. The float features him and a cross placed on plastic grass in front of him; he is presiding over the graveyard. And so it is no wonder that in the jerk and jolting pace of the parade he succumbs to the suggestion of his own death. A woman from the crowd cries out "'He looks stuffed'" (300), and he sees the image of his long-dead sister in front of him, walking down what he recognizes as the Chippewa "four-day road, the road of death" (300).

I'm dead now, he thought with calm wonder.
At first he was sorry that it had happened in public, instead of some

private place. Then he was glad, and he was also glad to see he hadn't lost his sense of humor even now. It struck him as so funny that the town he lived in and the members of the American Legion were solemnly saluting a dead Indian, that he started to shake with laughter.

The damn thing was that he laughed too hard, fell off the road, opened up his eyes before he'd gone past the point of no return, and found himself only at the end of the parade. He quickly shut his eyes again. But the road had gone too narrow. He stumbled. No matter how hard he called, his sister continued forward and wouldn't double back to help (300).

Russell's sense of humor literally keeps him alive. It yanks him out of the compelling presence of death into consciousness of the scene. And what a scene he makes in his mind's eye—a dead Indian paraded down Main Street. The idea gives him such pleasure that he is distracted and death gets away without him, much to his chagrin. Thus out of the beautiful vision at his moment of death, Erdrich has seen to it that Russell makes a joke. Death gets jilted in a similar fashion by Nanapush, the man who adopts Lulu, who is a father-figure to Fleur. To survive the consumption that long ago wiped out much of the tribe, he started a story, telling it to himself. "I got well by talking. Death could not get a word in edgewise, grew discouraged, and traveled on" (*Tracks* 46).

Russell is not the only one who hilariously represents the dead in the sugar beet parade. Sita Kozka, Mary Adare's cousin and longtime co-quette, through a disappointing career in marriage eventually loses her wits but not, appropriately enough, her looks. She grows dim, and on the day of the parade when Mary and Celestine drive in to pick her up so they can see Celestine's daughter named the Beet Queen, they find her "stand-ing upright in the yew bushes" (*The Beet Queen* 290). She is peeved, they as-sume. It turns out, in fact, that she is dead. The branches of the bushes have held her up, and Mary and Celestine have to untangle her. "We unhooked Sita's necklace from the twig and her head fell a fraction to one side so that she seemed, now, more alert and observant than she had been in weeks" (292–93). Their dilemma is that they are late for the parade, and there is nowhere to put Sita; rather than leave her alone in the house, they decide to take her with them, right in the front seat. Then in their rush to get to Argus, they get into the parade, perhaps at the very moment Celestine's brother Russell is laughing his way out of death. But this particular joke is on the women, who seem directed by fate (and their series of decisions) to land directly behind a huge, spray-painted cloth and Kleenex sugar beet and in front of the high school drill team. This is no solemn funeral procession. The attention they draw is minimal but nevertheless enough to make them tense, flanking the dead woman and waving to the crowd, including the local mortician, whose possible attention is an especially harrowing event. Their performance—and luck—under pressure is remarkable, much as it was when Sita had opened a refined dining restaurant in town and they attended the grand opening but ended up hustling back to the kitchen to replace the cook and helpers, who were struck down with food poisoning. Russell was with them then, and he understood how they could manage the complicated orders. "'No one out there understood the menu,' he explains. 'In case you hadn't noticed, the damn thing was in French'" (122). So they do relax like he says and "'cook it up the way you would at home'" (122). The way they handle that potentially devastating affair is practice, of sorts, for the absurd parading they do of her death in the sugar beet festival. Rather than have the death be a tragedy for them, they adapt to it—and enjoy in it what humor they can. Their resourcefulness puts them in a creative and comic relation to death. Erdrich celebrates their adaptability.[58] With the parade ride exquisitely orchestrated, down to the beautiful resting place under the fairground elms where afterwards they park Sita, Erdrich places the outrageousness of this incident beyond the control of even the principal characters. The joke, after all, is on them, and the sense of it is beyond them, though we can sense the comic order in which the craziest things are fitting. We trust Erdrich to surprise us with the unpredictability and beauty of that order.

If any character shows us how wild the world is, that person is Fleur. She has been tossed by fate recklessly and still made her own way. She has been betrayed more than once. The rape devastated the trust that she had had with the men at the Argus butcher shop—tenuous though it was, based on a card game; years later, Nector Kashpaw betrays her by using her tax money (for land by Lake Matchimanito) instead for Kashpaw land. The result is tantamount to rape—this time in the form of a logging company that plans to cut the trees and thus provide the government the money it demands from that land. Although at first Fleur does not know about the betrayal, when she hears the sound of logging, her reaction is im-

58. She celebrates that kind of adaptability in all her novels. Of *Love Medicine*, Gleason says, "Erdrich's characters keep chuckling, especially when—by rights—they shouldn't. But that is precisely the nature and function of *Love Medicine*'s compassionate humor: it heals, it renews, it integrates, it balances. It *belongs*, in short, where it should not" (71).

mediate—she puts on her skinning knife and loads her gun (*Tracks* 206–7). We do not underestimate her. To defend her place, she would do anything—direct action the first recourse. The betrayal came from within the tribe, however, so she cannot go and just fight the loggers. Without an obvious enemy, she is bewildered and thinks to die—of course in the lake. So she fills her pockets with rocks and walks in, only to have her lover, Eli, drag her out. Nanapush is there holding Lulu when Fleur dismisses Eli and curses Nector. It is the child, the new chance, and the curse that restore Fleur's hope. Nanapush recounts to Lulu that scene when the child spoke in her sleep.

> I don't remember what you said, but I know it was ridiculous, and made no sense, and that it made your mother laugh.
> She laughed out loud so rarely that I didn't recognize the sound of it at first, rich, knowing, an invitation full of sadness and pleasure. I could not help but join (214).

The sleeping child's nonsense words dissolve in Fleur the strain of trying to understand why the betrayal and the logging have happened. Some things are unaccountable. Were we to grapple with their logic, we would turn bitter, confused, stymied, immobile. Better to open up to the worst and feel the tug of the dangerous and absurd plot, where self-control is the only power we have. Laughing, Fleur regains that power, both accepting her situation and boosting her creative energy to deal with it. Nanapush is surprised at her energy.

> I thought that Fleur would fade now, react in dismay, that without Eli and surrounded by the lumber crews that labored with careless persistence, her heart would empty. I thought that since she had strolled into Matchimanito, determined to walk toward the cleft of bright water on the horizon, and since she had been dragged out by Eli, she would have no choice but to come live with us, to be there when Eli returned.
> Instead, she took strength (217–18).

Fleur's wild spirit is linked to her lake-lapped woods, her ancestral land. Knowing she shall be evicted once the loggers reach her, she enacts another kind of suicide—this one defiant, confident, and larger than herself. If they are going to kill her, she figures, she might as well do it herself; perversely, she survives by accepting a symbolic death and plotting it out in advance.

The weather portends drama. Weird light and thunder have been preceded by long days of eerie calm. Nanapush, going to visit Fleur, is rattled by it, but as he reaches her, she is confronting the logging crew, resisting eviction, and she is not rattled. The last of the trees stand around her cabin.

> Her face was warm with excitement and her look was chilling in its clear amusement. She said nothing, just glanced into the sky and let her eyes drop shut.
> It was then I felt the wind building on the earth. I heard the waves begin to slap with light insistence against the shore. I knew the shifting of breeze, the turn of weather, was at hand. I heard the low murmur of the voices of the gamblers in the woods (222).

Her humor is compatible with the wildness of the weather. The wind arises, as if to answer that last long laugh of hers when she had emerged from Matchimanito and heard Lulu speak inexplicable words from her sleep. The wind speaks clearly but inexplicably too.

> The men spun in surprise when the first tree crashed down beyond sight. Someone laughed nervously, another commented in rude tones and then there was a brief cessation among them. They listened. Fleur's hair ruffled and the hide across the fire flapped. Another tree, a large one, pitched loud and long, closer to where we stood. The earth jumped and the shudder plucked nerves in the bodies of the men who milled about, whining softly to each other like nervous cattle. They bit their lips, glanced over their shoulders at Fleur, who bared her teeth in a wide smile that frightened even those who did not understand the smiles of Pillagers (222–23).

Fleur has entered fate's wayward swing and suggested a lead in its dance. Whether she controls the wind or whether she just fits into its grand spontaneity is impossible to discern. Spiritually cleaved to her place, Fleur has a will that is indistinguishable from it in this instance. The wind comes right when she needs it to come. Nanapush speaking:

> One man walked quickly to the east, then stopped. A small tree went down and barred his path. Men climbed into their wagons, licked fingers to test the breeze. The next tree slipped to earth.
> It was then I understood.

> Around me, a forest was suspended, lightly held. The fingered lobes
> of leaves floated on nothing. The powerful throats, the columns of
> trunks and splayed twigs, all substance was illusion. Nothing was solid.
> Each green crown was held in the air by no more than splinters of bark.
> Each tree was sawed through at the base (223).

The final sentence is no less miraculous for being a prosaic answer. It is a
punch line, in fact, a huge joke that Fleur is playing at great sacrifice. She
has done the men's work for them and thrown it in their faces to terrify
them and to secure herself from despair. She has accepted the inevitable
only on her own terms, logging off her land in the spirit of its wildness,
and thus keeping that alive despite losing the trees. Such a sacrifice has no
logic, only the absurd sense that a sleeptalker's words might, words you
could laugh about because they are perfect—inexplicable yet fitting.
Because we remain with Nanapush and protected by Fleur throughout this
scene, Erdrich surprises but protects us too. Erdrich wants us to feel perhaps like Nanapush, who, the moment before the trees fall, says, "I looked
around, curious as one becomes in moments of such tension" (222). To
readers who are alert and alive to possibility, Erdrich remains a trickster we
trust.

Because we feel complicity with her, we see clearly into the world she
loves. It is a landscape both complex and vivid, focused on the human inhabitants with a kind of wide angle that picks up also physical features like
the weather, the land, the animals, and their spiritual implications.[59]
Erdrich's ecological household is mystical and exploratory. She believes it
to be wild, writing that wildness into the lives of her characters and suggesting the elusive, larger significance in their interactions. No one in her
fiction has a buttonhole on the truth. Each makes a version of it, and
Erdrich thrives on the layers of experience their stories make—each an
angle of insight as if up through water or through snowflakes or through
the branches of trees into the truth. Each story contributes to a well-
rounded perspective of the events that take place in fictional Argus, North
Dakota, and the Indian reservation. Erdrich wants to show this world to
us in that multifaceted way because she has the conviction that it is com-

59. Erdrich writes, "In a tribal view of the world, where one place has been inhabited for
generations, the landscape becomes enlivened by a sense of group and family history.
Unlike most contemporary writers, a traditional storyteller fixes listeners in an unchang-
ing landscape combined with myth and reality. People and place are inseparable"
("Where I Ought to Be" 1).

plex beyond what she can say. She needs many characters to say it, and even then no metaphysical answers come clear. But we learn much about attitude and beauty. We see Erdrich's loving portrayal of her characters' flaws and her exquisite care to show that painful experiences are exacted from them perfectly. June dies, yes, but she is transfigured. Her tragedy is only one of many shocking incidents that Erdrich makes beautiful by loving, loving even the hardships, being that open to ecstasy. She surprises us most by leading us wide-eyed into scenes that ought to make us cover our eyes but instead compel us to see with a new spirit, a new perspective.

Beauty attends wildness, which is the way the ecological household finds itself to fit together. She offers not answers but skills, in particular the skill to be funny and to act on the faith that the world has a comic order. That means taking pleasure in wildness, in the seeming chaos of a "design so vast it seem[s] unrepetitive up close" (*The Bingo Palace* 226). The spirit world certainly suggests to us that it has a sense of humor—it can come up with the wind when Fleur needs it, just as it can toss her back out of drownings in the lake. Its humor indicates a larger comedy at work in the world, a comedy that keeps balancing ecological and human changes and revitalizing itself through them. Comedy anticipates and ensures survival. Erdrich's humor shows us that survival through that comedy can be beautiful.

SHORT CUT

Coyote Newcomer, Sally Carrighar

Sally Carrighar's Coyote in *One Day on Beetle Rock* takes us far afield from Erdrich's Coyote-like Fleur. Yet her realistic perspective of the creature gives us a new way to view the struggle for survival as well as an introduction to the tenor of the struggle that occupies the farmers of Wendell Berry's concern. Coyote is one of the ten creatures figuring in Carrighar's loosely constructed plot of a day on Beetle Rock, Sequoia National Park, high in the Sierra Nevada Mountains of California. In mid-May, Mule Deer Buck led his herd up to the meadow at Beetle Rock. As he came, he recognized the Black Bear, Weasel, Deer Mouse, Chickaree, Steller Jay, Grouse, and Lizard and noted the presence of Coyote, whose kind had not resided there for more than three years. Beetle Rock is a granite outcropping far above the chaparral of the foothills. It tops out over a mile above sea level, just over the tips of sugar pines and sequoia, which stand in a grove along the Rock's edge. It is a new home for Coyote, who grew up in lower country around ranches where the grass was short and the mice seemed easy to catch. Carrighar focuses on a day in mid-June.

Coyote is hungry, having had little to eat: "for three days now there had been nothing in his stomach but a little grass. The cavern of his ribs seemed to hold only a craving. Pain stabbed in his joints. His eye sockets burned" (118). It is Coyote's own perspective that Carrighar the naturalist gives us—at least as she figures it might be for an enterprising Canid, in particular this individual who, despite his species' reputation for adaptability, has to learn for himself the cost of being a newcomer. This Coyote has been with his mate in the mountains for only three months, and he has not yet learned that the meadow, most strongly riddled with mouse scent, is not the best place to catch mice. He persists in hunting there.

The grass in which he waited for the mouse was taller than he. It brushed the sides of his face and bent under his belly. In the foothills, sheep had cropped the grass close; the Coyote could speed over it easily, and anywhere see to the roots. His method of stalking was adapted to that shorter grass. Here he was fairly drowned in the limber fibers, and his stalking motions, decisive and fine, so effective on the lowland range, repeatedly failed to capture the prey (*One Day on Beetle Rock* 118).

This is no mythical Coyote with supernatural powers. This is a nearly desperate predator, whose heart pounds at "a freshening of the mouse scent" (118) and whose hunger over the lean spring has escalated into starvation. A mouse would be a boon. When he catches one at the creekbank, he pursues that venue, immediately having "perceived an advantage there" (118) where no movement of thick grass forewarns mice of his pounce. Carrighar at once joins the Coyote and ranges omnisciently beyond him, punctuating the narrative of the creature's day with remarks of the following bearing: "Unless he learned more tricks of mountain foraging soon, he might be unable to catch any prey at all. Hunting required that one's powers be keen, even in country that was familiar" (119).

We follow Coyote, then, with Carrighar's mind, which endows the animal's situation with suspense beyond the Coyote's own experience of it; for his is the suspense of hunting and hunger alone, and hers includes the premonition that the animal could starve. It is the plunge through the naturalist's perspective into Coyote's experience that makes the details of his life eminently significant. Whether the location of a ground squirrel's burrow or the direction of the wind at the moment, the particulars can mean the difference between a catch or futile effort, food or continued famine. Coyote misses a squirrel twice, first hunting alone and then with his mate's help to play decoy. His failure after he has involved his mate carries an emotional burden:

> At the den, his mate would not be sleeping now. She would be waiting, watching feverish-eyed to see the Coyote come loping in with a fat squirrel, meat for all of them. He did not return to the family. With a blind homing impulse, a tormenting urge to be again in the brushlands, he loped down the surface of the Rock . . . (122).

Suggesting that coyotes have emotional responses, Carrighar augments the drama of the day—Coyote has a "family" that he cannot, we intuit, bear to disappoint. These are hard times. Carrighar never asks for us to feel identification with the Coyote: her boldest move is to accomplish that prima facie, delivering us onto Beetle Rock where the moon is up and a strong wind is blowing so that it seems natural and ordinary to be there with Coyote—howling, checking his pups outside the den, leaving to hunt. It seems perfect to learn the place from one who lives there—and who is also learning about it. The author's radical undertaking—to accompany omnisciently a wild creature of another species—is accomplished via quotidian detail, establishing a domestic appeal that tempers the unorthodoxy of cross-species identification.

Further accounting of what happened that day will convey a full taste of the dramatic style and domestic focus by which Carrighar prompts us toward Coyote. Here the domestic scene is a wild place, with no predictable comforts.

> The Coyote on Beetle Rock paused towards midnight to recover strength and to wait for the moon, due to rise from behind the eastern peaks. As he stood upon an angular boulder, thrust into the canyon from a cliff, the wind parted his fur. The wind was pouring over Glacier Pass and Mineral King, builder of thunderheads. It was flowing down and past the Coyote like a movement of the night itself (114).

This is home—at least Coyote's new home. Carrighar settles us in by giving us a tour, revealing the locations of the den "in a hollow formed by the tilted corner of a granite block" (115); the meadow, across the Rock from the den, which attracts Coyote because of its scent of mouse; the creek that passes through the meadow; the borders of the Rock, home to squirrels and chipmunks "where the forest broke away into thickets, brush, and the gray-leaved, bright-flowered gravel plants" (119); the way down where Coyote heads after he twice misses the squirrel and wants to be in the foothills, "down the surface of the Rock, past its upper and lower fringes of manzanita, into the oak thickets below, through dark groves of cedars and open stands of pines and firs rising obliquely from the steep slope" (122); the safe cranny under a sequoia toppled across a creek, where Coyote waits out the thunderstorm; the draw up a bank where he chases a deer and then finds weasel trails. This wild tumble of up-lifted, glaciated, evergreen- and meadow-sweetened Sierra mountain is now the domestic terrain of Coyote—and in searching to satisfy necessities (trying to assuage his hunger), Coyote comes to experience the difficult, dramatic landscape as home. We are initiated to it thus, concentrating on the domestic and in the process gaining an entirely nonhuman perspective of the mountainside.

The hunt is both a quintessential domestic activity for Coyote and wild dramatic action. As such, it torques our minds to redefine home and domesticity and shows again Carrighar making subtleties do bold work. From under the sequoia trunk after the thunderstorm passes, Coyote becomes alert to a peep below him.

> Soon he had discovered a fledgling, a bird he did not know. It was a mountain dipper, wren-shaped, gray, matching the water. On the edge of a stone, with its feet in the current, it continually squatted, down and up, to imitate the ripples and thereby escape notice. Yet it kept reminding its parents in a shrill voice that it wanted food. Except for its piping and the opening and closing of its orange mouth, the Coyote probably would not have seen it (124).

The fact that Coyote does not know the bird, missing what seems to be an easy catch because he does not know the bird's habits, reiterates that he is a newcomer. "Once more the mountain world had tricked him" (124), Carrighar writes, giving her readers, also novitiates to this territory, the opportunity to identify with the creature. Mealtime is strenuous, we see: Coyote sprinting after a deer, backing off when it turns to kick. Finally, with "the last of his energy blazing up as his need for food became unendurable" (126), Coyote locates a weasel burrow. "Frantically he began to dig. The wet earth crumbled beneath his paws. The scent was so fresh that he expected every scoop to disclose the nest" (126). But his meal is contested. The mother Weasel attacks to save her kits. She leaps at Coyote's face.

> The Weasel hung by her teeth from the Coyote's lip. She clawed for a hold in the fur of his throat. He flung his head to shake her off, but still she held. With a stronger swing he got free of her, ripping away the flesh she had gripped (126).

We want Coyote to eat the weasels. We want him to get the doe also, which he pursues once he consumes the two tiny weasel kits. Anything but starvation. We are on Coyote's side. The final hunt scene, anticipated by both Coyote and his mate to be a relay chase—foothill style—of the nervous doe, ends abruptly when the doe falls to a cougar. The coyotes do not even have a chance to start their chase—and what a relief! Coyote knows the cougar's habits—knows how to clean up following its kills. So the cached meat, after the cougar has eaten, falls to the *Canis latrans* scavengers, who transfer it to their own hiding place and eat well, finally, for the first time in months. Coyote leaves to follow the cougar on its hunting circuit.

▼ ▼ ▼

"THIS IS A DANGEROUS BOOK, FULL OF DISTURBING POSSIBILITIES," WRITES Robert C. Miller, director of the California Academy of Sciences in 1943 when *One Day on Beetle Rock* was published. His introductory note to the book specifies what those dangers might be: the young could want to become naturalists, and adults might be drawn to the mountains.

Carrighar's is a dangerous book because it is boldly sympathetic and enlists us emotionally on behalf of the creatures—the characters—whose day she recreates. By choosing to tell stories (narration rather than explication), she taps our imagination and can thus best cultivate our concern for the denizens of the place. Her strategy to fictionalize produces an affective and ecologically effective natural history, entirely unorthodox. Giving attention to Beetle Rock itself and to the overlapping lives of creatures, she demonstrates that meaning on that mountain is far from human-centered. Thus her book is dangerous because, in assuming to involve us in its imaginative exercise of participating in the lives of animals, it shakes us free of an entirely human perspective. We join new domestic routines. Despite how different the animals' homes are from human ones, we are not excluded from them. We see what thrills, challenges, and disturbs the creatures. We come to care.

Besides being boldly sympathetic, the book is comic as well. Weasel, not Coyote, is the first animal whose story Carrighar tells; and so before we are nervous about Coyote's hunger, we know Weasel's passions and dilemmas. We understand Beetle Rock to be a busy household. Only with detachment can Carrighar sympathize with each of these ten Beetle Rock residents, committing herself to them even as they oppose one another. Her ability to be passionately ambivalent is evidence of her comic skill. So, too, the book's structure is comic because all the creatures are protagonists of their chapters, influencing the nature of the place, changing it and being changed by it.[60] The large mind Carrighar has to enact a day of such manifold character enables her to portray pleasure and grief about a single event—about, for instance, the Coyote's encounter with the Weasel. The

60. With her focus on animals, Carrighar gives new context to Northrop Frye's assertion that the final society formed by comedy is inclusive (*Anatomy of Criticism* 164). Beetle Rock is fully populated but comes to include also the new Coyotes—having many heroes, it accommodates them all in the fashion of comedy, according to Joseph Meeker (33).

comic success of the book depends on its alternating points of view—its obvious ambiguities—which render the world wayward and mysterious even as it is being opened, in glimpses, to our ken. Taken down to its minutest detail, we are launched as if aloft into the thunderstorms that sometimes come cracking down over all of Beetle Rock, or over the Weasel, in particular.

> As the canyon trembles with the shocks hurled on its sides, the Weasel in the fir hole weaves and sways. This at last is a weasel's forest—lights, sounds, scents, intensified to the limit of excitement.
>
> Too soon the storm began to pass. The Weasel felt its going. She detected the first crumbling of the violence—the delay in the thunder, which then broke slowly, lacking its earlier, full, murderous crack. It rolled out longer, a sustained, reverberating roar.
>
> The lightning flashes came less often, and were paler, weaker, a suffused white-green. This was only a pretense of danger. The rain was ceasing; in diminishing waves it was departing down the mountain. Finally there was only water dripping from the leaves.
>
> A break in the clouds showed high blue, and below, in the canyon, sunshine tinted a misty feathered slope. The storm was over. The Weasel's world had fallen away (24–25).

So we have a measure of Weasel's predilections before she discovers the Coyote at her den. The scene is horrifying:

> she uttered a shrill cry at her first sight of the burrow. Over it crouched a great fur body, the Coyote digging to the nest.
>
> His paws worked fast, scattering clumps of mud to both sides. His haunches twitched, and his nose moved impatiently across the fresh-cleared earth. The tiny Weasel instantly attacked. She sprang for the face of the Coyote, where she caught with her teeth through his lower lip. The Coyote yelped. He swung his head to try to shake the Weasel off. Still she clung. Desperate, he gave his head a great jerk and the Weasel was hurled to the ground with his torn flesh in her mouth.
>
> She leapt again for his face. But he was ready; she barely missed death between his snapping jaws. Again she tried. This time she felt the grazing of his teeth. Hopeless now, but wild with grief, she crouched in the hollow center of a log, out of his reach. The Coyote resumed his dig-

ging, his sidewise glance on the little head, all fangs and scarlet tongue, and glittering eyes.

The two young weasels were still in the nest when the Coyote, with a last quick scoop, uncovered them. Each was soon quieted, as their mother's cries tore through the soft bright air. The Coyote was deliberate at his meal. When he finished, he walked off slowly across the Rock. The Weasel watched him disappear below its rim.

She continued to stare at the cleft where he had vanished until the frenzy died from her eyes. Then she came down off the log, her body but a loop of limp flesh. She growled to call her three remaining kits, who had hidden in the thicket, and led them to a pile of boulders at the end of a gully. In its crevices she saw them curl themselves for sleep. And then the Weasel too lay down, with her tail across her face (25–26).

The Weasel is passionate, and we sympathize with her. We can also see the scene from the Buck's point of view: "The Weasel was shrieking, jays were squawking overhead, and a ground squirrel piped a shrill whistle" (186). "Fear," according to the Grouse, "circled out from the Coyote" (42). Yet we know also, apart from Weasel's reckless despair and the impact that the hunt has all across the Rock, Coyote's final impatience to get a meal. There are no villains here but instead a series of heroes, each introducing us to Beetle Rock from a new angle. The "willing tension" that Carrighar says "keeps a wilderness society stable" (9) is a quality that her own intimate perusal across species lines creates. Effective because it is flexible, transformative, and visionary, her understanding of this place communicates both information about it and the wild spirit it has. She succeeds because she is comic, not deigning to settle on any particular perspective in evoking the life of Beetle Rock. And success means that she has created a dangerous book, challenging and powerful enough to drum us awake, making us perhaps as alert as she says the members of the Rock are in being "ready to leap, to chase, to freeze, to threaten, to love, or to step aside—in an instant" (10).

As a newcomer who adapts to the mountains, Carrighar's Coyote makes changes in the place and contributes to the new balance it achieves. Beetle Rock's equilibrium is comic, and Carrighar's portrayal of it as such is successful in the same way that Wendell Berry is successful in creating a picture of the farming community that faces and absorbs tragedies without becoming tragic.

▼▼▼

Wendell Berry

Maintaining Household Jokes

FARMER AND PROFESSOR, RURAL HOMEBODY AND SOPHISTICATED WIT,
Wendell Berry stands uniquely placed in the tradition of Southwest humor
to conflate its conventional incongruities between gentleman narrator and
rural protagonist. His ear and voice have been cultured by a close-knit
farming community in the Outer Bluegrass of Kentucky, Henry County,
where the Kentucky River flows northwest as it nears the Ohio. His has
been an extended vocal family. "As a child I heard a lot of the Bible, a lot of
hymns, a lot of sermons, and a lot of storytelling, joking, and talk, both
black and white," Berry has said ("A Question a Day" 40). Additionally, his
voice has been cultivated by education at the University of Kentucky and
by teaching appointments at Stanford, UK, and New York University. His
is a literary voice—with a formal, measured pace and a politeness so thor-
ough one almost misses the humor. "I'm wary of trying to deal with the
issue of literary influences, because of my fear that I won't remember them
all and my suspicion that I don't even know them all" ("A Question a Day"
40–41). Balancing his reasons between fear and suspicion, Berry's answer
is poised and self-deprecatory. He is poking fun at himself, presenting his
fallible, flawed, deficient character. The humor is ensconced in the sedate
parallel structure of the sentence and in the nature of the event, an interview featuring him—what fun, then, to undercut himself. Berry's answer
reveals the quiet style of his humor and, in continuing, his habit to be thor-
ough rather than flippant. He replies that his work focuses on a particular

place, and so he has looked to other writers also interested in place ("A Question a Day" 41).[61]

In 1964, Berry and his wife, Tanya, chose to return from his successfully incipient sampling of academia in Europe[62], New York, and California and go back to Kentucky to buy a farm and settle in the same community where Berry grew up. Berry's literary voice is insistently rural. And incisive. Expect the polite tone to preclude strong opinion and prepare for the surprise when Berry's elegant prose, as it often does, turns cutting. His remark on the U.S. Census of 1993 displays characteristic snap: "American farmers, who over the years have wondered whether or not they counted, may now put their minds at rest: they do not count. They have become statistically insignificant" (*Another Turn of the Crank* 9). Playing the word *count* for all it can render, colloquially in terms of worth and literally in terms of numbers, Berry is sharply humorous about the status of farmers. Farmers—Berry included—still exist; their struggle has not been obliterated by the census numbers. Berry is rawly amused that the farmers' desperate position is immeasurable and now officially invisible.

The same sharp humor marks the narrative comment in "Fidelity" when Danny Branch, about to abduct his comatose father, Burley, from the hospital to go home for his death, has the fortune to be inconspicuously present when the emergency room is crowded, "for it was now the tail end of another Friday night of the Great American Spare-Time Civil War" (*Fidelity* 122). Certainly our country's driving record is masochistic. Berry points to that tragedy with humor because he wants to awaken his audience to the problem. He counts on humor as much as fact or logic to stimulate and persuade us. Given Berry's voice and his concerns, we expect neither a quiet, docile disappearance of the farming population into the "statistically insignificant" nor the silence of tacit approval for the speed and shape of progress in modern America. Given Berry's humor, we expect to be elicited into the fray.

The effort of his fiction and nonfiction has been to tell of people's relation, especially agricultural relation, to the land. In this story, the issues of cultural and ecological destruction are clearly wedded, and they are urgent because they are personal. The farm population is declining, young people

61. Homer, Dante, Spenser, Shakespeare, Milton, Pope, Marvell, Thoreau, Jewett, Williams, and Rexroth can be numbered among his literary influences.
62. Berry won a Guggenheim in 1961.

leave, and development and careless use consume productive land. That is, you see your neighbors go, you lose the young crowd to college and cities, you watch the new highway or poultry plant tear up countryside you used to hike through. With personal losses wrought by a centralized economy of global proportions, Berry faces tragic, perhaps hopeless, circumstances. But he takes the attitude that one of his characters, Andy Catlett in the novel *Remembering*, professes—that sometimes even a losing argument should be made (87). He responds to tragedy intimately and resourcefully, in the end sustaining courage through his faith that the world is comic, an optimistic reading of our state of affairs that depends on faith, since it is not corroborated by much contemporary evidence. His delicate, fierce, and joyful use of humor attests to the varied ways he maintains a comic perspective.

Driven more by the impulse to teach than to entertain and compelled to argue against what he abhors, Berry uses humor selectively—when it suits the purposes of his argument in nonfiction and when, in his fiction, it suits the characters or situation. Although his *oeuvre* is not often funny, it does show that he can be funny. He always *employs* humor, rarely displaying or showcasing it, inevitably making a point. To the extent that he uses humor, he exercises his comic perspective and ensures the vitality of it—matching the elegiac tone in his work. Of his ten works of fiction, six dwell significantly on death, particularly the deaths of old men. A humorous tone dominates only two of his book publications (both fiction): *Watch With Me: And Six Other Stories of the Yet-Remembered Ptolemy Proudfoot and His Wife, Miss Minnie, Nee Quinch* (1994) and *The Discovery of Kentucky* (1991).[63]

Berry's effort to maintain a comic perspective is manifested in the difference between humor in his fiction and nonfiction. The more focused Berry is on argument—in the effort of his nonfiction to critique the thoughtless modernization, centralization, and specialization of society—the less playful or funny his humor is, the more it tends toward irony, sarcasm, or parody. In the rhetorical fighting mode that places him most starkly against the forces he opposes, his humor can be almost desperate. Its tone of sad outrage registers how grave and overwhelming the threats to community and nature are that Berry has chosen to face. In fiction, sympathy characterizes his humor. The style is hopeful and less anxious since Berry stands here within a world he has created, where the survival of his values is imaginatively possible and his comic perspective is buoyed. A

---

63. *The Discovery of Kentucky* is a long short story, published independently as a chapbook.

more detailed overview of humor in Berry's nonfiction shows how it struggles against tragic circumstances.

In the essay "Waste," Berry takes on the excesses of industrial production. Railing against the way our goods become trash, he writes, "I confess that I am angry at the manufacturers who make these things. There are days when I would be delighted if certain corporation executives could somehow be obliged to eat their products" (*What Are People For?* 127). The very politeness with which Berry issues his idea for returning waste to its source—a version of the desire to "cram it down their throats"—gives his anger a sheen of humor. We do not laugh, for neither the situation nor the humor calls for that, but we feel the tap of surprise and recognition that humor can impart. Through this verbal alarm, Berry awakens us to the often hazy connection between the institutionalized production of waste and the people who profit from it and are responsible for it. Yet the responsibility has other tragic dimensions, and humor allows Berry to convey the gravity, depth, and complexity of it. The fact that his violent suggestions are presented formally—he "would be delighted" if they were "somehow [to] be obliged" to consume their products—implicitly acknowledges that violence against CEOs would abet violence rather than improvement. The blame for the waste problem lies also with us consumers, rural and urban people alike. Berry's humor concisely conveys the insidious magnitude of the problem as well as his sad outrage over it—on some days, "the Ohio, whose name (*Oyo* in Iroquois) means 'beautiful river,' [is] so choked with this manufactured filth that an ant could crawl dry-footed from Kentucky to Indiana" (*What Are People For?* 126).

When Berry exaggerates, he does so fiercely, turning a tall-tale style toward modern environmental horrors. The ant can traverse a river, and people can eat mechanically. In "The Pleasures of Eating," he raises the specter of tragic dissociation between people and their food.

> The food industrialists have by now persuaded millions of consumers to prefer food that is already prepared. They will grow, deliver, and cook your food for you and (just like your mother) beg you to eat it. That they do not yet offer to insert it, prechewed, into your mouth is only because they have found no profitable way to do so. We may rest assured that they would be glad to find such a way. The ideal industrial food consumer would be strapped to a table with a tube running from the food factory directly into his or her stomach (*What Are People For?* 146).

In summing up—"Perhaps I exaggerate, but not by much"—Berry forces the negotiable tall-tale limit between fact and fantasy out beyond what most of us would have willingly imagined for ourselves. He feeds us an unattractive image of our automatization, acknowledging his exaggeration in order to insist to those who might dismiss the picture altogether that exaggeration is the least part of it.

Henri Bergson has asserted that the primary impetus to laugh is provided by rigid or automatized behavior that shows humans acting like machines; this laughter, he says, is a type of survival mechanism that highlights and scorns characteristics deleterious to adaptation and social flexibility (471–77). Berry replicates this psychology when he shows us how unpalatable our "industrial eating" is. And he persists with an imaginative furor that is fierce more than funny: "Like industrial sex, industrial eating has become a degraded, poor, and paltry thing. Our kitchens and other eating places more and more resemble filling stations, as our homes more and more resemble motels" (147). In stylizing the horrors he perceives, Berry finds the comic distance that allows him to fight back and deliver his readers into the fray.

Berry's essays titillate because they maneuver us to understand our situation and the situation of culture, agriculture, and character differently than we perhaps ever previously did. He realigns conventional history: "The first and greatest American revolution, which has never been superseded, was the coming of people who did *not* look upon the land as a homeland" (*The Unsettling of America* 4). His style is unforgettable. He employs the panache of the tall-tale raconteur and underwrites it with devastating seriousness. As he avers in "The Pleasures of Eating," "Perhaps I exaggerate, but not by much": he titillates because he uses the language of exaggeration yet insists on its truth. He draws a new boundary through the territory of fact and fantasy that the tall tale establishes. Furthermore, the context has changed from that of the traditional tall tale—rather than the terrifying wilderness, the "free" market of a centralized economy holds sway. Berry characterizes that progress:

Once the revolution of exploitation is under way, statesmanship and craftsmanship are gradually replaced by salesmanship.* [*In a footnote he explains, "The craft of persuading people to buy what they do not need, and do not want, for more than it is worth."] Its stock in trade in politics is to sell despotism and avarice as freedom and democracy. In business it sells sham and frustration as luxury and satisfaction. The "constantly expanding market" first opened in the New World by the fur traders is still expanding—no longer so much by expansions of territory or population but by the calculated outdating, outmoding, and degradation of goods and by the hysterical, self-dissatisfaction of consumers that is indigenous to an exploitative economy (*The Unsettling of America* 11).

If we agree or partly agree with this critique, we may, upon recognizing the effrontery Berry has to define our world thus, feel the kind of nervous delight that taboo-breaking humor imparts. He attacks business as usual. If we do not agree, we are taken on the ride nonetheless, with Berry dispensing with all the customarily honored words. For instance, fearing that farmland will be destroyed by corporate ownership, he writes, "If it does happen, we are familiar enough with the nature of American salesmanship to know that it will be done in the name of the starving millions, in the name of liberty, justice, democracy, and brotherhood, and to free the world from communism" (*Unsettling* 10). Berry is fierce because he cannot be simply funny about what he sees to be tragedy. His comic vision both points to that tragedy and saves him from gloom. It results in his outrageous entry to matters of course, wherein he critiques what others accept as normal: "There is nothing more absurd, to give an example that is only apparently trivial, than the millions who wish to live in luxury and idleness and yet be slender and good-looking" (*Unsettling* 12). Is there, we question, inconsistency in that wish? Given the socialization that has led us to expect that both conditions are possible—in fact that health and beauty *accompany* wealth and luxury—we stumble over Berry's indictment of this assumption. He calls for consistency between livelihood and character, equating our work with our person and showing that if we live destructively (in idleness and luxury), we make ourselves crabbed and unattractive. Berry knows well his deviance and enjoys the complexity of it, throwing hitches into mainstream parlance. His nonfiction is "funny" because he plays the flamboyant anarchist with the sincerity of a loyalist. He presents our assumptions to be shams and levelly maintains a provocative style that insists upon the gravity of the situation. Humor is his final resource in defying the modern juggernaut; it keeps his attitude healthy, serving as a boundless source of courage.

▼ ▼ ▼

HUMOR IS ALSO HARBINGER AND EVIDENCE OF CELEBRATION. IT SHOWS people to be glad, in some fashion, of their condition—or at least glad of their awareness of that condition. So when in *The Discovery of Kentucky* the Port William neighbors, playing Kentucky pioneers (complete with Kentucky Pride whiskey) in the inaugural parade for the governor, see the float "Forward With Kentucky Education" that features a log cabin opposed to "a modern classroom with a lot of equipment and no books," their fun with it is immense. Jayber Crow, the barber, incites them.

> The truth was upon me, as Kentucky Pride was within me, and I made a gesture from the cabin to the classroom to the float that said, KENTUCKY—OPEN FOR BUSINESS. "We've come a long way," I said, "to be first in folly."
>
> "Now, hold on!" Mush Cotman said, attentive to the Kentucky Pride within himself. "Wait a damn minute! Ain't we supposed to be smarter 'n Alabama?"
>
> "Arkansas, ain't it?" Burley said (21).

Berry's fiction shows humor in this transformative vein—sympathetic and positive. Although it deals with issues as critical as his nonfiction does (in this case the exploitative notions to develop Kentucky economically) and it critiques them from the same principles, it does so without the dire tone of the nonfiction humor. It escapes bitterness by being funny.

Berry accomplishes this style of humor because his fiction imagines a world, the rural community of Port William and Hargrave on the Kentucky River, that is hopeful—that manifests his interests and usually struggles toward his values. This world is a source of strength for Berry. Since the late fifties he has been developing it, or, indeed, addressing it; for this fictional world is modeled on the Port Royal community where Berry lives today and where both the maternal and paternal sides of his family for four to five successive generations have lived. In the Coulters, the Catletts, the Feltners, the Penns, and the Proudfoots, Berry has created characters through whom he can imaginatively rework his largely forgotten ancestral connections to the place, filling in his ancestry via a fictional route. Beginning with essays in *The Long-Legged House* (1969) and *The Unsettling of America* (1977), he has persistently stressed the idea that we have not yet "arrived in America." His fiction is an effort to complete that arrival. The effort is predominantly personal, arising from his desire to be a "placed" person: "I saw that if I belonged here, which I felt I did, it was not because anything here belonged to me. A man might own a whole county and be a stranger in it. If I belonged *in* this place it was because I belonged *to* it. And I began to understand that so long as I did not know the place fully, or even adequately, I belonged to it only partially" (*Recollected Essays* 42, 52). Berry understands his arrival to be a practical and spiritual exercise. His fiction shows it also to be an imaginative discipline, with every work of fiction he has published—from 1960 to 1997[64]—dealing with the Port William membership (as Berry calls those who belong to that land). Berry persists in constructing this fictional world largely because he continues to "arrive" in his own place: his writing is an outcome of that homecoming discipline.[65] His fiction gives us an intimate and manifold entry into a long-settled community.

In *Nathan Coulter*[66], *A Place on Earth*, *The Memory of Old Jack*, *The Wild Birds: Six Stories of the Port William Membership*, *Remembering*, *The Discovery of Kentucky*, *Fidelity: Five Stories*, *Watch With Me*, *A World Lost*, and *Two More Stories of the Port William Membership*, we find that humor is serious business—it is deeply meaningful to the community. In this last volume, jokes about the small, sweet watermelon that Elton Penn should not eat during a hot afternoon cutting tobacco are actually an invitation to eat. The workers, in making humor out of a simple thing, reinforce their solidarity to cope with a tough job. Much the same solidarity in humor unite Danny Branch and the aged Wheeler Catlett when the old man drives them the right direction home but the wrong way in the interstate's emergency lane. Their common understanding through humor helps them ride out the incident and survive. In the five novels, four collections of short stories, and one chapbook, we learn about loss and survival in the world Berry has labored over with exquisite concern and grace. We experience the celebratory humor of *Watch With Me*, stories that have the flavor of an epic past, recounting the hyperbolic exuberance of the Proudfoot clan; the exaggerated shyness of Ptolemy and Miss Minnie when they want to begin courting;

64. In 1997, Gnomon Press in Frankfort, Kentucky, published two of his newest short stories in a slim volume entitled *Two More Stories of the Port William Membership*.

65. Pages 76 to 81 in *Recollected Essays* concern Berry's initial choice to move back to Kentucky despite his faculty position at New York University and despite the assumption of many that such a return would come "at the price of intellectual death." He writes, "When I lived in other places I looked on their evils with the curious eye of a traveler; I was not responsible for them; it cost me nothing to be a critic, for I had not been there long, and I did not feel that I would stay. But here, now that I am both native and citizen, there is no immunity to what is wrong" (80).

66. Berry revised both *Nathan Coulter* and *A Place on Earth* for their republication by North Point Press in 1985 and 1983, respectively. References here are based on the revisions.

the hopeless circles they make driving through Louisville, attempting to find the fair; and the solemn vagrant boy and his father, whom they feed and go to desperate measures to make laugh, accomplished at last by Ptolemy's antic spilling of buttermilk down his shirtfront. We see humor in the attitude that sustains characters through hard times. We see humor as fun and tough, necessary and luxurious. We respect the humor that has the longevity and buoyancy to propel characters through loss and apparent tragedy and accomplish Berry's successful homecoming in Port William. Humor helps take Berry home.

Consider the role he gives humor in *The Wild Birds*. The first story involves newly married Wheeler Catlett setting off to rescue his Uncle Peach from another drunken spree in Louisville. Uncle Peach has been a trial to his family all his life and increasingly so as he gets older. In both his relationships and his handyman work, he is dependent and incompetent.

> He never married, for the reason, according to him, that he could never accomplish a short courtship; no woman who came to know him well enough to make up her mind about him would make it up in his favor (7).

> Whatever he has done with, for the day or the moment, he dropped wherever he was, until he built under his feet a sort of midden of lumber, scraps, and tools, in which whatever he needed at any given moment was lost (9).

Although his failures trouble him and his family, here Uncle Peach hosts not a somber story but a comic one, making comedy essential to conveying the story's lessons and moral grace. From the start, Berry establishes the comic tone, recounting the phone call that Wheeler makes from his office to his bride. Both are quick-witted.

> "Hello," Bess said.
> "Would this be the beautiful young widder Catlett?"
> "Herself. What did he die of?"
> "Love, of course."
> "For me?"
> "For you."
> "Well, wasn't that sweet!" (4–5)

The serious information that follows this playful exchange takes a comic shape because Wheeler and Bess have just been funny and can bestow that attitude on other concerns. "Bess, my star client, Uncle Peach, requires my services at Louisville" (5). Humor shows their intelligence at liberty to be creative; in a psychological sense, it demonstrates that they are free—articulate about their situation and capable of having an uninhibited perspective on it. The linguistic fooling around is essential play, crucial to evoking the larger context that puts a particular burden (rescuing drunken Uncle Peach) in place and makes it easier to handle. When Wheeler was seventeen and frustrated with his mother's tireless accommodations for Uncle Peach (her brother), she tries to explain her devotion to him: " 'blood is thicker than water,' " she tells Wheeler. He turns her moral cliche into mockery by the bounce of a feminine rhyme, replying, " 'Blood is thicker than liquor.' " She, however, does not use the humor to distance herself from her brother with scorn; instead, she defuses her son's anger by accepting the sad and comic plight that she is attached to Uncle Peach despite his horrifying habits. Her answer is calm and open: " 'Yes,' she said. 'Thicker than liquor too' " (10). Likewise, Berry's humor with Uncle Peach is gentle and sustaining. In describing how the young lawyer Wheeler came to take over responsibility for Uncle Peach, Berry tells it this way:

> He was perhaps made eligible to come into this inheritance by the ownership of an automobile, which, as it turned out, proved the finest windfall of Uncle Peach's entire drinking career. It meant that he could get drunk in complete peace of mind. He could go clear to Louisville, spend all his money, exhaust his credit, ruin his health—and then Wheeler would come and take him home in the car, paying off whatever creditors might stand in the way. It was a grand improvement over the horse-and-buggy days (13–14).

That is, Berry tells it in a funny way—not because the situation has a good or happy ending or because any of the characters involved are pleased with it but because it demands humor in order for Uncle Peach to remain beloved. Berry's prose conveys the tone of the family's relationship to Uncle Peach—necessarily a complex comic attachment if they are to cope repeatedly with his worst mistakes and still love him.

Distance enables humor, yet Berry's humor, in paradoxical style, returns us to his subject with love. Humor enacts a homecoming of consciousness because it gives us the distance to see back into our original state of mind. Such a return is corollary to our long-term commitments when, as Berry says, we choose again what we have already committed ourselves to.[67] "Thicker Than Liquor" is explicit about the distance necessary to humor. Wheeler becomes increasingly impatient with Uncle Peach as the day wears on and the possibility of returning to Bess by nightfall diminishes.

> Wheeler usually put up with Uncle Peach by finding him funny, which was easy enough, for Uncle Peach's life and conversation were rich in absurdities, and Wheeler's involvements with him invariably made good stories. But underlying the possibility of laughter was the possibility of anger, and he was close to that now (21).

Capable of transforming trouble, humor sometimes nevertheless escapes us. When, on the train home, Uncle Peach grows mightily and loudly sick, the public spectacle is almost unbearable for the young man. Berry writes, "And yet, in the very midst of it, Wheeler knew that it was rare. It would make a good story, as soon as he could get out of it. But it was not funny now" (22). The prospect of humor pulls Wheeler through a difficult time. He endures ignominy partly on the faith that he will achieve distance, that a story will prevail, that the situation itself will be subsumed in the routine that returns Wheeler to his wife at night—the prospect of normalcy helps render the immediate trials comic. The moral effort in the story to take care of family—to love Uncle Peach beyond his faults—succeeds because of comic skill. Humor and a faith in humor enable moral action.

Like Wheeler, Berry has an eye for the inclusive story but cannot always "get out" of the events of Port William far enough to revel in that story. He has been primarily concerned with eliminating distance—establishing the membership of people to land in Port William—and his determination to make the place alive has psychologically aligned him to it, shunting much humor aside. Furthermore, his determination to evoke intimacy has often made him a chronicler rather than a member: the humor that arises is often observed in the characters and not primarily intended to amuse us. With Berry participating solely as the narrator, his humor is filtered by description so that we are more conscious of the distance we have alongside Berry in observing the comic moment than we are of the quirk of perspective the

---

67. His poem "The Wild Rose" casts the idea thus: "and once more I am blessed, choosing / again what I chose before" (*Entries* 15).

characters themselves felt, launching the fun. This is the case in "A Jonquil for Mary Penn" when the women who have gone out picking blackberries must cross a barbed wire fence on the way home, and all pass without hitch except the last, Josie Tom, who has successfully held the wires apart for the others. She gets hung up—and begins to laugh.

> "Josie Braymer," she said, "are you going to just stand there, or are you going to unhook me from this shitten fence?"
> And there on the ridgetop in the low sunlight they danced the dance of women laughing, bending and straightening, raising and lowering their hands, swaying and stepping with their heads back (*Fidelity* 71).

More than humor, we absorb the beauty of this scene. The characters are enjoying the fun, but we are with Berry standing in attendance of a time-less and intimately timely moment. His description does homage to it. So his desire for communion inspires a reverential attitude that forestalls our complete participation in the lively world he has created. Though Berry in-tends for his narrative visit among characters to create intimacy on a com-munity scale, the effect of it is instead distancing, that of witnessing humor rather than enjoying it . Especially in early novels such as *A Place on Earth* and *The Memory of Old Jack*, Berry is too psychologically close to the charac-ters and the effort to raise a full community into fictional life to be able to be funny. He continually tells us what happens that is funny without trans-lating the humor into a funny narrative and allowing it to be wild—on the loose in his readers. He controls it. Despite this and despite the fact that the burden of his fiction lies with loss, the community's survival that now wends through ten works of fiction compels comedy. Once Port William is established, Berry can begin to replace his narrative distance with psycho-logical distance, stepping back far enough emotionally from his commu-nity in order to go to it again, arriving into it beside his characters so the fun escapes none of us.

The comic genius to "get out of town" in order to know and tell the truth of it for Berry involves the dual process of creating the town and emerging from it to look around clearly. Humor succinctly embodies this process, first setting the scene where common understandings are possible, then taking us out of our attachments far enough to know them, and finally delivering us back in the significance of those attachments with the knowl-edge that our relationships are provisional, mutable, and precious.

From the start, with his earliest fiction, Berry embeds in Port William the means to get out of town. Burley Coulter is that means, a man who hunts and fishes as much as he farms (he helps others rather than running a farm of his own), who never officially marries, who has the willfulness and humor that make him a Coyote figure in Port William—"wayward," as Berry puts it. In choosing a person whose tendency to head for the woods embodies his social iconoclasm, Berry replicates in fiction his philosophy about how to change institutional stagnation.

> If change is to come, then, it will have to come from the outside. It will have to come from the margins. As an orthodoxy loses its standards, becomes unable to measure itself by what it ought to be, it comes to be measured by what it is not. The margins begin to close in on it, to break down the confidence that supports it, to set up standards clarified by a broadened sense of purpose and necessity, and to demonstrate better possibilities (*The Unsettling of America* 174).

Applied to agriculture, as Berry uses it in this instance, this philosophy encourages the practical handiwork of laying out field plots so that trees and wild edges flourish, choosing crops that are diverse, and growing a mixed variety of these crops. Such farming escapes the peril of agribusiness "orthodoxy" as it shows up in monoculture crop production. Human communities also may work according to the comic principles of the small-scale, diversified farm, or they may mire in orthodoxy, whose hermetic concerns set up the conditions for revolt. Berry sees no need for such polarization: "The remedy is to accommodate the margin within the form, to allow the wilderness or nature to thrive in domesticity, to accommodate diversity within unity" (*Unsettling* 178). He wants the form to be flexible so that it can change without collapsing—wildness ought to inform farming as much as rebels ought to be included in society. Berry brings the wild into the heart of Port William through Burley. He is marginal to the household economies but central to the membership of characters, central to the health of their community—a symbolic ombudsman to the ecological household. Berry lauds the inclusion of wilderness in farming practices as a "graceful, practical generosity toward the possible and the unexpected, toward time and history" (179), and he ventures that generosity in his fiction by giving Burley a place to muster what trouble he may.

From the start, Burley is funny. Because he is loved in the community and because he strays roguishly away, he inadvertently rescues it from dullness and, worse, orthodoxy. The community stretches to accommodate his humor and predilections. Burley appropriately occupies the outskirts of Berry's narrative focus, never emerging fully into view as a title character but influencing the community atmosphere from his childhood to death. *Watch With Me* shows him as a boy. At Goforth School's fall festival where recitations by students distinguish their scholastic progress and where Ptolemy Proudfoot has gone to court the schoolteacher, Miss Minnie, Burley falters over his poem, which Miss Minnie has chosen particularly for him because it is "masculine, robust, locally applicable, seasonally appropriate, high-spirited, and amusing." She wants him to shine. Instead, failing even her prompting, he quits trying to pretend.

> Miss Minnie was reading desperately, trying to piece the poem together as he dismembered it, but he had left her behind and now he was stalled. She looked up to see an expression on his face that she knew too well. The blush was gone; he was grinning; the light of inspiration was in his eyes.
>
> "Well, drot it, folks," he said, "I forgot her. But I'll tell you one I *heard*" (*Watch With Me* 17–19).

Fluent in vernacular idiom as fully as he is inarticulate in the academic, Burley could deliver a good one, the audience knows; Miss Minnie, however, gracefully maintains the mark of her decorum on the event and thanks him back down to his seat. The incident highlights Goforth's perhaps most unaccomplished student, but rather than diminishing Miss Minnie's achievements, it augments them—at least for Tol Proudfoot. Tall, awkward, strong, and formally as inept as Burley, he is dumbfounded by little Miss Minnie's brave, gregarious propriety. That she "stopped that Burley Coulter and set him down" makes Tol's heart "swerve like a flying swift" (20). So the boy's failure not only indicates the bond that he has with the audience, who know how folks speak and would undoubtedly find that talk more amusing than literary pretension, but it also gives Tol further cause to fall in love with Miss Minnie. Burley's waywardness draws the community together.

Burley's influence continues far beyond his youth. In *Nathan Coulter*, the adult Uncle Burley early on shows up drunk. His waywardness has its price. Responding to his nephews' friendly greeting, he is cordial: " 'Well now,' he said, 'good morning, boys.' He let go the door to wave to us and fell down in a pile" (34). He is not funny here to any of the folks present, for the adults on the scene are worried and grieved, and the boys are baffled.

But it is partly Burley's penchant to risk himself that enables him to try new things and be consciously funny. For example, he collects his mother's ducks, her embroidery hoops, a tank for water, and his nephews to head to the Fourth of July carnival and set up a booth. There he capitalizes—dime by dime—on the ducks' name-touted talent for ducking: they avoid every hoop that folks toss at them from a tantalizingly close distance. Comically ingenious, Burley has pockets full of dimes when the ducks begin to tire and people win their money back. To curtail complete ruin, he turns the game over to his nephew so he can play the shooting gallery next door, from where he has an angle to shoot the ducks, eventually finishing off his game to the amusement of the crowd. No one cavils that he has prematurely ended their chance to win back the dimes. They admire his quick thinking. Burley's ingenuity nevertheless carries with it a social cost that marginalizes him (*Nathan Coulter* 66–71, 80–82).

In a style as similarly creative as his carnival game, Burley deals with the game warden who suspects him of dynamiting fish. Burley had not done so. But with no way to prove his innocence, Burley instead takes the warden out with him in the boat, ostensibly to get the fish that the warden ostensibly wants to buy. Burley has packed the leftover dynamite. Once out on the water, he lights the fuse and lays it at the bottom of the boat under the warden's feet. To save himself and them all, the warden snatches it up and throws it into the water himself, which, of course, kills fish. They all gather up the catch, and the warden, who now shares complicity in the crime, does not prosecute. Together, Nathan and Burley watch him leave.

> "It's a shame we had to mistreat him," Uncle Burley said.
> I knew how he felt. There was no reason for what we'd done, except that we'd all wound up together in the same mess. We'd been having a good time, and now we'd ruined it. "It takes the pleasure out of fishing," I said (*Nathan Coulter* 133).

Again, the comedy here goes beyond humor or fun. For his carnival stint, Burley had caught the holy outrage of his family; for the fish tragedy, he suffers from his own and Nathan's remorse. As a role model to Nathan, he is a complicated hero—an independent character that Robert Torrance defines as a comic hero, both triumphant and abhorred.

> Because society almost invariably looks askance at his subversive unconstraint . . . (festivity being an inveterate stranger to boundaries), he

will also normally appear comic in a more negative sense through the derision that his dissent elicits from those who uphold the social order. In the resulting conflict, or *agon*, he proves himself a hero by courageous perseverance, resourceful intelligence, and a more or less conscious acceptance of the inevitable risks that he chooses to run in his willfully comic challenge to the deadly seriousness of his world (viii).

Seriously employed in Berry's fiction, Burley's comedies give Nathan a way to learn the boundaries, norms, legalities, and proprieties of his world. That is, Nathan learns that the territory you enter to cross the line of accepted behavior is highly charged—his uncle's creativity can be profitable and dangerous. Nathan learns that adult play must be undertaken consciously because it has consequences.

Berry sees to it that, in his dying, Burley unites the community in comically defiant style against the values of modern, technological society. In the hospital, sanguinely considered by the medics to be in a coma rather than to be dying, as his family knows him to be, Burley occasions a nervy scheme by his son, Danny Branch, to abduct him from the hospital. This title story of *Fidelity* is redolent with humor, much of it inspired by the collective outrage the Port William membership has come to feel over the economic "progress" that endangers them and their place. Wheeler Catlett's son calls the hospital after the abduction: "'This is Henry Catlett. I have a little law practice up the river here at Hargrave. I hear you've mislaid one of your patients'" (137). The hospital supervisor does not appreciate the jibe and does not know that Henry wants to talk to the detective not to find out who the kidnapper might be but to learn what the authorities know so that he can better protect Danny Branch. Port William knows what has happened and aligns itself against the hospital and detective alike and, in fact, against all that they represent. On his night drive to the hospital, Danny figures that his patched-together truck might not hold up at interstate speeds (Burley has called the old Dodge "'a loose association of semi-retired parts, like me'" (115).). So he contemplates his options. "'If she blows,' he thought, 'I'll try to stop her crosswise of both lanes'" (116). This may be a temporary Luddite pleasure, but it is indicative of the guts Danny has to act on the confidence that he and his kind know better than medical professionals how Burley should die. Danny takes the tubes from his father's nose and the IV from his arm, and carries him out as if a corpse to head for familiar woods, explaining where they are so Burley is comfortable and aware.

This drama of his death and burial takes place in relative obscurity while the public action involves the orchestrated baffling of Detective Kyle Bode. First Henry Catlett deflects him by broadening the context of what the incident means. The country lawyer tells Bode,

"You're here to represent the right of the state and other large organizations to decide for us and come between us. The people you represent will come out here, without asking our opinion, and shut down a barbershop or a little slaughterhouse because it's not sanitary enough for us, and then let other businesses—richer ones—poison the air and water" (165).

The detective retorts, "'What's *that* got to do with it?'" His objection does not succeed in changing the debate; he continuously hears from the community that context has everything to do with it. After Henry, Wheeler, too, elaborates on Burley's family connections and membership to the area. They complicate the law by holding themselves to higher standards than it, asking, for instance, as Wheeler does, " "To whom and to what does Burley Coulter belong?'" (174). Bode tries to insist on atomizing the affair, explaining in confessional mode, " 'all I know is that the law has been broken, and I am here to serve the law.' " Wheeler's response is beneficent and patient.

"But, my dear boy, you don't eat or drink the law, or sit in the shade of it or warm yourself by it, or wear it, or have your being in it. The law exists only to serve."
"Serve what?"
"Why, all the many things that are above it. Love" (175).

The comic and kindly humbling of Bode involves showing him unprofessionally interested in the dog that comes up in conversation about Burley. The description that Mart Rowanberry gives Bode of a blue tick hound is fine evidence for nothing Bode can use. By the time all the loved ones of Burley have gathered in Wheeler's office, Bode is literally ushered helplessly into the community context where his law has no relevance and is, in fact, foolish. Danny Branch then arrives, spotlessly clean and smiling into the gathering, completing the comic triumph of Burley's death and Port William's independence.

Berry's seriousness about his moral world, where people ought to and do care for each other and the land, might warrant it to be a grave world, but instead Port William is intensely comic. The relevance of humor is paramount to community dynamics and survival. It is deadly serious, for instance, when Ernest Finley's attraction to Ida Crop is curtailed by the return of her husband, prompting Ernest to commit suicide. But when pixilated Jayber, Burley, and Big Ellis decide to fill his yet empty grave with the drunk Whacker (it is Armistice night, much celebrated except in the mourning Feltner household), there becomes a way to bear Ernest's death and World War II without remaining in the tragedy of the deaths. Mat Feltner is sitting up with Ernest's body when he is alerted by "the approaching clamor of Whacker's funeral procession":

> At first it seemed only a fitful last resurgence of the festivity, an indecipherable mingling of shouts and laughter, but as it drew nearer he made out the measured heavy beat of a dead march and, above it, the strained wailing of a dirge.
>
> Mat's first impulse was to take the irreverence of it as an affront. . . .
>
> But that they went by singing, voices raised in the rhythm of loss and grief with unabashed glee, seemed to Mat to change the night, to start it toward something else—though he was not able to say what (*A Place on Earth* 299).

The turn out of mourning comes not because mourning is over but because it has been placed. The drunks have obliviously taken the first precipitous leap out of one "story" into the next—into the amassed stories that make the context for any one story. Burley and company's mock funeral rites—the in fact dangerous lowering of a big man into a six-foot hole—rejoins the presence of death to the giddy atmosphere the Armistice inspired. Their comedy initiates a way to live into the deaths of kin and countrymen, literally reveling in them, and so to get out of them also—sober up into a world transformed by play even as it assumes seriousness. By virtue of promoting creativity, humor facilitates survival, encouraging people to cope with new and tough situations or to deal with old troubles in innovative ways.

▼ ▼ ▼

ANOTHER ROUTE TO BERRY'S HUMOR ANGLES THROUGH ANARCHY INTO comedy. Comedy as a plot (the loss and recovery of equilibrium) and attitude (the acceptance of change and mystery) often differs from what we find funny; for instance, Coyote can be comically troublesome without being funny. As the traditional Old Man or as the free-wheeling woman in Le Guin's "Buffalo Gals," Coyote's main role is anarchist, not necessarily humorist. However, myth puts her in a comic plot, so we associate all her provoking indiscretion with humor. Comedy never comes entirely devoid of humor, and humor cannot be extricated completely from comedy. Each provides a nonlinear route to the other. In developing arguments, Berry uses humor to augment his defiance, but he more often takes on the role of anarchic Coyote—if the contentious word *anarchy* were to mean what bioregional enthusiast and humorist Jim Dodge articulated, "Anarchy doesn't mean out of control; it means out of *their* control" (8). Anarchy fits comedy like a glove, pointing out a direction for change. Although making humor is not Berry's main technique in pressing for reform, it fits his style as a Coyote figure—anarchist, trickster, revolutionary. Berry is comic de-spoiler of the notion of progress, a notion both pervasive and insidious, quartered not only in Congress and corporations but also in the conscious-ness of most Americans, who assume that industrial and technological modernization promotes their well-being.

Berry has different standards, minority ones. In elevating the old-fashioned goal of community health as a preeminent standard, Berry is an anomalous underdog. His satiric preface to *Sex, Economy, Freedom & Community* recognizes the fight. "Dear Reader," it opens, "This is a book about sales resistance." Cleverly enjoining the allure of progress with the hawking of false promises, Berry establishes his role: "The first duty of writers who wish to be of any use even to themselves is to resist the lan-guage, the ideas, and the categories of this ubiquitous sales talk, no matter from whose mouth it issues" (xi). When asked in a 1993 interview about how to improve education, Berry replied, "My approach to education would be like my approach to everything else. I'd change the standard. I would make the standard that of community health rather than the career of the student" ("Field Observations" 58). He distrusts the hype—the "sales talk" of modern America—that purports to deliver a better future but in fact does nothing practical.

Berry is revolutionary in his refusal to participate in the assumptions of contemporary culture. Paul Merchant writes, "In a world of rapid turnover, immediate gratification, and headlines, he is a traditionalist, tak-ing the long view. He is not fashionable, because he has resisted the very tendencies in national life that contribute to fashion" (2). Merchant is right to conclude that Berry as a writer and thinker "resists simple classification"

(2). Indeed, he is hardly even a "traditionalist" because he does not believe that an adequate tradition has yet existed in the United States. Countering the claim that his vision may be regressive and nostalgic, he says, "There is no time in history, since white occupation began in America, that any sane and thoughtful person would want to go back to, because that history so far has been unsatisfactory"—we have lacked, of course, "stable communities well adapted to their places" ("Field Observations" 59). In an increasingly urban and frenetic society, Berry's vision is revolutionary because it is rural and unhurried. Or unharried. He has been schooled to practice this style: "You see, when you farm, it does not make any difference how wound up you are. If you are going to grow corn, you have got to slow down to the speed of corn" ("The Art of Place" 33). Strangely enough, then, his provocation to the mainstream is sometimes no more aggressive than the styled practice of slowness, caution, and care.

As such, he is sufficiently pugnacious to rile up contention. Berry plays his revolutionary Coyote role with a suave and modest mien. "I thought once I was going to become a modern person, but it turns out that I'm not one," he has said. "Keeping up with the times is the least of my interests" (Aprile 19). Despite the fact that he has kept up with the direction of the times, which is evident in his numerous works of nonfiction, his characterization is apt. He is decidedly not modern, a fact that seems to provoke less furor from readers than his avowed contentment about it. For instance, when Berry's brief essay "Why I Am Not Going to Buy a Computer" first appeared in *Harper's*, readers wrote in angry. They objected to the fact that the author's wife is his "best critic" in a "literary cottage industry," as Berry describes it, where she types his drafts; they objected to the moral valence Berry gave his decision to avoid coal-generated power as much as possible. They felt judged, and they did not appreciate it. Berry not uncommonly has this effect on readers, who shy at the context that he raises around his decisions: it is a moral context based on different standards than that of the mainstream, and as such, it poses a frightful threat to the assumptions of most people. This is a sampling of their letters:

Wendell Berry provides writers enslaved by the computer with a handy alternative: Wife—a low-tech energy-saving device.

I would be happy to join Berry in a protest against strip mining, but I intend to keep plugging this computer into the wall with a clear conscience.

I have no particular desire to see Berry use a word processor; if he doesn't like computers, that's fine with me. However, I do object to his portrayal of this reluctance as a moral virtue. Many of us have found that computers can be an invaluable tool in the fight to protect our environment. . . . Perhaps Berry feels that the Sierra Club should eschew modern printing technology, which is highly wasteful of energy, in favor of having its members hand-copy the club's magazines and other mailings each month? (*What Are People For?* 172–74)

The tone of Berry's essay—not sarcastic and not arch toward others—in general differs from the tone of these letters. The essay shows him to be strongly committed to personal principle. It does not play the game of abstraction or dissociation by which we normally cushion our consciences from local or global problems and thus make our lives comfortable. Berry chooses to write longhand because he does not want his writing to be dependent on electricity, which comes cleanly into our homes but wrecks a part of the greater household in providing this convenience. By his personal example, Berry insists that our ideas ought to have meaning in our lives—ought to have relevance to how we live. The following is a sampling of Berry's reply to his detractors, whom he politely calls "correspondents":

My correspondents are certain that I am wrong and that I am, moreover, on the losing side, a side already relegated to the dustbin of history. And yet they grow huffy and condescending over my tiny dissent. What are they so anxious about?

I can only conclude that I have scratched the skin of a technological fundamentalism that, like other fundamentalisms, wishes to monopolize a whole society and, therefore, cannot tolerate the smallest difference of opinion.

If some technology does damage to the world—as two of the above letters seem to agree that it does—then why is it not reasonable, and indeed moral, to try to limit one's use of that technology? *Of course*, I think that I am right to do this.

One of the letter writers described me as "a fool" and "doubly a fool," but fortunately misspelled my name, leaving me a speck of hope that I am not the "Wendell Barry" he was talking about. Two others accused me of self-righteousness, by which they seem to have meant that they think they are righter than I think I am. (*What Are People For?* 175–79)

If people take umbrage at Berry's moralism and the practical use he makes of it, they have usually believed it to be antagonistic and failed to match his good humor. He is moral trickster in having a sense of humor about his beliefs. That is, he retains some distance from them, acknowledging that they are in flux and may change. Via humor, he is able to maintain both his attachments and a healthy perspective—the "distance" that is not abstraction or lack of commitment but awareness of context. Humor gives Berry the distance from his morals and norms so that he can see himself *inside* them, *choosing* a mannerly life. "The Joy of Sales Resistance," preface to *Sex, Economy, Freedom & Community*, illustrates his comic skill.

> As I understand it, I am being paid only for my work in arranging the words; my property is that arrangement. The thoughts in this book, on the contrary, are not mine. They came freely to me, and I give them freely away. I have no "intellectual property," and I think that all claimants to such property are thieves. I am well aware that you cannot give your thoughts to someone who will not take them, and I am prepared for that.

> An essayist not only has no right to expect complete agreement but has a certain responsibility to ward it off. If you tell me, dear reader, that you agree with me completely, then I must suspect one or both of us of dishonesty. I must reserve the right, after all, to disagree with myself.
> But however much I may change my mind, I will never agree with those saleswomen and salesmen who suggest that if I will only do as they say, all will be fine. All, dear reader, is not going to be fine. Even if we all agreed with all the saints and prophets, all would not be fine. For we would still be mortal, partial, suffering poor creatures, not very intelligent and never the authors of our best hope (xviii-xx).

These are neither the ideas nor the language of a moral fundamentalist; instead, they demonstrate Berry's willingness to proffer his vision and play with it, poking fun at himself. Thus he retains the "speck of hope" that he is not the "Wendell Barry" his correspondent lambasted. The moral trickster, a rare breed that includes Berry, is not necessarily funny but highly self-aware, conscious of the limits that his or her moral world projects and quick to investigate from all angles.

Knowing how inclusive his investigations are helps us understand his comic worldview. Berry's definition of community, with its insistence on the importance of nature, is best characterized by its comedy.

> If we speak of a *healthy* community, we cannot be speaking of a commu-
> nity that is merely human. We are talking about a neighborhood of hu-
> mans in a place, plus the place itself: its soil, its water, its air, and all the
> families and tribes of the nonhuman creatures that belong to it. If the
> place is well preserved, if its entire membership, natural and human, is
> present in it, and if the human economy is in practical harmony with the
> nature of the place, then the community is healthy. A diseased commu-
> nity will be suffering natural losses that become, in turn, human losses.
> A healthy community is sustainable; it is, within reasonable limits, self-
> sufficient and, within reasonable limits, self-determined—that is, free of
> tyranny (*Sex, Economy, Freedom & Community* 14–15).

The comedy in this passage has nothing to do with tone but is invested in the structure of the community he describes. That community is inclusive and egalitarian, bound by limits that direct its changes. It is a wild but cer-tainly not lawless community; its health lies in its adherence to comedy. Most important to this concept of community is Berry's assertion "*All* neighbors are included" (15).[68] By envisioning a membership that includes nonhuman nature, Berry chooses a context large enough so that ecological concerns give him an uncanny perspective.

> From a human point of view, the difference between the mind of a
> human and that of a mountain goat is wonderful; from the point of view
> of the infinite ignorance that surrounds us, the difference is not impres-
> sive. Indeed, from that point of view, the goat may have the better mind,
> for he is more congenially adapted to his place, and he would not en-
> danger his species or his planet for the sake of an idea. As I see it, then,
> the condition of mystery inescapably implies the necessity of restraint
> ("A Question a Day" 41).

68. According to Joseph Meeker, comedy assumes, "that survival depends upon finding accommodation that will permit all parties to endure" (33). Northrop Frye emphasizes that, in comedy, the final society that results is inclusive (*Anatomy of Criticism* 164).

The world is comic because it hosts so many different points of view. The combination of them all into one inclusive community creates mystery, according to Berry, hence his word *Creation* to describe this world. *Creation* connotes that the power and consciousness of the world exceed the human mind. Berry's comic vision, which prompts him to survey a situation from different perspectives, alerts him to possibilities that may be beyond his capacity to fathom. He knows that he does not know it all—Creation goes beyond his grasp. Creative enough to see the comic construction of this world, Berry also is committed enough to pursue the practical ramifications that a comic worldview ought to have on its human members. Since we can never know the world well enough, we should live attentively, as if to give the rest of Creation plenty of room. Eminently concerned with how we live in the world, Berry emphasizes practice, livelihood, discipline, and household economy. We hear less from him about the ambiguities and mystery that attend Creation—and even less about the faith and levity that help people entrust themselves to inexplicable forces—and so his work contrives to obscure its comic foundations.[69] He is explicit about his concerns.

> Moral value, as should be obvious, is not separable from other values. An adequate morality would be ecologically sound; it would be esthetically pleasing. But the point I want to stress here is that it would be *practical*. Morality is long-term practicality (*A Continuous Harmony* 165).

Wendell Berry deserves the reputation of being a moralist, for he wants to see people live respectfully on earth. However, it is the comic underpinning of his moral impulse that keeps Berry lively—poised to use humor and accept ambiguity.

Berry's comic worldview is shaped by what he calls a "tragic sensibility," a sensibility that makes the tone of much of his work elegiac and drives his humor to be fierce or delicate, usually eschewing the absurd or ridiculous. Northrop Frye has written that tragedy is implicit or incomplete comedy, especially in terms of the Christian plot, which incorporates death in the larger scheme of redemption and resurrection ("The Argument of Comedy" 64–66). One can also say that the ecological "plot"

---

69. Characteristic of the sympathetic response to Berry are the assessments of Wallace Stegner and Gregory McNamee, who both consider Berry to be a radical opposed to the dominant order and describe his work with such words as integrity, responsibility, and propriety—which are most attentive to his seriousness (47–52; 90–102, respectively).

is also comic because every natural change or death participates in the on-going drama of adaptation and survival.[70] Speaking of tragedy, Berry em-phasizes the living we must do: he focuses on loss but demands survival. Tragedy, he says, is "at the heart of community life."

> The tragic sensibility simply accepts mortality as an inescapable condi-tion. In a sense, it is the necessary counterbalance to the tradition of see-ing the other as a living soul; it applies a sense of time and finitude to our relationships.
>
> The tragic sensibility sees and accepts that as we live we are going to live into the deaths of people we love; and it accepts that the condition of our love for those people is that we will lose them—or that they will lose us ("The Art of Place" 32).

This is the "heart" of community life because community consists of rela-tionships that attach people and places, and people's attachments in-evitably put them at risk. His notion of "tragic sensibility" refers more to the attitude we must practice to bear losses than to loss itself. Thus his tragic sensibility is a comic skill because it recommends that we commit ourselves to the beloved things that inevitably change.

> What we're really talking about is faith, the faith being that if you make a commitment and hang on until death, there are rewards. The rewards come. Nobody has ever said that this was easy to do, but I think that everybody who has done it has done it out of this faith that there are re-wards. My experience suggests very powerfully to me that there are re-wards ("Field Observations" 53).

Or as he said in another interview, "If we'd stayed in New York, we'd have gone to a lot fewer funerals. But we wouldn't have loved as much or been loved as much as we have" (Aprile 19).

In *The Comedy of Survival*, Joseph Meeker writes that the comic mode "depends less upon particular ideologies or metaphysical systems than tragedy does. Rather, comedy grows from the biological circumstances of life. It is unconcerned with cultural systems of morality" (22). Or with heroism. Although Berry is concerned with "cultural systems of morality,"

---

70. Joseph Meeker describes this best, aligning comedy with ecological "accommoda-tion" and evolution (26–27, 33).

he advocates modest, unheroic practices that "accommodate necessity," as Meeker says comedy and ecology do (30). For example, Berry speaks about planning his daily work.

> I can't help but notice, and I've been noticing for a good many years now, that my plans almost *never* work out. The day almost *never* exactly fits the plan. Some days depart *wildly* from the plan. So I conclude that even though you're going to make plans, if you're a live human being, one of the things you must learn to do is to take them lightly. . . . Make plans that are appropriately small ("Field Observations" 54).

Berry avoids the inflated notions of human self-importance that Meeker says create the absurd, vain, and ecologically destructive tragic plot. In fact, Berry sees the tragic plot unfortunately replicated in the environmental movement's focus on "planetary" versions of environmental problems.[71] He advocates instead a quotidian return to "the scale of our competence"—the local, where we address issues because of love. Again, Meeker: "To people disposed in favor of heroism and idealistic ethics, comedy may seem trivial in its insistence that the commonplace is worth maintaining" (26). To Berry, the commonplace may be the most powerful force we have, and it includes love: "Love is never abstract. It does not adhere to the universe or the planet or the nation or the institution or the profession, but to the singular sparrows of the street, the lilies of the field, 'the least of these my brethren.' Love is not, by its own desire, heroic. It is heroic only when compelled to be. It exists by its willingness to be anonymous, humble, and unrewarded" (*What Are People For?* 198–200). Insisting on small scale and modest aims, Berry subverts grand-sounding "cultural systems of morality" and shows that proper etiquette is not hardpan moralism but comic practice—necessary to survival, crucial to accommodating ourselves to place and circumstance.

Because morality for Berry is not abstract but rather created by people in a place acting in relation to others, place acquires a heightened significance as the practical site of morality. Thus embedded in nature, morality requires

---

71. Environmentalists are, however, neither uniform nor humorless. On starting Earth First!, Dave Foreman writes, "Radicals frequently verge on a righteous seriousness. But we felt that if we couldn't laugh at ourselves we would be merely another bunch of dangerous fanatics who should be locked up—like oil company executives. Not only does humor preserve individual and group sanity, it retards hubris, a major cause of environmental rape, and it is also an effective weapon" (20).

faith, for such morality cannot be explicated without arriving at the mysterious and miraculous presence of Creation. Commitment to such a world
requires a leap of faith. Berry does not have entirely rational terms to describe this world, for which he nonetheless encourages us to behave well,
but he is acquainted with the faith that will put him in relation to it.

> What I hold out for is the possibility that a man can live decently *without*
> knowing all the answers or believing that he does—can live decently
> even in the understanding that life is unspeakably complex and un-
> speakably subtle in its complexity (*A Continuous Harmony* 57).

> I understand [the Creation] to be a harmonious and beautiful whole. I
> am very happy to honor it. However, that the whole exists is not some-
> thing anybody is ever going to know for certain. We sense that the
> whole exists because we have experienced the intricacy, wonder and
> mystery of its parts ("The Art of Place" 29).

He emphasizes the uncertainties of knowing the world and the necessity of
acting on the faith that it is worth living for. Faith that presupposes mystery, committing itself consciously to that mystery, is comic. Berry chooses
marriage as a motif fundamental to comedy to embody such faith and to be
a metaphor for people's relation to the land. That motif is inherently comic,
uniting two in one, amalgamating perspectives, proposing new life.
Necessary to marriage and to Creation, faith helps keep us committed to a
changing thing, whether a spouse or nature. Berry may be a moralist, but
the comic element of his faith is overlooked by his critics, those who support him and those who find his down-home loyalties to place and marriage parochial or moralistic.[72] Fundamentally, Berry is making a gamble,
choosing to confer meaning upon the mysterious nonhuman world.

> Nothing is meaningful or valuable alone; to assign meaning and value
> to anything alone is, I believe, what used to be understood as 'idolatry.'
> Nothing can be its own context. Meaning and value are not generated

72. In defense of Berry's didactic work, Lionel Basney shows that Berry has evoked
"what is essential, and alive" in a literary tradition that extends at least to the Romantics,
a didactic but also imaginative tradition concerned with the applicability of art to people's lives (174–75). Carl Esbjornson praises Berry as an "upholder of moral standards"
(160) who has written literature that benefits community health because of "its most didactic function of remembering" (169).

by parts, but are conferred by the whole. The only safe contexts are, first, natural order and, second, a human culture formed in respect for natural order (*Standing by Words* 181).

To acknowledge that our own meaning is not under our control but instead dependent on ecological context—which Berry calls "natural order"— demonstrates his proficiency at dealing with ambiguity. His didacticism shows him to be hopeful, taking the courageous effort to conceive of and point out household rules that go with living in Creation. Berry's step to commit himself to an ambiguous universe is a comic one, a leap of faith.

Accomplishing a moral life takes practice, and humor is eminently suited to serve that process. As it glimmers in Berry's work through his narrative persona, and as it breaks free in stories and scenes that can make us laugh, humor shows not a lapse in sincerity but imaginative triumph— Berry succoring enough certainty of his creation to turn it loose. It is not easy for him to overcome the writerly dignity of being Port William's patriarch—and he never forgoes his poise—yet the persistence of humor in his most serious fictional moments shows it to be inseparable from his moral vision. Both his morality and humor issue from faith: faith that the particular tragedies of our immediate circumstances partake of a larger, comically inclusive story; and faith in an ethical life—"the possibility that a man can live decently *without* knowing all the answers, or believing that he does" (*A Continuous Harmony* 57). Humor completes Berry's morality by helping to keep it from completion, saving it from orthodoxy. That is, reminding us that the unlikely or unknown is part of the moral life—that those variables keep us humble and flexible. Berry's faith in Creation entails the need to be funny. The foundation of values he has established in fiction vivifies Port William only to the extent that it prepares the way for a more complete faith—the ability to play the moral limits for their humorous potential, thus keeping the faith honest to the mysterious Creation.

SHORT CUT

▼▼▼

Coyote Seer, Gary Snyder

Gary Snyder's debt to Coyote is that of an original thinker to a creative precursor. In selected poems, he takes liberties to imagine where the creature might yet go, using Coyote as an avatar of the wild and a witness to the fate of human civilization. His "Coyote Man, Mr. President, & the Gunfighters" shows Coyote to be serious about his trickster-reformer role, much as Berry is serious about employing his humor, and the polyphonic Coyote in "A Berry Feast" suggests the versatile perspective-taking that Rachel Carson accomplishes to comic effect in her work.

Coyote edges through Snyder's poems as if he were glimpsed on the move and has the respect of the poet to remain the vagabond, forever tripping through this world and beyond. Coyote is a wild creature we have taken to heart and transfigured in our stories. He is a visitor to our realm and always has an exit out, for he has never been completely what we have said. He is wild, magical, and elusive, and Snyder portrays him as such.

In "Through the Smoke Hole," Coyote is there at the center of the house where the smoke leads to outside and inside worlds—he is making the trip. His trickster cousins, the Raven and Magpie, fly up and out, but he "falls thru; we recognize him only as a clumsy relative, a father in old clothes we don't wish to see with our friends" (*The Back Country* 125). Not very alert to other worlds, we do not know how to see the transport between them. Coyote is hard to know because we keep seeing ourselves in him—the clumsy relative—the part of us that we would prefer to avoid anyway. If we do come to know Coyote, it will be because we have learned enough about ourselves to distinguish where we and he diverge and to acknowledge how we coincide with him, sharing parts of each other. Wild Coyote will not be followed.

We too have a wild nature, our most fearsome resemblance to Coyote. It is that nature we want least to recognize because we know the least about it; it frightens us, gesturing as it does at the way through the smoke. "The Call of the Wild" tells that story of our fear. The old man in the poem's first section who hears "the Coyote singing / in the back meadow" is an eighty-year-old rancher, miner, logger, and Catholic. He asks a federal trapper to kill the coyotes. Those not so encumbered by a

lifetime of controlling nature respond differently. Of the fate of these coyotes, the poet says sadly, "My sons will lose this / Music they have just
started / To love" (*Turtle Island* 21). His boys feel a native amity with the
coyotes that the Catholic Californian does not—the howling that makes its
own contrapuntal harmony touches and thrills the children. Yet because
these coyotes might be exterminated, the children may not develop a taste
for such music, and they may fail to match it with the wildness within
them.

Even people in search of harmony fail to find it if they are insular, unattached to the worlds that permeate their life. Coyote's world, for instance.
At least the Californian heard the coyotes'"singing"; folks who come to the
woods to practice their own inner harmony are missing the point that it includes a world of things—inner harmony entails focusing our attention beyond ourselves. These "ex acid-heads from the cities / Converted to Guru
or Swami" do not even hear the Coyote, so how can they know if he makes
music? Fully distracted with themselves, they "Do penance with shiny /
Dopey eyes, and quit eating meat" (21). They do not live where they are—
their "oil-heated / Geodesic domes" are "stuck like warts / In the woods"—
and even their dreams are displaced, dreams "of India, of / forever blissful
sexless highs" (21). The harmony they aspire to is fake, ersatz peace
achieved through oblivion rather than awareness.

> And the Coyote singing
>> is shut away
>> for they fear
>> the call
>> of the wild.

> And they sold their virgin cedar trees,
>> the tallest trees in miles,
> To a logger
> Who told them,

> "Trees are full of bugs" (22).

Such folks do not know themselves, nor do they know much of the natural
world around them. In truth, the tallest and the oldest of the cedars were living proof of their healthiness. The logger's appeal to the people's fear of the
wild (including insects) succeeds because they had not explored or studied

or tarried in their woods long enough to know for themselves how beautiful the trees were. So they lost what could have helped enlighten them.

Finally, in the poem's third and last section, government institutionalizes people's fear, deciding to make the war against nature "all-out" because "Defeat / is Un-American" (22). Snyder imagines that people take off to "special cities in the sky" (23) from where they can keep their distance from the earth and bomb it into submission. Their fears are munificent.

> And they never came down,
>   for they found,
>   the ground
> is pro-Communist. And dirty.
> And the insects side with the Viet Cong (22).

Such paranoia, all to this end:

> blinding sparrows
> breaking the ear-drums of owls
> splintering trunks of cherries
> twining and looping
> deer intestines
> in the shaken dusty, rocks (22).

The creatures and the earth are innocent, but, though this is obvious in the poem, equally obvious is the intransigence of the people's misplaced ferocity. The conclusion is not hopeful.

> A war against the earth.
> When it's done there'll be
>   no place
>
> A Coyote could hide (23).

It is a lament for the avatar of the wild, the Coyote. The envoy is not hopeful either.

> I would like to say
> Coyote is forever
> Inside you.
>
> But it's not true (23).

The wilderness that ought to be out there in the back meadow or further beyond us is not what we can replace. Nor can Snyder promise that we shall always keep Coyote inside us, for the wildness that continually offers itself up in our bodies we ourselves suppress—and the burden of his poem shows that we are successful at this. People who fear the unknown in themselves also try to eliminate mystery in the world (who can know why Coyote sings?) because it reminds them of their own fearsome wildness. A war such as "The Call of the Wild" reports is—in the ecological household—personal, domestic, and genocidal.

Coyote is interested in humankind's dilemma to come to terms with its place on earth. Usually in the midst of the fray, he can be a victim or a hero. Snyder knows him as an interlocutor between the human and non-human. In the same prophetic vein as "The Call of the Wild," "Coyote Man, Mr. President, & the Gunfighters" foresees the likely outcome of our nation's bellicosity. The prose poem opens with a statement of the problem: "Mr. President was fascinated by gunfighters" (*Left Out in the Rain* 206). He invites them in the thousands to the White House—"his White House"—where they practice shooting. But the shootouts in fact are far more than practice: casualties in dead and wounded men exceed one hundred a year. It is violence as entertainment—bloody sport. And someone, finally, objects enough to want to remedy the situation. It is the senator from the Great Basin who makes this move, offering "A basket of turquoise and a truckload of compost" to anyone who can stop the gunfights at the White House. These rewards are precious—and unique. We know their value, while at the same time we understand that such rewards are not the ones that would be offered in our day: they are not money or credit or a vacation. Instead they are material wealth, useful to improve the garden, fashion jewelry, or barter; and the fact that they are esteemed as rewards suggests that this is a different time than our own—where senators are identified by their region rather than state and much else has changed. When Coyote Man is called on to reason with the president, he immediately turns down the turquoise (the item most like money in value) and tells the senator, "'you'd owe a million wild ducks'" (206). Not that a coyote could ever hope to eat so many or want that many ducks for himself—no, he does not say that the senator would owe *him* those ducks but simply that he would "owe." Coyote Man is committed to a world bigger than the one he can realistically occupy. His motives are not selfish.

To be granted an interview with the president, Coyote Man must have a uniform and know how to shoot a gun. As the senator says, all the gunfighters who are invited to the White House "wear starched uniforms and have shaved cheeks; they glare fiercely, and speak in staccato sentences about ballistics and tactical deployment" (206–7). The requirements do not trouble Coyote Man in the least: he says he can handle a revolver and he agrees, "'I'll get me the uniform of a gunfighter'" (207). Informal and colloquial, his speech distinguishes him from the class of self-important, rigid gunfighters who perform for the president. Nonetheless, Coyote Man is game, adaptable to the demands of the situation, and he speaks the right language when the president asks him what his skill is, replying "'My shooting strikes and kills at every shot, and doesn't miss at nine hundred miles'" (207). He claims a magical talent and seems to deliver on its promise, hitting, in the trials, three dozen of the president's gunfighters, whereupon he is scheduled to meet the survivors for further dueling. But the most magical of his talents is his tongue, for he takes the liberty to answer the president's ever-practical question about his choice of revolvers by embarking on a metaphysical description of the three kinds of revolvers that he has. It is a gamble. The president could throw him in jail—or have him shot—but Coyote Man is ready to follow through on the respect he has earned and attempt to end the gunfights. Ostensibly he will speak Mr. President's language by describing his revolvers: the surprise is huge when he talks not about short or long barrels but the make of a "revolver of the cosmos," of mankind, and of the state. The first fits this description:

> "The Milky Way is its grip, the solar winds, the barrel. Its bullets are stars, it sights by the beams of pulsars. It spits out planets and bathes them, spinning, in heat and light. The ninety-two elements aim it; the secrets of fusion fire it. Wield it, and countless beings leap into life and dance through the void. Conceal it, and whole galaxies rush into nothingness. When this revolver is manifested the whole earth flourishes, the skies clear, the rivers sing, the gardens are full of squash and corn, the high plains rich with Bison. This is the revolver of the cosmos" (208).

All of this leaves the president "at an utter loss." Coyote is outlining the power inherent in the harmonious order of the universe—the mysterious order whereby the far-flung heavenly bodies conspire to endow bounty on the earth, plenty of squash and corn, plenty of Bison. This is the much-sung wealth of North America; Coyote comes out of native traditions into this one, which is a nightmarish projection of a twentieth-century preoccupation with guns, violence, and aggression. As would seem fitting, Coyote passes at his liberty between these traditions, this time bringing Native American wisdom about the real and metaphorical connections in the universe to bear on Mr. President. The revolver of the cosmos is as positive a symbol of the power in the universe as is the revolver of mankind positive about the potential of human enlightenment. Coyote further instructs the president.

> "The revolver of mankind? The twelve races are the grip; the three thousand languages the barrel. Forged in the Pliocene, finished in the Pleistocene, decorated with civilization, it aims for knowledge and beauty. The cylinder is the rise and fall of nations, the sights are the philosophies and religions and sciences, the bullets are countless men and women who have pierced through ignorance and old habits, and revealed the shining mirror of true nature. It takes its model from life itself, and trusts in the four seasons. Its secret power is the delight of the mind. Once grasped it brings harmony and peace to the planet; like a thunderbolt it destroys exploiters, and dictators crumble like sand. This is the revolver of mankind" (208–9).

This is a weighty lecture to deliver to a man programmed to know guns only literally. The Coyote's revolver has intangible targets and creative, peace-loving ends. It further expands and transforms the context of gunfighting that Mr. President has defined so narrowly and confined himself inside. Coyote Man is intent upon revamping the president's worldview so that he will want to change his behavior; he appeals to the histories of the universe and mankind in the attempt to place the president in a reality more comprehensive than that of the White House. In fact, Coyote Man wants to make Mr. President's power seem ridiculous, and he clinches that with his account of the revolver of the State, obviously recognizable as the kind of gun that fascinates the president.

> "It is used by men in starched uniforms with shaved chins who glare fiercely and speak in staccato sentences about ballistics and tactical deployment. On top it blows out brains and splinters neckbones; underneath it spits out livers and lungs. Those who use this revolver are no different from fighting cocks—any morning they may be dead or in jail. They are of no use in the councils of mankind. Now you occupy the office of Mr. President, and yet you show this fondness for gunfighters. I think it is rather unworthy of you" (209).

Snyder has chosen a fitting cast of characters to represent contemporary problems. His Coyote Man has leapt not only from native North American cultures to a White House scandal but he also plays a larger cross-cultural role as the star character in this creative reproduction of a third-century BC Chinese text, "Discourse on Swords" (from Burton Watson's translation). Who would be better suited than Coyote to be this cultural ombudsman? Snyder has picked the North American figure most likely to be disarmingly persuasive, relevant, and magical, and has employed him as a wise trickster, who unmasks destructive practices. Coyote puts the president in clearer relation to the wider world.

Coyote plays a similarly positive but less structured role in "A Berry Feast" (*The Back Country* 3–7). He is truly the interlocutor here, speaking the languages of people and creatures and serving as the presiding character of a poem ripe with voices and manifold action. He is again important in Snyder's imagination of the other worlds that might come after this one—or emerge in it. Just as the colonizing berry bushes are harbingers of that world, Coyote evinces a tenacity that promises to last through all that may pass. A description of him is this poem's first stanza:

> Fur the color of mud, the smooth loper
> Crapulous old man, a drifter,
> Praises! of Coyote the Nasty, the fat
> Puppy that abused himself, the ugly gambler,
> Bringer of goodies (3).

Coyote is himself as multifarious a soul as the world he inhabits, which in this poem is where bears eat berries and deposit the remains (seeds fertilized) on the trail, where the mythical woman married to a bear raises "half-human cubs" (3), where suburbanites face the forest (felled for their developments) in the grain of their pine-planked homes, where cats drink breast milk a woman squeezes for them (4), where huckleberries persist in a logged woods (5), and where a traveler finds a bright room to eat breakfast at night in an unfamiliar town (6). Coyote has this crazy world's fortuitous, random, interconnected style because he was raised in it, talking and interbreeding. "K'ak, k'ak, k'ak! / sang Coyote. Mating with / humankind . . . " (3). This modern (and mythical) world is often violent—at cross-purposes with itself—and Coyote sometimes tumbles out the loser. Or so it happens that he is "Coyote: shot from the car, two ears, / A tail, bring bounty" (4). For all that, he is an insatiable survivor: he has a flair for the comeback.

> —and when Magpie
> Revived him, limp rag of fur in the river
> Drowned and drifting, fish-food in the shallows,
> "Fuck you!" sang Coyote
>   and ran (5).

Huckleberries, too, though at a different pace (the growing seasons) and by different means (through the digestive tracts of their consumers), run, spreading through meadows, valleys, pine woods, gullies. Pioneering in places only marginally fertile, they bring with them the host of creatures who make meals of them: the huckleberries portend wildness, the influx of interdependent lives whose story is more complicated than anyone's but Coyote's. "A Berry Feast" is Snyder's evocation of that complexity, the myriad voices of creatures and people; the presence of death, birth, and resurrection; the shared food; the intersection of wilderness and civilization; the intercourse of mythologies with the present and of species with each other. The feast is communal, but only those who share shall participate in it. In the end, longevity and health go to those who fully give themselves up to the round of the food chain. The huckleberries are the clear leaders here, for they have much to offer: their sweet nutritious fruit is bountiful food for others. In turn, those creatures whose appetites are plumped with the berry carry its seeds with them wherever they go. Thus the huckleberry moves felicitously on. The animals' territory is the berry's, and the berry is also a pioneer, seeded ahead (by water, wind, or serendipity) into places that will draw its animal counterparts.

The final scene is futuristic. It is a new day. Much has changed—in the way that change has of being completely natural, fitting in seamlessly to the previous order. The spunky Coyote is present to usher in the day with his sharp cry.

> Coyote yap, a knife!
> Sunrise on yellow rocks.
> People gone, death no disaster,
> Clear sun in the scrubbed sky
>   empty and bright
>
> Lizards scurry from darkness
> We lizards sun on yellow rocks (6).

Lizards remain when people are gone—as does the Coyote. We are treated to the view as these creatures see it.

> See, from the foothills
> Shred of river glinting, trailing,
> To flatlands, the city:
>   glare of haze in the valley horizon
> Sun caught on glass gleams and goes.
> From cool springs under cedar
> On his haunches, white grin,
>   long tongue panting, he watches:
>
> Dead city in dry summer,
> Where berries grow (7).

The view is Snyder's projection of the fate of cities and people, if they be stingy in spirit or jealous of their part in the harvest of all things. Lacking generosity, people will not flourish, and their city will die along with them—to be retaken by huckleberries and wilderness. So Snyder prophesies, encouraged at his work by the Coyote who lurks in myth and in flesh somewhere at his side. Snyder's Coyote is a survivor, and his example of adaptation and tenacity anticipates the nature of survival propounded by Rachel Carson.

FIVE

Rachel Carson

Upholding the Comedy of Survival

NATURE AS RACHEL CARSON INTRODUCES IT TO US IS AT ONCE AS familiar as a homebody we have grown up knowing and as unsettling as a mysterious stranger, Coyote hastening by. Carson has embraced the wildness in nature, and much of her effort in getting us to know nature involves preparing our senses to know what she cannot tell us, what she does not know. She believes that our emotional response to nature is our most direct route to understanding the beautiful and baffling world. Her inclusion in this book on humor is fitting because of her comic vision, not because there is much humor in her work.

Carson did have a personal sense of humor, inclining toward the mischievous; still, the most significant connection to humor in her work is her comic vision. It gives her distance as well as intimacy with nature, and it enables her to write with an empathetic imagination without presuming to superimpose herself on her subject. Carson believes that comedy as a pattern for change is essential to survival in nature. She wants nature to be free to exercise its comic, quirky mutability, and she wants to partake of its spirit. To do so, Carson must recognize the ordinary and be prepared for the extraordinary: she must be a well-schooled scientist who knows how to play. To cultivate playfulness in her work, she uses her imagination freely to create narratives based on the scientific fact and to place herself at different vantage points than customarily assumed by the scientist or observer. Her play is a literary, scientific endeavor to absorb herself in her subject: it is disciplined by comedy because she depends on the comic skill to be detached from her subject as she embraces it.

This simple and sophisticated approach to nature is a gift to readers, yet it has never won the attention it deserves. Carson is most well-known for her final book, *Silent Spring*, which had extensive public-policy ramifications. *Silent Spring* focused debate in the country on pesticides, and her argument against them gained popular support despite the threat it posed to the status quo. A presidential commission investigating the concerns Carson raised agreed with her, although there was a panicky uproar from chemical industries that denounced her and her work.[73] It was unprecedented that DDT would be banned, unprecedented that one book could effect such change. And so it is no wonder that her gift of playful inquiry has been subsumed in the fervor over *Silent Spring*.

For all her public acclaim, notoriety, and influence, Carson was a private person, a shy person. How she came to harbor a passion for nature compelling enough to write herself into the public eye and eventually fame is a story that can best begin with her posthumously published *The Sense of Wonder*. Written in the fifties and published in *Woman's Home Companion* as "Help Your Child To Wonder," the essay reassures adults about their role in guiding children to explore and know nature. It gives us much of her philosophy about play, especially how play is valuable to us all our lives. Carson herself had no children and never married, but she adopted her grandnephew, Roger, in 1957.[74] In *The Sense of Wonder*, Carson describes her walks and adventures with Roger, reflecting on the importance of their time together outside and their pleasure in what they saw. She talks about Roger learning rapidly, remembering more about the woodlands and shore than he would have, Carson is sure, were he enjoined from the start to remember. Her narrative shows Roger learning successfully because he is allowed to play and explore in the company of an adult who is a fellow adventurer. The story is positive and appealing. Her descriptions of wet-weather outings ("A rainy day is the perfect time for a walk in the woods"

73. In May 1963, the President's Science Advisory Committee issued its report, *The Use of Pesticides*, which recommended reforming pesticide laws and eliminating the most dangerous of the pesticides, including DDT.
74. Indeed, she had serious domestic concerns—by age twenty-nine, she supported her mother and two nieces. She had earned a master's degree in marine biology in 1932 and had secured a job with the federal Bureau of Fisheries in order to ensure security for her family.

30) or treks on the beach during a gale, coupled with plentiful photographs from the rocky Maine seacoast where she had a house, provide an exemplary adventure, a prompt to the reader to be adventurous as well. Parents need not be intimidated, Carson shows; they need not be bird-watchers or naturalists or experts to teach their children about nature. Parents can be as wacky and playful as she has been with Roger, seeing in the tiny spruce seedlings Christmas trees for the squirrels or bugs or rabbits. We learn from her that teaching is the least significant part of the adult's role with children out-of-doors. Attitude and joy are far more important as a formula to encourage children's innate reactions.

> A child's world is fresh and new and beautiful, full of wonder and excitement. It is our misfortune that for most of us that clear-eyed vision, that true instinct for what is beautiful and awe-inspiring, is dimmed and even lost before we reach adulthood. If I had influence with the good fairy who is supposed to preside over the christening of all children I should ask that her gift to each child in the world be a sense of wonder so indestructible that it would last throughout life, as an unfailing antidote against the boredom and disenchantments of later years, the sterile preoccupation with things that are artificial, the alienation from the sources of our strength (42–43).

She knows how that alienation might be forestalled.

> If a child is to keep alive his inborn sense of wonder without any such gift from the fairies, he needs the companionship of at least one adult who can share it, rediscovering with him the joy, excitement and mystery of the world we live in (45).

So Carson encourages us to play in order to inculcate in ourselves and children an emotional foundation from which further learning will precipitate. For facts to become knowledge and for knowledge to have "lasting meaning," she says, intellectual inquiry must be emotively inspired. By being playful, children and adults help keep each other happy and lively.

Carson's talk was revolutionary, setting more trust in children than professionals or parents might be expected to and looking to feelings as the rubric for developing knowledge. Her trust in children is focused on the style of awareness that playing encourages—their sense of wonder. She touts that sense as essential to human development, an unfailing resource, buoy, and creative energy needed by people throughout their lives.[75] Those who have it "are never alone or weary of life" (88). Most importantly, she links that sense of wonder with nonhuman nature and makes an imaginative leap in asserting the nexus between human happiness, health, and the wild world.

> There is symbolic as well as actual beauty in the migration of the birds, the ebb and flow of the tides, the folded bud ready for the spring. There is something infinitely healing in the repeated refrains of nature—the assurance that dawn comes after night, and spring after the winter (88–89).

Her evocations of nature throughout the book artistically demonstrate what her exposition conveys—that nature is standard, source, and inspiration for humans because of its seasonal repetitions and surprises.

Carson's recommendations to parents have more than personal authority. In 1959, the results of a study that Edith Cobb conducted concerning creative thinkers, childhood experiences, and nature had surprising similarities to Carson's ideas.[76] Cobb found that people who are gifted as adults have usually been able to retain connections with the "genius of childhood," tapping what she calls a child's "plasticity of response." The "plasticity," or freedom from a conditioned response, involves the imagination, play, and creativity that liberate children from the mundane (123). Cobb argues that the "middle-age range" in children (say from five or six to eleven or twelve years) is particularly important as a creative source, which adults can plumb through memory, because children then are developing a consciousness of themselves as well as a relationship to the world.[77] Children want, she says, above all "to make a world in which to find a place to discover a self" (125). In other words, their instinct is to look outward, exploring the environment in curiosity and necessity. Their effort

75. Johan Huizinga has extensively examined the characteristics and significance of play. He values play as a "culture-creating force" necessary to "real civilization" (211).
76. Cobb's study was first published as an article in *Daedalus* 88 (1959) : 537–48; it appeared as a book in 1977. Quotes here are from its reprinting (in revised form) in *The Subversive Science* (1969), eds. Paul Shepard and Daniel McKinley.
77. In *Playing and Reality*, D. W. Winnicott asserts that playing, in allowing people to be creative, helps them know who they are (53–54).

toward self-consciousness is not self-centered but ecological, an exploratory look around the big house, having the healthy balance that Paul Shepard asserts in *Nature and Madness* is critical to being "Me in a non-Me world" (34). A person's acceptance of the ambiguities in identification with and difference from the nonhuman world is a sign of maturity, Shepard says (13). Without such a resolution between ourselves and nature, he continues, we are incomplete and unhealthy. Cobb's work, published with the title "The Ecology of Imagination in Childhood," points to that resolution as the creative locus in human development. Not just the gifted, she says, should enjoy the child's "plasticity of response"; instead it "must be recognized as a common human need in adapting to life and society" (123).[78] Carson, too, found in a child's sense of wonder the essence of later energy and joy. Her book, then, is as much a prompt to adults about playfulness in their own lives as it is a guide for them about taking children out-of-doors.

Although focused on the story of the child Roger, *The Sense of Wonder* reveals to us the childhood inspiration Carson maintained as an adult. The essay is not autobiographical, yet the ideas and passion of the author about the creative value of nature speak to the outdoor upbringing she must have enjoyed. Carson was raised in Springdale, Pennsylvania, where her parents settled in 1900, keeping a few barnyard animals—pigs, chickens, a cow, rabbits—and harboring a host of wilder ones in the sixty-five acres of woods and fields beyond their house. Separated in age from her siblings by eight and ten years, Carson had plenty of solitary time. The family's property at the edge of town was huge enough (for a little girl) always to afford a new place to explore: so she often played alone and found companionship in the creatures and the outdoors. There were books too. Her mother, Maria McLean Carson, read aloud to the children, whetting her youngest daughter's desire to read independently. This skill she acquired in first grade; by fourth grade, she knew she wanted to write for a living (Sterling 22–23). A story she wrote in second grade and illustrated with a decorative border shows that her literate imagination was continuous with her outdoor interests. In a child's cursive script:

78. Two articles by Louise Chawla published in 1986 and 1990 in *Children's Environments Quarterly* point out methodological shortcomings in Cobb's work and suggest that environmental memories are important primarily in those with artistic creativity who enjoyed a sense of social security as children. Rather than refuting Cobb's claims, Chawla qualifies them.

The Little Brown House

Once upon a time, two little wrens were hunting a little house to set up housekeeping. All at once they saw a dear little brown house with a green roof. "Now that is just what we need," said Mr. Wren to Jenny. (Photo illustration, Sterling)

Literacy gave Carson a new way to explore the outdoors, a route for the imagination that could not only translate voices in nature (as it did for Mr. Wren in this story) but also be a partner to the girl in her childhood adventuring. As an adult author, she wrote that "to keep alive his inborn sense of wonder" a child must have an adult with whom to share discoveries about the world. For Carson herself, that companionship was provided as much by books and writing as by her mother or another adult. Her sense of wonder came to be invested in literacy as well as in nature.[79]

These two interests inspired and influenced each other, and so as a junior in college she decided to switch her major from literature to biology (leading her to remark that at last she had found what she wanted to write about). Her talents culminated in four books: *Under the Sea-Wind*, *The Sea Around Us*, *The Edge of the Sea*, and *Silent Spring*—as well as numerous articles and *The Sense of Wonder*. What the books show is that her aesthetic sense permeated her scientific concerns. Carson articulated her creative ethos on occasion, as she did in 1952 in her acceptance speech for the National Book Award: "If there is poetry in my book about the sea, it is not because I deliberately put it there but because no one could write truthfully about the sea and leave out the poetry" (Brooks 128). In this case both her aesthetic and scientific interests go back not to a childhood association with the sea, for she encountered it for the first time as an adult in her early twenties, but to a fundamental emotional bond with nature. Affection became medium for Carson in the fluid association she made between intellect and aesthetic. Because Carson was a writer before she became a biologist, her scientific endeavors were imbued from the start with an artistic focus. Indeed, we can learn a great deal about her science from an explanation she gave of her approach to writing.

79. Biographer Linda Lear says that the turn-of-the-century nature-study movement highly influenced Maria Carson in raising her youngest daughter. The movement encouraged parents to help their children to appreciate nature in order to develop their moral, aesthetic, and community sensibilities (13–15).

The writer must never attempt to impose himself upon his subject. He must not try to mold it according to what he believes his readers or editors want to read. His initial task is to come to know his subject intimately, to understand its every aspect, to let it fill his mind. Then at some turning point the subject takes command and the true act of creation begins. . . . The discipline of the writer is to learn to be still and listen to what his subject has to tell him (Brooks 1–2).

Her writerly sensitivity is indicative of a pervading and forceful ecological sensibility that served her well. As Paul Brooks wrote in his preface to the twenty-fifth anniversary edition of *Silent Spring*, "She had an emotional response to nature for which she did not apologize" (Carson xiii). To be emotional as a scientist is conventionally unacceptable—a breach, it would seem, in professionalism. Yet for Carson, emotion is the groundwork for other pursuits, an essential foundation that inspires in her writing the respect to "be still and listen," paying attention to what one has taken as a subject.

The ecological sensibility that her respectful listening encouraged is foremost a style of perception—it is her adult version of a sense of wonder, and, as such, it is bold, intuitive, and playful. Whether doing research or imagining other creatures, she sought to look beyond isolated data and to understand context; she lingered over domestic connections between organisms and their environment; she witnessed their cosmopolitan relation to the world.[80] For instance, she added a unique touch to the pamphlet series about eating fish that she wrote during World War II, pamphlets that encouraged civilians to diversify their diet and thus better cope with food shortages. At the time, from 1943 to 1945, she was the assistant to the director of information for the Fish and Wildlife Service. Besides the requisite dietary and culinary information about the fish, the "Food from the Sea" pamphlets featured a story—the life story of each fish. Carson explained this presentation in her introduction to the series:

Before we can try new foods, we must know what they are. Our enjoyment of these foods is heightened if we also know something of the

---

80. In *Playing and Reality*, D. W. Winnicott shows that playing helps people come to creative terms with their relation to the world. Carson's work has this function of play—it forever seeks to put characters and place in relation to each other.

creatures from which they are derived, how and where they live, how they are caught, their habits and migrations (Sterling 106–7).

With similar predilections, Wendell Berry writes in "The Pleasures of Eating":

> A significant part of the pleasure of eating is in one's accurate consciousness of the lives and the world from which food comes. The pleasure of eating, then, may be the best available standard of our health. . . . Eating with the fullest pleasure—pleasure, that is, that does not depend on ignorance—is perhaps the profoundest enactment of our connection with the world. In this pleasure we experience and celebrate our dependence and our gratitude, for we are living from mystery, from creatures we did not make and powers we cannot comprehend (*What Are People For?* 151–2).

Berry and Carson perceive that the satisfaction in eating issues from full acquaintance, the extensive knowledge of a food's history. But whereas Berry stays religiously shy of the nonhuman mysteries of other creature's lives (remaining the humanistic observer, steward, and grateful recipient), Carson plunges in with the faith that her empathetic imagination wields. She takes the creature's point of view yet retains her human vocabulary, fashioning a style of dual perspectives. *Under the Sea-Wind* features just such writing:

> The gnawing pang of hunger was a sensation new to Silverbar. A week before, with the others of the sanderling flock, she had filled her stomach with shellfish gathered on the wide tidal flats of Hudson Bay. Days before that they had gorged on beach fleas on the coasts of New England, and on Hippa crabs on the sunny beaches of the south. In all the eight-thousand-mile journey northward from Patagonia there had been no lack of food (55).

Carson's affections make her bold, and her knowledge gives her reason to be bold. She can speak of the diet of sanderlings, their migration, their hardiness. The author's ecological sensibility thus has the playful result of Silverbar the sanderling leading us unerringly into her world, where we are graciously deposited. Carson is perspicacious to effect the crossover by making us imagine how Silverbar and the other creatures feel. Guided by sensory information, we find easy transport into the bird's world. We participate in the world of sensation, activity, and emotion that other creatures share, a kinship Carson is sensible of and that makes her writing intimate and, in terms of shifting perspective, comic.

The fact that Carson had an ecological sensibility meant that she was a maverick.[81] In his preface to *Rachel Carson at Work: The House of Life*, Paul Brooks acknowledges how much she was ahead of her time.

> When she began writing, the term "environment" had few of the connotations it has today. Conservation was not yet a political force. To the public at large the word "ecology"—derived from the Greek for "habitation"—was unknown, as was the concept it stood for. This concept, however, is central to everything that Rachel Carson wrote. Few of us have dwelt with such awareness and understanding in the house of life (xi).

Her uncanny insight into the house of life issues from her wisdom to be playful. So she rearranges the evidence of our evolution to show us those connections that make the world a household.

> When they went ashore the animals that took up a land life carried with them a part of the sea in their bodies . . . each of us carries in our veins a salty stream in which the elements sodium, potassium, and calcium are combined in almost the same proportions as in sea water . . . our lime-hardened skeletons are a heritage from the calcium-rich ocean of Cambrian time (*The Sea Around Us* 13).

Carson gives us a unique scientific genealogy, connecting people with the ocean so that knowledge of our primordial kinship may cleave us

---

81. Assessing Carson's most famous book in *Since Silent Spring*, Frank Graham, Jr., concludes that it caused a turmoil because it had ecological rather than economic casting (53). As such, it appealed to a sensibility that did not associate nature primarily with monetary value, and so it disturbed many people's utilitarian assumptions. Scholars invariably note the ecological perspective that Carson brings to her work. Roderick Nash's discussion of Carson in *The Rights of Nature* (78–82), Bill Devall and George Sessions in *Deep Ecology* (94), David Orr in *Ecological Literacy* (86–87), and Vera Norwood in *Made From This Earth: American Women and Nature* (142–71) all look to Carson's ecology as the primary feature of her writing. Norwood says that she was a maverick by extending women's traditional concern for the home to nature and encouraging environmental activism to care for this larger "home." In this way, Carson's ecological sensibility politicized women's relation to nature.

emotionally closer—establishing a briny consanguinity between all. In the ecological household, Carson supposed us all to be distinct yet related.[82] This vivid representation of facts is both playful and effective—we remember it, and we are prepared for the author's further insights. The poetry that she says is necessary to the truth about the ocean is necessary because poetry addresses the mystery of our connections, tapping in us the nonintellectual instinct we have to see kinship, feel relation, and identify the family.

So Walt Whitman figures the sea as "the fierce old mother incessantly moaning" (58) in "Out of the Cradle Endlessly Rocking," and it is "Sea of the brine of life and of unshovell'd yet always-ready graves" (81) in "Song of Myself." Carson never pretends that we can abstract our consciousness from ourselves or ourselves from the greater household; she believes that we can know ourselves in the natural phenomena we study, completing the scientific with the intuitive. Playfulness and poetry are routes to the intuitively felt truth. Henry Beston, whose *The Outermost House* (1928) was a beloved and influential book to Carson (Lear 101), expounds,

> *Creation is here and now.* So near is man to the creative pageant, so much a part is he of the endless and incredible experiment, that any glimpse he may have will be but the revelation of a moment, a solitary note heard in a symphony thundering through debatable existences of time. Poetry is as necessary to comprehension as science. It is as impossible to live without reverence as it is without joy (220–1).

Carson's sensitivity to "the endless and incredible experiment" results in her lyrical writing and her creative research. As a scientist, she is respectful, playful, attentive, and joyful. Those emotional responses secure her work practically to the ethical world, for they allow her to imagine what her research indicated, to convey the sense of those results poetically and empirically, and to see what they meant in terms of human relationships and responsibility. Carson's love of nature emboldened her to be in the service of a moral and creative world—in the service of the truth, as she intuited it.

82. Since comedies ritually bring together people in marriage, Carson is identifying comic form in our primordial relationships; she is recalling the ancient marriage that helped create us.

▼ ▼ ▼

WITH HER MAINE SUMMER-HOME NEIGHBOR DOROTHY FREEMAN, WHO became the writer's beloved friend, Carson shared her personal and professional thoughts. In letters dated November 4 and 5, 1957, Carson explained the niche she considered her writing to occupy.

> Apparently I have never made it clear that I consider my contributions to scientific fact far less important than my attempts to awaken an emotional response to the world of nature.

> when I say I don't think the scientific aspect of my writing is most important, of course I should qualify and explain. I mean, I don't think straight scientific exposition is my "contribution" to the world. It is, I agree, what you call lyricism. But if that lyricism has an unusual quality it is, I think, because it springs from scientific fact and so rings true (*Always, Rachel* 231–32).

Fact alone falls short of truth, Carson would maintain, for facts require feeling to complete them, to assimilate them in our lives. We can hear that feeling ring in her prose.[83] Her first book, *Under the Sea-Wind*, is redolent with her empathetic brand of ecological literacy. From the beginning we perceive it in her description of a South Atlantic island at dusk, made dramatic by the appearance of a large bird, a black skimmer, here called Rynchops, who remembers the island from previous migrations and has returned to feed. Rynchops dips close to the water along the shoreline: "Yet so quietly did he approach that the sound of his wings, if sound there were, was lost in the whisper song of the water turning over the shells on the wet sand" (5). The image of a silent bird coursing over sibilant surf tantalizes our senses, and Carson gracefully hooks us. Though Rynchops, the particular bird that she imagines came to the island that night, might never have existed, his kind has: his habits are accurately described, and, most importantly, we readers believe that Rynchops is real and did as Carson reported.

83. Carol Gartner has studied the literary quality of Carson's prose and notes that its poetic oral quality is the result of careful work by the writer; its effect, she posits, is to give us the feelings that we might have in the presence of the ocean or other natural things (56–57). For instance, Carson's prose typically features grammatical parallels and repeated rhythms so that the sentences surge to a climax just as the ocean builds and rocks itself out in waves (98).

Her play with scientific fact is aimed not at fantasy but at our deliverance into the actual natural world. Furthermore, that she names Rynchops gives him personality and substance. Seeing, as we do, with the plethora of sensory information she provides, we believe in the truth of the scene.

Truth, too, of just the same sensory-specific quality attends her description of the phalaropes, birds who have migrated to the Arctic to nest. Both the cock and hen have been alerted to a fox trotting nearby; both go to the water and circle, pretending to feed "until the air came clean again, untainted by the musky smell of fox" (67–68). As unaccustomed as we are to being preyed upon, humans can nonetheless identify with the powerfully simple image—the invisible event—of the air "coming clean," clearing, harboring no more danger, the predator gone. The truth in Carson's scientific writing is based on fact and perfected by lyricism in its appeal to our senses, for we believe in what we have experienced. Although Carson explained to Dorothy Freeman that scientific fact gives her writing its ring of truth, her use of sensory details gives us more immediate access to the natural world.[84]

Thus we come to a closer look at what Carson means by the truth in her writing. That truth is based on facts but goes beyond a literal interpretation of them. As noted, she creates creatures like Rynchops and scenes like the encounter between the fox and the phalaropes. These may not have existed, yet she makes us believe they did. They are true to us because we have seen them by the grace of Carson's lyricism. In our sensory response, we participate in the world she describes: it rings true because we have seen and felt it happen.

Carson's literary efforts to write the truth about nature are a form of play—effective in making us feel and believe. It is instructive to note how playing—always an act of "make-believe"—creates its own truth, for in much the same way Carson's lyricism delivers us to "a true sense of the world," in Henry Beston's words. First a cautionary note about play from Johan Huizinga: "Play lies outside the antithesis of wisdom and folly, and equally outside those of truth and falsehood, good and evil. Although it is a non-material activity it has no moral function. The valuations of vice and virtue do not apply here" (6). Whatever truth is established in the make-

---

84. In a review of *Under the Sea-Wind*, Henry Beston also resorts to a notion of truth to describe Carson's achievement: "Some spiritual instinct has shaken itself free and has refused to take the scientific vision of nature as complete. . . . It is Miss Carson's particular gift to be able to blend scientific knowledge with the spirit of poetic awareness, thus restoring to us a true sense of the world" ("Miss Carson's First" 100).

believe world of play, it is hermetic, utterly unlike the dualistic distinctions between truth and falsehood or good and evil that occur in the outside world. Playing is a thing apart, establishing its own world and yet belonging in this world. Again, Huizinga: "Into an imperfect world and into the confusion of life it brings a temporary, a limited perfection" (10). Playing takes us to a place that is free, safe, and creative. David Miller writes, "Sometimes we play so well that we simply forget we are playing. We think our play is reality. It is" (173). It is not merely an escape; it is its own free world, reality structured in time and place and governed by its own order.[85] When children or adults enter together into play, they can know the freedom of a thousand perfect possibilities. Their world happens—it is true—because they participate in it; they make and believe it. It is true as long as their imagination maintains it.

Likewise, Carson writes the truth when she poetically describes the sea or imaginatively traces the nocturnal route of Rynchops because she is appealing to the quality of mind that graces a person playing. Her storytelling and specific sensory details entice us to join her. We believe in Rynchops because she makes us see, feel, and imagine his life. The exciting twist to Carson's play is that she leads us not apart from the world but deeper into it so that nature and the lives of animals have domestic clarity. Whereas we might have known nature before from an observer's distance, following Carson's lead we gather close and go in. And so we experience it and participate in the truth of Carson's lyrical portrayal.

If we hear her prose ringing true, we also hear its clear moral imperative, clear, that is, in the content of what she writes rather than in any explicit dictum. In *The Rights of Nature*, Roderick Nash notes that quality in her work: "The marine ecology books[86] profess no overt environmental ethic, but they testify on almost every page to the author's awe in the face of the vast community of life centered on the oceans" (79). Implicit in her attentions to the seemingly insignificant beach flea as well as to the gull, the eel, the shad, and countless others is the conviction that each creature deserves space at sea and a place in our consciousness of the marine world. More is at play here than overwhelming awe or even sympathy. Her moral impulse is complex beyond what Nash indicates, though awe and other emotions do prompt her responses to nature and thus influence the ethical convictions she develops. The moral imperative we hear is comic for the

---

85. Huizinga gives play these characteristics (7–13).
86. Her first three.

following reasons. She believes in our need to stand in relation to the non-human world, which flourishes because of the changes and reestablishment of biological equilibrium that drive its evolution. Thus, in order to know the world, we need to develop comic skills; to wit, we should have the sympathy to love the world as it is and the detachment to love the world as it shall change. Carson wants us to make comic skills the center of our environmental ethics so that we are prepared to respect nature's caprice, the comedy that ensures survival.

"Environmental ethics" as a term blossomed after "natural resources" and "conservation"; it seemed to appear from a different template, a less utilitarian one than the others. Its usage corresponded with the Western mind's incipient awareness that nature has value, standing, and rights independent of humankind.[87] Aldo Leopold has given some of the earliest and most perspicacious testimony in pursuit of an environmental ethics. In *A Sand County Almanac*, he writes, "The evolution of a land ethic is an intellectual as well as emotional process" (263), a close match to Carson's insistence in *The Sense of Wonder* that attitude and affection are more primary to knowing nature than formal education. Leopold, again: "It is inconceivable to me that an ethical relation to land can exist without love, respect, and admiration for land, and a high regard for its value" (261). With emotion and intellect being key ingredients of environmental ethics, adds N. Scott Momaday in "An American Land Ethic": "We Americans need now more than ever before—and indeed more than we know—to imagine who and what we are with respect to the earth and sky. I am talking about an act of the imagination essentially, and the concept of an American land ethic" (103). Carson might add that we need also to imagine ourselves in relation to the ocean to figure out who and what we are. With emotion, intellect, and imagination conspired to form such an ethic, one might, in the spirit of Carson's play with Roger, reword the term better to suit Carson's work. Thus environmental ethics can mean ethics of the household: how we ought to live in and treat our home, our beloved places, for all places are beloved, each a home to something. The issue is how we should act there, in everyone's home: Household etiquette written large.

Comedy is essential to that etiquette, since it would require a balance between all parties. Comedy would keep human arrogance under control,

---

87. The Deep Ecology movement, with roots in the 1970s, and the history detailed in Nash's *The Rights of Nature* (1989) attest to that development. Deep Ecology is a name for the idea that the biotic community includes humans but does not pander to them or include them more than any other natural thing.

for no household hangs together long if some members get an uppity atti-tude. Carson's exercise of comedy is apparent in her ability to identify with nonhuman creatures and simultaneously to wield a wide-ranging perspec-tive of them. Her comic aptitude is fully contemporary, although some nature writers have taken Carson's "mild" or old-fashioned anthropocen-trism to mean that Carson is a somewhat outdated (if esteemed) predeces-sor in the field.[88] They perhaps miss her genius for comedy, which is as great a contribution to human relations with nature as her warning about pesticides is to the health of nature. We can look for her genius in her imag-inative and heartfelt style of ecology: the contrary twist that comedy en-dows to her sympathies.

The opening scenes of that south Atlantic island in her first book exem-plify this twist. Carson plays with our sympathies, giving us a comic glimpse of a world that is dear to her. She describes a "run of spawning shad, fresh from the sea" (16) who have lingered beyond the island for sev-eral days before making their way in past the island toward the estuary. Many have never yet returned from the sea, where they grew large, eating shrimps and amphipods; in order to mature at sea, they left the fresh water of the river as young fish, "scarcely as long as a man's finger" (17). Their re-turn recalls those "dimly remembered" (17) beginnings, as they go "feeling their way along the streams of less saline water that served them as paths to the river" (16). From Carson we learn also that between their initial run to saltwater and the return to spawn, the shad elude human ken—their ways are mysterious, they themselves "disappeared." She speculates:

> Perhaps they wintered in deep, warm water far below the surface, rest-ing in the dim twilight of the continent's edge, making an occasional timid journey out over the rim beyond which lay only the blackness and stillness of the deep sea. Perhaps in summer they roved the open ocean, feeding on the rich life of the surface, packing layers of white muscle and sweet fat beneath their shining armor of scales (17).

Carson piques our curiosity, interests us in the welfare of these fish, and manages to give a material description of them that clearly shows their high economic quality without sounding at all utilitarian. Instead, we feel that their succulent, fertile bodies are beautiful. We like the shad.

88. With a tone of chagrin, Snyder (*A Place in Space* 164) and Nash (*The Rights of Nature* 80) note Carson's occasional utilitarian tendencies.

Shift to fishermen. The one who lives on the island has, like the other locals, learned from his father and grandfather how the shad come in toward the west bank of the river when they enter the estuary. This fisherman does not own gill nets himself but has them in common with another fisherman. We learn also that the gill-net fishermen have been crowded out of the best spots by those who have the means to afford fixed gear—pound nets—and that there has been at least one local fight between these two classes of fishermen. The gill netters are in the minority and, in a sense, on the run. Hence, we are provoked to some sympathy for the island fisherman and his type.

Turn then again to the shad and, now, also to the fishermen's gill nets.

About midnight, as the tide neared the full, the cork line bobbed as the first of the migrating shad struck the gill net. The line vibrated and several of the cork floats disappeared under the water. The shad, a four-pound roe, had thrust her head through one of the meshes of the net and was struggling to free herself. The taut circle of twine that had slipped under the gill covers cut deeper into the delicate gill filaments as the fish lunged against the net; lunged again to free herself from something that was like a burning, choking collar; something that held her in an invisible vise and would neither let her go on upstream nor turn and seek sanctuary in the sea she had left (20).

Carson is explicit and detailed. She chooses to narrate the struggle of the first of the doomed shad, and in so revealing that it was female and four pounds, she appeals to our strongest sympathetic impulse: we respond to individuals, especially those we are acquainted with. This roe shad's agony and confusion affect us more strongly than would the fate of an entire school of shad, had we merely been told that they had swum into gill nets and died. Carson engages our sympathies for the individual and then extends them to the whole migrating lot and beyond.

The cork line bobbed many times that night and many fish were gilled. Most of them died slowly of suffocation, for the twine interfered with the rhythmic respiratory movements of the gill covers by which fish draw streams of water in through the mouth and pass them over the gills. Once the line bobbed very hard and for ten minutes was pulled below the surface. That was when a grebe, swimming fast five feet under water after a fish, went through the net to its shoulders and in its violent struggles with wings and lobed feet became hopelessly entangled. The grebe soon drowned. Its body hung limply from the net, along with a score of silvery fish bodies with heads pointing upstream in the direction of the spawning grounds where the early-run shad awaited their coming (20–21).

With our sympathies hurtled in the direction of the shad and other misfortunates who hit the nets, we feel little alliance with the fishermen.

Yet Carson does not allow us to be settled with easy sympathies. Next we hear about the eels. They live in the estuary, fishing and robbing the fishermen's gill nets. And since they are unable to catch shad unaided, the nets provide a fantastic opportunity.

As the eels poked their heads out of the holes under the roots of the marsh grasses and swayed gently back and forth, savoring eagerly the water that they drew into their mouths, their keen senses caught the taste of fish blood which was diffusing slowly through the water as the gilled shad struggled to escape. One by one they slipped out of their holes and followed the taste trail through the water to the net (21–22).

The eels have a full meal, so the shad's demise satiates another creature. In this manner, Carson draws us nearer to equilibrium, and we feel its calm as she returns to a bird's-eye view—this is Rynchops again coming into action, providing perspective—of the fishermen pulling in their nets. They find the shad carcasses, and they are bitterly angry. Given that we are imaginatively with Rynchops, we feel nothing as the men below curse and hurl the skeletal shad overboard. When the skimmer leaves them and their pitiful catch of a "half-dozen shad" in their boat, "Already gulls were gathering on the water where the gill net had been set, screaming their pleasure over the refuse which the fishermen had thrown overboard" (24). So opens the first chapter of *Under the Sea-Wind* in the full comic fashion of shifting perspectives, with Carson collecting and focusing our sympathies, and then diffusing them, leaving us with a satisfying and challenging manifold vision of the island.

The steady reserve by which Carson flicks from empathy for shad to fishermen and shad to eel and gull suggests neither amorality in nature nor ambivalence from her but instead the comic intelligence that distinguishes her environmental ethics. She is above all committed to ecological balance, which is itself a changing thing. How that balance changes is of utmost concern to her, for she wants to protect the process from destructive human interference. Her passion to preserve nature for its own purposes fuels *Silent Spring*. In it, she rebukes humans for their ignorance and gall to use DDT and other pesticides carelessly, and she emphasizes balance: "Future historians may well be amazed by our distorted sense of proportion. How could intelligent beings seek to control a few unwanted species by a method that contaminated the entire environment and brought the threat of disease and death even to their own kind?" (8). Her embrace of change in nature makes her anything but ambivalent about balance. In a televised debate she wryly skewered a chemical industry spokesman's cockeyed assumption that people have already controlled the balance of nature: "Now to these people apparently, the balance of nature is something that was repealed as soon as man came on the scene. You might just as well assume that you could repeal the law of gravity" (Sterling 183).[89] With a humorous flair, Carson insists that ecological balance be free to continue its comic course, unimpeded by humans.

It was perfect that Carson, as a devotee of Albert Schweitzer's work, particularly his call for a "Reverence for Life," received the 1963 medal in his name from the Animal Welfare Institute. Deeply honored, she forbore the debilitation of cancer and a recent heart attack to prepare a speech and accept the award in person. In the speech, with a grace that defied her personal suffering, she speculated on what triggers the experience of reverence,

> perhaps the sudden, unexpected sight of a wild creature, perhaps some experience with a pet. Whatever it may be, it is something that takes us out of ourselves, that makes us aware of other life.

And she asserted the need for ecological balance.

> Dr. Schweitzer has told us that we are not being truly civilized if we concern ourselves only with the relation of man to man. What is important is the relation of man to all life. This has never been so tragically overlooked as in our present age, when through our technology we are waging war against the natural world. It is a valid question whether any

89. The program, called "The Silent Spring of Rachel Carson," was aired on CBS News April 3, 1963. In her introduction, she explained that the public had already heard about the value of pesticides, so in her work she had "set about to remedy the balance there" (Lear 449).

civilization can do this and retain the right to be called civilized. By acquiescing in needless destruction and suffering, our stature as human beings is diminished (Brooks 315–6).

It is part of Carson's practice as a writer and a thinker to "take us out of ourselves," restoring our sense of balance by putting us a little further out in the natural world than we might have gone without her. To Aldo Leopold's famous statement of land ethics, she has much to add. In 1949, Leopold wrote, "A thing is right when it tends to preserve the integrity, stability, and beauty of the biotic community. It is wrong when it tends otherwise" (262). In that statement Carson would read ecological stability to mean a kind of comic reshuffling, the cut deck continually being changed and restored to equilibrium. Such equilibrium is a dynamic state, much like the stability of a family, whose babies are born and old people pass on. Carson is morally committed to a changing thing. The qualities constant to her ethos are patience and humility and playfulness. She desires to preserve the evolutionary comedy of the biotic community, with the understanding that that comedy has the dynamic integrity of the wild, moving in beautiful and surprising ways.

Comic morality, then, is a term for human respect of wildness at work, its mix and matching of manifold parts. It is not an unqualified acceptance of change or trendy style or relativism; comic morality requires more wisdom and imagination than that, suggesting the step a little beyond ourselves, where we might see the world from other than anthropocentric eyes. So the emphasis in Carson's writing on a sense of wonder—our "plasticity of response"—manifests itself in her playful presentation of the world as animals or insects or birds might deal with it and as it appears in light of geological processes. New perspectives modify values, Carol Gartner says, in describing the effect of Carson's perspective-changing technique (117). Carson challenges us to be flexible—to see the comic plot and not be unsettled by it but to fit in by recognizing that even in flux personal standards do exist. The etiquette appropriate to the ecological household includes all those skills that it takes to maintain our own households—love and perseverance ad infinitum—and requires also the imagination to see that all our households are linked. The standards, then, are ordinary household etiquette and a stake in the world's greater mysteries. The practical outcome of a sense of wonder can be, as it was for Rachel Carson, a respect for the wild balance of things and ethical behavior based on that respect.

▼ ▼ ▼

CARSON PUT PLAYFULNESS INTO HER BOOKS BECAUSE SHE INVESTED
herself emotionally in her subject and allowed herself to be tweaked or baffled or surprised as it, she has written, "takes command and the true act of
creation begins." Comic skill keeps Carson creative by reminding her that
one perspective is always modified by another and larger mysteries inform
them all. Such an understanding keeps her telling the truth when it might
be tempting instead to romanticize. For example, over the South Atlantic
island where Rynchops cruises, the full moon, when it rises, has this effect:

> The sea, that gleamed with the moon's lambent silver, drew to its sur-
> face many squids, dazed and fascinated by the light. The squids drifted
> on the sea, their eyes fixed on the moon. Gently they drew in water and
> expelled it in jets, propelling themselves backward away from the light
> at which they gazed. Moon-bewildered, their senses did not warn them
> that they were drifting into dangerous shoals until the harsh grate of
> sand brought sharp awakening. As they stranded, the hapless squids
> pumped water all the harder, driving themselves out of even the
> thinnest film, onto sand from which all water had ebbed away (*Under
> the Sea-Wind* 39–40).

She is faithful to the full picture, the one where moonstruck squid die and
where beach fleas eventually get the remains of a bass who has eaten a
ghost crab who was preying on the beach fleas. Although her description
of the crab piques our affections for him (he "was a creamy tan, matching
the sand so closely that he was all but invisible when he stood still. Only
his eyes, like two black shoe buttons on stalks, showed color" (*Under the
Sea-Wind* 32), she insists on the fictive truth that this crab was far from his
burrow when the swirling birds overhead and the fisherman on the beach
startle him to dash into the surf—and there be eaten. Her comic skill here
does not mean that she finds his fate humorous or even that she prefers this
twist in the run of events; instead, it enables her to show the pulchritude of
loss and continued life in the vital swapping that fuels the food chain.
Rather than let herself be splayed out emotionally after the characters, she
is poised, occupying them all.

  The comic skill that helps her tell a truth that may be painful but is
nonetheless beautiful makes her bold about the way she tells her story. *The
Sea Around Us* opens with this flair:

> Beginnings are apt to be shadowy, and so it is with the beginnings of that great mother of life, the sea. Many people have debated how and when the earth got its ocean, and it is not surprising that their explanations do not always agree. For the plain and inescapable truth is that no one was there to see, and in the absence of eyewitness accounts there is bound to be a certain amount of disagreement (3).

Carson did not know that her second book would be a record-breaking national best-seller and recipient of the 1951 National Book Award.[90] Her first book, which appeared on November 1, 1941, inauspiciously before Pearl Harbor, had occasioned little response, and Carson had no assurances that her next book would improve that record. About the publication of *Under the Sea-Wind*, she later commented, "The world received the event with superb indifference" (Brooks 69). She was courting that same indifference with her second book. The gamble apparently inspired her spunk, for her project was no less ambitious than to describe the ancient incipience of the ocean, to tell a history of the seas, and to provide what might be called a scientific biography of the ocean. It is indicative of the spirit of play invested in her entire book that she so candidly at the start acknowledges that her story will be at odds with other accounts of the ocean's formation. Not reticent of the gamble, she lays out her *modus operandi*. "So if I tell here the story of how the young planet Earth acquired an ocean, it must be a story pieced together from many sources and containing whole chapters the details of which we can only imagine" (3). Her attitude is humble (recognizing that her story is part of a family of stories) and bold (expecting our complicity with her in imagination and speculation). Both qualities suggest that playfulness conditions the way she writes. It makes her at once easy and challenging to read—"For although no man was there to witness this cosmic birth, the stars and moon and the rocks were there, and, indeed, had much to do with the fact that there is an ocean" (3). Lacking human presence, the rocks and celestial bodies were the first witnesses, Carson implies; she thus makes players of the raw materials, as if they were sensible participants in the geological turmoil, a move that elevates them above the status of mere objects for the scientist's study. In this way, humbling and emboldening comedy fashions in her work a point of

90. *The Sea Around Us* stayed on the *New York Times* bestseller list for nonfiction for eighty-six weeks and won a slew of awards and honorary degrees for Carson, among them the John Burroughs Medal and fellowship to England's Royal Society of Literature.

view that ranges beyond that of the scientist or even the poet, resurrecting in modern mien an ancient, trusting, and compelling—perhaps best characterized as childlike—mind.

Furthermore, Carson's comic skill keeps her alert to the ambiguities of the natural world and human knowledge of it. She is comfortable on the cusp of understanding and mystery. In *The Edge of the Sea*, she pursues an account of the meaning promised by innumerable biotic riddles but affords ample attention to the magic, mystery, and beauty of nature. Carson honors the mysteries that her science assays to resolve, doing so with the pithy and prosaic: "We can only ask these questions; we cannot answer them" (210); "our knowledge is encompassed within restricted boundaries, whose windows look out upon the limitless spaces of the unknown" (177). And with the exquisite "The floor of the cave was only a few inches below the roof, and a mirror had been created in which all that grew on the ceiling was reflected in the still water below. Under water that was clear as glass the pool was carpeted with green sponge. Gray patches of sea squirts glistened on the ceiling and colonies of soft coral were a pale apricot color. In the moment when I looked into the cave a little elfin starfish hung down, suspended by the merest thread, perhaps by only a single tube foot. It reached down to touch its own reflection, so perfectly delineated that there might have been, not one starfish, but two" (3). She wants to know nature yet also knows she cannot know it all; blessed with such wisdom, she is at peace with ambiguity, forever clarifying her relation to the abounding mystery.

In her work on *The Edge of the Sea*, Carson collaborated with Bob Hines, an artist who had been on her staff at the Fish and Wildlife Service when she was editor in the Information Division. Much of her research for the book was done in the field—at the shoreline—where she would collect and study specimens and Hines would draw them. Their close association gave Hines a picture of her informal side. For example, she initiated calling the specimens they collected "wee beasts." Hines has reflected that Carson "had a subdued sense of humor. The impression of her laughter is more vivid than any detail of its causes. They were small unmemorable things. All I can remember is her beautiful tinkling laugh in moments when she felt strongly the enjoyment of being alive. It was good to hear her laugh" (Sterling 135). Luckily he remembered a modicum of details, recalling the time when she gave the crabs she had collected the names of three acquaintances of theirs from the Fish and Wildlife Service. And the two of them, while working at Key West, sent Shirley Briggs a postcard about their recent adventures in the water—the octopus they had reportedly shaken hands with. Carson wrote, "He was a baby about ten inches long, and he did seem reluctant to part" (Lear 232). More than most, Hines recognized the playfulness that informed her professional work. Hines also helped with the logistics of research for *The Sea Around Us*; he carried the loads of books she needed back and forth from the Department of Interior Library and many others. With comic sweetness and characteristic grace, Carson inscribed his copy of the book, "To Bob Hines, who bore many of the burdens connected with the writing of this book" (Sterling 124). The pleasure she had in their camaraderie she acknowledged by making an inside joke, answering the spirit of their friendship in kind with a witty recognition of her debt to him.

Hines can speak also to the official comportment that equally describes Carson. According to him, she was an adept and firm administrator. Her steady rise to the position of editor of Fish and Wildlife Service publications in 1949 corroborates his praise. Hines remarked, "She didn't like shoddy work or shoddy behavior. She was just so doggone good she couldn't see why other people couldn't try to be the same. She had *standards*, high ones" (Sterling 111). Those standards were such that biographer Linda Lear calls her a "perfectionist" in the office (125). Even so, the energy with which she performed her work was not superhuman. Bureaucratic burdens were sometimes frustrating enough to have been stultifying, and had she been ground down by them, her creative vision would have suffered. Instead she maintained a certain freedom of mind because she and others in her workplace created an atmosphere that nurtured humor. With artist-illustrators Katherine Howe and Shirley Briggs (hired by the Department of Interior in 1944 and 1945, respectively), Carson developed strong friendships that succored them all from complacency. For lunches they would often gather with other co-workers and Bert Walford, Carson's supervisor, in the office that Carson shared with him, where against regulations they would use a hot plate in the closet to make tea and Nescafe. Lear quotes Briggs's diary: "Our clandestine Nescafe sessions break the monotony. Lock the door and huddle around furtively. Kay [Katherine Howe] opened the door a crack to take something from the messenger and Walford thinks we should have a floozy wrapper to slip on at such times" (124). The group also threw their humor into critiques of various reports or publications. Again, Briggs:

[Carson's] qualities of zest and humor made even the dull stretches of bureaucratic procedure a matter for quiet fun, and she could instill a

sense of adventure into the editorial routine of a government department. My office adjoined hers, and this gave me an inaccurate and heady
view of government life. . . . Intransigent official ways, small stupidities,
and inept pronouncements were changed from annoyances into sources
of merriment. Nothing could pass the wry scrutiny of that gathering and
still seem unsurmountable or too frustrating . . ." (Brooks 77–78).

Briggs knows well the role of humor in enabling one to discover new perspectives. As a cartoonist, she acquired the task of portraying "amusing office episodes"—"the hilarious side of frustrating government routine"
(Briggs Letter 1997); and so by choosing the funny angle into affairs that
beleaguered them, she helped her colleagues find satisfactory passage
through difficult times. What Briggs calls Carson's "fund of quiet fun"
(Letter 1997) was important in sustaining the author through office work
that was frustrating because it absorbed time that she wanted to spend
writing.[91] On a more philosophical level, that fund of fun underwrote her
creative freedom to be a scientist with ecological sensibility. Briggs is canny
to remark that humor in nature writing is important for its effect of "en-
forcing a sense of proportion and some psychic distance from events"
(Letter 1997), yet the most remarkable facet of Carson's comic capacity is
its incorporation of detachment with emotional alliance and ethical commitment. In Carson, "psychic distance" meets creaturely affection—and
the result is powerfully beautiful nature writing, instructive in its surprise,
joy, and respect. Her descriptions in *The Sea Around Us* of the surface of the
ocean exemplify the style Dorothy Freeman called lyrical.

The face of the sea is always changing. Crossed by colors, lights, and
moving shadows, sparkling in the sun, mysterious in the twilight, its as-

91. However, her employment gave her opportunities to travel and do research that
would not otherwise have been possible. In a letter to a friend, she expresses her frustration over these matters: "I know that if I could choose what seems to me the ideal existence, it would be just to live by writing. But I have done far too little to dare risk it. And
all the while my job with the Service grows and demands more and more of me, leaving
less time that I could put on my own writing. And as my salary increases little by little,
it becomes even more impossible to give it up! That is my problem right now, and not
knowing what to do about it, I do nothing. For the past year or so I have told myself that
the job (for the first time in my years with the Service) was giving me the travel I wanted
and could not afford on my own and that, temporarily, was compensation for its other
demands" (Brooks 77).

pects and its moods vary hour by hour. The surface waters move with the tides, stir to the breath of the winds, and rise and fall to the endless, hurrying forms of the waves. Most of all, they change with the advance of the seasons (29).

It is lyricism bound to a coterie of facts.

A hard, brilliant, coruscating phosphorescence often illuminates the summer sea. In waters where the protozoa Noctiluca is abundant it is the chief source of this summer luminescence, causing fishes, squids, or dolphins to fill the water with racing flames and to clothe themselves in a ghostly radiance. Or again the summer sea may glitter with a thousand moving pinpricks of light, like an immense swarm of fireflies moving through a dark wood (32).

It is lyricism dependent on the comic flair of Carson's imagination, making possible unique metaphorical context for scientific fact.

Autumn comes to the sea with a fresh blaze of phosphorescence, when every wave crest is aflame. Here and there the whole surface may glow with sheets of cold fire, while below schools of fish pour through the water like molten metal. Often the autumnal phosphorescence is caused by a fall flowering of the dinoflagellates, multiplying furiously in a short-lived repetition of their vernal blooming (33).

Her comic skill not only delivers us via distinctive tropes into a new feel for the facts but also gives us a perspective of ourselves.

Man, in his vanity, subconsciously attributes a human origin to any light not of moon or stars or sun. Lights on the shore, lights moving over the water, mean lights kindled and controlled by other men, serving purposes understandable to the human mind. Yet here are lights that flash and fade away, lights that come and go for reasons meaningless to man, lights that have been doing this very thing over the eons of time in which there were no men to stir in vague disquiet (34).

In Carson, the comic skill that gives her psychic distance from her own kind allows her to see the distance we maintain from the natural world and to know ways in which she might bridge that distance, bringing us across a cultural divide so that we may be at home in nature.

▼ ▼ ▼

TO ACCOMPLISH SUCH GRAND-SCALE HOME-COMING, CARSON CHOOSES to be a storyteller, making herself a folklorist of science. She is interested in a plethora of stories, whether research from the international community of scientists or the singular experience of a mackerel who is inconspicuous in a school of foraging mackerel; and she strives mightily to know how to tell these stories. When she speaks for other creatures or describes the sea, she assumes the role of translator, having let the subject absorb her and "take command" and thus being able to host it—conveying the poetry innate to the sea or the spontaneous reactions of wild creatures in their world. She is a folklorist because she wants to pass these stories on to us. In telling them correctly, she entices us into play mode so that we participate in the stories. She trusts in the value of them as templates for our continued survival on earth and for the sophistication of our aesthetic sense, helping us to see the beauty in wild things and the necessary place that all things beautiful have in making our household complete. In addition, Carson is a folklorist of science because she believes that facts and research need a community of people to complete them—that community alone makes the connections that distill science in our lives and work and thus make new findings meaningful. As a folklorist, she has a comic eye on her own profession and a loving attachment to the ecological household where human lives find greater context.

Hers was a unique literary project—to draw readers into the life of the marine world so that our understanding of it would be sensory and intuitive as well as intellectual. In order to bring creaturely sensibility closer to human ken, she has to coax us out of our habitual modes of perception. About *Under the Sea-Wind*, she writes,

> To get the feeling of what it is like to be a creature of the sea requires the active exercise of the imagination and the temporary abandonment of many human concepts and human yardsticks. For example, time measured by the clock or the calendar means nothing if you are a shore bird or a fish, but the succession of light and darkness and the ebb and flow of the tides mean the difference between the time to eat and the time to fast, between the time an enemy can find you easily and the time you are relatively safe. We cannot get the full flavor of marine life—cannot

project ourselves vicariously into it—unless we make these adjustments in our thinking (Brooks 34).

Guided by an instinct for identification, she treads between human and nonhuman perspectives, the kind of route Coyote takes.[92] Carson continues:

On the other hand, we must not depart too far from analogy with human conduct if a fish, shrimp, comb jelly, or bird is to seem real to us—as real a living creature as he actually is. For these reasons I have deliberately used certain expressions which would be objected to in formal scientific writing. I have spoken of a fish "fearing" his enemies, for example, not because I suppose a fish experiences fear in the same way that we do, but because I think he *behaves as though he were frightened.* With the fish, the response is primarily physical; with us, primarily psychological. Yet if the behavior of the fish is to be understandable to us, we must describe it in the words that most properly belong to human psychological states (Brooks 34).

In strategizing how best to identify with other creatures, Carson makes plain how fully committed she is to reaching her audience. She will go beyond the strict dictums of science in order to communicate a full sense of what the facts mean. Stories help her transform data in this manner and offer her readers wild surprises, as does the appearance of an eel as protagonist, in the final section of *Under the Sea-Wind.*

Stuck with the reputation of being a sly and sinister character, the eel is less likely to enjoy our sympathy than the other creatures she spotlights in the book—the skimmer, sanderlings, and a mackerel. In one passing reference to an eel in the book's first section, Carson herself seems to perpetuate the stereotype of eels, referring to the eyes of a conger eel as "small" and "malignant" (95). In the last section, however, she proves the eel to be fascinating, tenacious, and compelling, one whose life in both freshwater ponds and deep ocean waters represents a migration as powerful and mysterious as the sea. Carson as folklorist introduces us to the eels thus: "There is a pond that lies under a hill, where the threading roots of many trees—mountain ash, hickory, chestnut oak, and hemlock—hold the rains in a

92. Commenting on the personalism with which Carson worked, Brooks surmises, "She felt a spiritual as well as physical closeness to the individual creatures about whom she wrote: a sense of identification that is an essential element in her literary style" (Brooks 8).

deep sponge of humus" (209). This is a storybook entrance into an attractive, interesting world. We learn that two streams bring down water into the pond, that cattails and rushes and willows grow at its edges, and that in springtime herons come to feed on the small fish and minnows who live there. It is called Bittern Pond, after the herons. Our first indication of the tale's unusual point of view occurs when Carson places this waterway in relation to others: "From Bittern Pond to the sea is two hundred miles as a fish swims" (210). She orients us down in the water, judging distance by how it would be there. And still we do not know she plans to focus on eels; she tells us gently.

> Every spring a number of small creatures come up the grassy spillway and enter Bittern Pond, having made the two-hundred-mile journey from the sea. They are curiously formed, like pieces of slender glass rods shorter than a man's finger. They are young eels, or elvers, that were born in the deep sea. Some of the eels go higher into the hills, but a few remain in the pond, where they live on crayfish and water beetles and catch frogs and small fishes and grow to adulthood (210–11).

Nothing could be sinister about such a scene or about glassy baby eels. Being thus lavish with detail, Carson absorbs us in the world of the eels without giving us a chance to harbor habituated responses to the creature. She benevolently tricks us out of our assumptions and surprises us with altogether new loyalties and understanding.

Carson cleaves us to the sensory life of the eel, in particular Anguilla, who arrived in Bittern Pond ten years earlier as an elver and now knows all its customary tastes, hiding places, and food—from frogs and crayfish to the occasional water rat toppled off the bank. Storms in November unsettle this eel, and Carson tells us that the creature "savored the strange tastes and smells in the water" (212), water that has percolated through the forest uplands, acquiring the bitters of fallen leaves and the smooth richness of humus. Just as the eel is newly stimulated by the season, we are insinuated for the first time into an eel's life—and so, Carson finely associates us both by awakening us simultaneously.

This November the water strikes Anguilla differently than it ever before has. She forgets hunger and begins instead to hunger for someplace else. That Carson uses "food hunger" in describing Anguilla's change of appetite—her desire to move on—bestows upon us a sensory equivalent by which we can imagine the compulsion to migrate. Anguilla wants to go somewhere dark and warm.

> She had known such a place once—in the dim beginnings of life, before memory began. She could not know that the way to it lay beyond the pond outlet over which she had clambered ten years before. But many times that night, as the wind and the rain tore at the surface film of the pond, Anguilla was drawn irresistibly toward the outlet over which the water was spilling on its journey to the sea (213–14).

We are drawn there too, now caught up not only as we imagine the eel to be but also inspired by curiosity, for Carson has laid a strong hint of a plot, and we, who are driven by our own unique appetite for stories, follow it. The way is unfamiliar for both eel and reader, yet there is surety in the migration. "Anguilla followed the stream, feeling her way by the changing pressure of the swift water currents. She was a creature of night and darkness, and so the black water path neither confused nor frightened her" (214). Currents and dark water constitute a "path" in Carson's translation of the eel's experience into more humanly familiar terms. Carson transports us to the wild by giving it to us with a domestic mien. And with sensory clarity. She never mitigates the full effect of the wildness in experiences that typically occur without human attendance. The continued tale of Anguilla's run to the ocean has that sensory challenge.

> As the river widened and deepened, a strange taste came into the water. It was a slightly bitter taste, and at certain hours of the day and night it grew stronger in the water that the eels drew into their mouths and passed over their gills. With the bitter taste came unfamiliar movements of the water—a period of pressure against the downflow of the river currents followed by slow release and then swift acceleration of the current (224).

To eels whose eyes are being enlarged and snouts compacted, "perhaps in preparation for a descent along darkening sea-lanes" (226), novel stimuli are exciting and compelling. They pass toward a tantalizing unknown: "The eels lay deep under water, savoring the salt that grew stronger hour by hour as the wind-driven wall of sea water advanced into the bay" (227). In the plot that Carson has caught us all up in, we are, like the eels, invested in a mysterious thing. The eels are free and wild because where they want to go is what they have submitted to.

> Soon after the tide turn, the seaward movement of the eels began. In the large and strange rhythms of a great water which each had known in the beginning of life, but each had long since forgotten, the eels at first moved hesitantly in the ebbing tide. The water carried them through an inlet between two islands. It took them under a fleet of oyster boats riding at anchor, waiting for daybreak. When morning came, the eels would be far away (228).

Once they are taken by the pull of the tide, it irrevocably moves them. Theirs is the freedom of necessity. We too have that freedom, following Carson's lead, compelled by her narrative, drawn into a wilder world than we might have ever expected to know.

As a folklorist of science, Carson is successful in giving us more than we expect, expecting more from us than we might think we could imagine, and initiating us into the ecological household, where we were not aware we wanted to go. Carson is ever ready to identify helpful correspondences. The oceanography equipment following World War II that took undisturbed samples of the ocean floor up to seventy feet long she prosaically describes as working "on the principle of an apple corer" (*The Sea Around Us* 76). With such core samplers, oceanographers could study the sedimentation and geologic history of the ocean floor. On the subject of sediments, Carson is eloquent.

> Every part of earth or air or sea has an atmosphere peculiarly its own, a quality or characteristic that sets it apart from all others. When I think of the floor of the sea, the single, overwhelming fact that possesses my imagination is the accumulation of sediments. I see always the steady, unremitting, downward drift of materials from above, flake upon flake, layer upon layer—a drift that has continued for hundreds of millions of years, that will go on as long as there are seas and continents.
>
> For the sediments are the materials of the most stupendous "snowfall" the earth has ever seen (75).

This imagery transforms the facts of erosion and sedimentation and gives way to a vivid scene:

We may think of the abyssal snowstorm in terms of a bleak and bliz-zard-ridden arctic tundra. Long days of storm visit this place, when dri-ving snow fills the air; then a lull comes in the blizzard, and the snowfall is light. In the snowfall of the sediments, also, there is an alternation of light and heavy falls. The heavy falls correspond to the periods of mountain building on the continents, when the lands are lifted high and the rain rushes down their slopes, carrying mud and rock fragments to the sea; the light falls mark the lulls between the mountain-building pe-riods, when the continents are flat and erosion is slowed. And again, on our imaginary tundra, the winds blow the snow into deep drifts, filling in all the valleys between the ridges, piling the snow up and up until the contours of the land are obliterated, but scouring the ridges clear. In the drifting sediments on the floor of the ocean we see the work of the "winds," which may be the deep ocean currents, distributing the sedi-ments according to laws of their own, not as yet grasped by human minds (79–80).

Her storytelling approach to science sparks our imagination and facilitates our understanding. So, too, when she wants to give us an image of the depth of the ocean, the shelf near the abyss where all is quiet and where the eels disappear (beyond human tracking) to do their spawning, she de-scribes it in bucolic language as the place "where fish herds browsed in the blue twilight, on the edge of the deep sea" (*Under the Sea-Wind* 254). As readers assumed to be accustomed to cows or sheep in "herds" that "browse," we are implicitly being asked to imagine fish meandering with the same casual necessity—a hundred fathoms below the surface, below where our senses usually focus. Carson passionately wants us to know the wild world, and she uses bold and playful stratagems to accomplish that goal.

A serious and dedicated student, meticulous lab researcher, "perfection-ist" office worker, and supporter of her mother and nieces and grand-nephew, Carson would not have called herself a folklorist, certainly not one with tricks up her literary sleeve. Yet, according to Shirley Briggs, Carson had that spunk. Of all her colleague's cartoon work, Carson was most delighted with the melodramatic depiction of her that Briggs made after the publication of *The Sea Around Us*, when Carson became famous and suddenly subjected to people's curiosity about her. The cartoon, enti-tled "Rachel as her readers seem to imagine her," showed an Amazonian large woman poised boldly before a wild sea. In assessing Carson's appreciation of the cartoon, Briggs comments that Carson's mother, Maria, shared with her daughter "the same rather mischievous sense of humor" (Letter 1997). Many readers wanted to assume that she was male since they could not believe a woman could have such scientific proficiency. Carson recalled,

> Then others assumed that, since I knew enough to write *The Sea*, I must be gray-haired and venerable. One of my unknown correspondents wrote that I was probably just what he was looking for as a wife—except that to have learned all I put in the book must have taken a long time and perhaps I was too old for him. I think I could have qualified, but that was one of life's opportunities I passed by (Brooks 132).

Carson was wry—quick to enjoy whatever humor this public interest occasioned. A trickster motif is fitting for the author's career—her unprecedented fame—and her literary skill.

If Carson bucked gender roles in the mid-twentieth century by writing authoritative books on the sea, she stepped altogether clear of them in writing *Silent Spring*. With it, she became a radical in the scientific community, using her connections and her expertise toward activist goals, which meant critiquing the widespread reliance on chemical pesticides and also implicitly critiquing the collusion between scientists and the chemical industry in advancing these chemicals. She was defending the health of the home-place, not the home as a constricted sphere where women were expected to contain their energies in the fifties but the ecological household— the natural world as the home to which we all belong. Thus, within the tradition of women's concern for homelife as well as the tradition of women writing in domestic metaphors about nature (Norwood 148), Carson developed revolutionary attitudes. She heeded women's calls of anger and distress over the spraying of pesticides, and she spoke out in protest.[93] The fact that she spoke from inside the scientific community directly to the outside world—the public who she felt ought to be warned about the dangers of pesticides—meant that she chose to flout the conventional route of professional dialogue.[94] As Vera Norwood writes, "By

93. A January, 1958, letter from Olga Owens Huckins about the DDT that killed birds in her yard helped inspire *Silent Spring*.
94. David Orr writes, "Scientists of the quality of Rachel Carson or Aldo Leopold are rarities who must buck the pressures toward narrowness and also endure a great deal of professional rejection and hostility" (87).

granting status to the worries of ordinary citizens, many of whom were women, Carson empowered people to question the authority of scientific figures in government and industry" (169). She was a maverick, a folk hero, unafraid to challenge business as usual.[95]

Carson's mischievous sense of fun, her genteel trickery, and her comic perspective are the keystones of her ability to be a survivor of her attachments. She was playful and bold to practice knowing so many creatures intimately; her identification with her subjects has meant that her writing about them excels in imagination and intimacy. Just as important to her ability to write lovingly about the marine world, the shore life, and the birds is her knack for remaining unattached, for only with this reserve can she keep all her attachments intact. The creatures she knows consume each other—their dependence on one another irrevocably completes the exchange of matter that creates energy. Were Carson to favor certain parts of that life, she would be less the scientist and more the romanticist. Instead, she turns a quintessentially comic eye on her beloved biotic world; she loves it for itself and for its changes—for becoming more than what she knows it to be. This is what she calls "the spectacle of life" as it evolves. In *The Edge of the Sea*, she expounds on her interest in the spectacle.

> Underlying the beauty of the spectacle there is meaning and significance. It is the elusiveness of that meaning that haunts us, that sends us again and again into the natural world where the key to the riddle is hidden. It sends us back to the edge of the sea, where the drama of life played its first scene on earth and perhaps even its prelude; where the forces of evolution are at work today, as they have been since the appearance of what we know as life; and where the spectacle of living creatures faced by the cosmic realities of the world is crystal clear (7).

Though no cosmic meaning is transparent, Carson has continued to stand in the presence of the spectacle because it affirms the fact that a larger plot than we know exists. Carson partakes in the need for that relation: connection to things greater than ourselves is fundamentally comforting, even when that spectacle is a changing thing. About one aspect of the spectacle she has studied so much—the shoreline—Carson is mystical:

95. Donald Worster says that with *Silent Spring* Carson "inaugurate[d] the literature of ecological apocalypse" (23).

in my mind's eye these coastal forms merge and blend in a shifting, kaleidoscopic pattern in which there is no finality, no ultimate and fixed reality—earth becoming fluid as the sea itself (*The Edge of the Sea* 249-50).

Her faith in life involves the comic leap of believing in something beyond what she knows.

For as the shore configuration changes in the flow of time, the pattern of life changes, never static, never quite the same from year to year. Whenever the sea builds a new coast, waves of living creatures surge against it, seeking a foothold, establishing their colonies. And so we come to perceive life as a force as tangible as any of the physical realities of the sea, a force strong and purposeful, as incapable of being crushed or diverted from its ends as the rising tide (250).

The value in Carson's comic perspective, her ability to be attached and committed yet not devastated by changes, culminates in her unprecedented accomplishment with *Silent Spring*. If we choose not to look at the resounding popularity of *Silent Spring* or at the astounding clarity with which she conveyed to a general audience the significance of hydrocarbons; if we choose to leave unspoken the considerable ramifications that *Silent Spring* has had on government policy, ecological health, and on people's attitudes and empowerment;[96] if we choose instead to focus on the fact that during her struggle with cancer she compiled the condemning evidence against deadly pesticides and wrote a positive and affirming book, we see the power of a comic perspective in her accomplishment.[97] Without that perspective, Carson may not have had the energy to complete *Silent Spring*, for without it, the devastating blow that DDT and other pesticides are systemic threats to the environment might have seemed unsurmountable. We owe the existence of *Silent Spring* partly to the comic skills Carson developed in her first three books. Detached enough to assemble the facts and see her way—our way—through them, yet attached enough to write with loving concern, she imagined that balance in the ecological household could be restored. Hers was faith underwritten by a practice of believing

96. Some of the books that document this legacy include *Pesticides and the Living Landscape*, *Since Silent Spring*, *Silent Spring Revisited*, *The Recurring Silent Spring*, and *After Silent Spring*.
97. Paul Brooks in an introduction to *Silent Spring*: "So she succeeded in making a book about death a celebration of life" (Carson xiii).

that comedy—change and equilibrium restored—ensures survival. Her courage was driven by comic spunk. Seeing that, we may learn what Carson most dearly wanted to convey—that the beauty of the world is comic—and that, given a chance, we shall stand in wonder of it and always be at home.

▼ ▼ ▼

Making Sense of Humor in North America

THE BEST WAY TO SEE BACK INTO THESE ACCOUNTS OF THE WRITERS and their humor is to go through Coyote, the way we came. Among the Wishram people of the Columbia River, tales of the way things started show that Coyote has always been there. He seems wiser than the first people, suggesting that their arrival occurred when he was already a savvy, mature creature with all his talents. He is curious about people— more worldly than they are. He has definite ideas about the way they should live.

The time that Coyote was traveling up the river and saw a man dive from his boat and come up with two sturgeons, one in each hand, he figured he could steal one of the fish from the man's canoe. He does so, but the man finds Coyote's hiding place and scolds him. Coyote has never been scolded before by a man with no mouth, speaking with a sound deep in his nose. So when he cooks the fish and the man cannot eat it but wants to, Coyote cuts a mouth open in him, freeing the man to speak and eat. Then all the mouthless people of his village come to Coyote for their mouths to be made. They want to give him a woman in payment, but he does not take one (Ramsey 49–51).

That is what Coyote can be like for the Wishram—self-assured, opinionated, heroic, cunning, hungry. Should he bestow some blessing, it is likely to be painful. He is bad, as the mouthless fisherman says, but he also wants to make things as they should be, as he sees they would fit best in that place. Since he knows the place well, he is certain that the people who live there must eat fish. By giving them mouths, he makes that diet possible.

In a Wishram story of the first pregnancy, Coyote is also like this: He finds a man trying to carry firewood between his legs—tripping and somersaulting—and helps him out, showing him how to fashion a rope from hazel-brush and carry the bundle on his back. He even carries the wood for the man back to his home and his reputedly pregnant wife. Coyote sees that the wife is not pregnant; she has only a splinter in her finger, infected. He removes the sliver and proceeds to show her how to make a child. Then, indeed, she is pregnant, and Coyote gives the man the child as his own (Ramsey 51–52).

Coyote seems to have extended business with people. Keeping an eye on them affords him no end of work, intrigue, and pleasure. Even after they need no help to make babies, he remains sexually interested in the women, as he is in many other female creatures. We do not hear exactly what the husband thought of Coyote's solicitations upon his wife, but we can expect that he was anxious to play that role himself. What do the Wishram think of Coyote? Though he is a hero to them—teaching them also how to catch salmon—he is certainly a trial, always insinuating himself into their affairs, tricking them too.

The Wasco–Warm Springs people, also of the Columbia River, tell of the five pretty sisters who were bathing and washing clothes in the river. Coyote spotted them and, desiring them all, plotted to change himself into a baby and float down on a papoose-board to them. In that manner, he satisfies himself with four of the girls but fails to fool the fifth because she notices first his penis, which he has forgotten to change when he became a baby (Ramsey 52–53). Coyote is morally challenging. We cannot say he is just bad because he is better and more useful than that. In fact, he is useful particularly when he is bad because then we can see what we question or disapprove of and, rather than ignore it, can identify and laugh about it. Coyote is not always funny, but nevertheless it takes a sense of humor to accept him as both the hero and the mendicant, understanding that the internal foil of his characteristics is necessary to his magic, power, and realism.

Native to North America, Coyote and the host of stories that accompany him give us local entrances into our place. In "The Incredible Survival of Coyote," Gary Snyder writes, "There is something to be learned from the Native American people about where we all are. It can't be learned from anybody else" (*A Place in Space* 156). We contemporary people may be independently becoming native in terms of knowing our places, but that education requires the good attitude that Native American stories demand of us. Acquiring that attitude is a matter of practice, involving how to pay attention, listen to voices other than our own, grow familiar with animals and plants, love what we cannot control, accept the contradictory truths the world offers, believe in Coyote as a fool and a hero. The practice to have that expansive attitude comes powerfully from Coyote stories, for even if we learn nothing from the specific adventures he pursues, we are still left with the fact that this rambunctious creature is as good as he is bad. To embrace such a morally challenging figure as Coyote, we are bound to develop our sense of humor. What we can learn from Native Americans, then, that we cannot learn from anyone else is the profound role of humor in helping us have cooperative and successful relationships with a place and with each other. No wonder Louise Erdrich called humor the "primary ceremony" across all the tribes. Humor helps people entertain paradox and see creative ways to be in relation to it. Humor prepares us to accept surprise and inconsistency in the ecological household and thus makes us adaptable, enhancing our chances of survival. Coyote is one of many tricksters throughout world folklore. They have come from around the globe and apparently have been everywhere on their journeys, an indication of their ubiquitous usefulness to all people. If people can cope with a trickster, they know how to live without a program of answers or responses—they know how to be spiritually, practically, and imaginatively resourceful.

Humor in North America has been around long before the pathogens, weeds, and domesticated animals of European settlers arrived, leveling the wild playing field as they did so that the settlers themselves were only a subsidiary wave of the "ecological imperialism" that swept across the continent.[98] When the settlers did move in, they further remade the New World, taming nature until it had a familiar character. Wilderness was shunted back. Less effort was spent on getting along with the place than in getting on, expanding trade and the economic reach of personal households. The distinctive humor that Americans developed—outrageous exaggeration—was a humor of colonization rather than wisdom based on nature such as Coyote tales are. Settlers exaggerated what their logging,

98. Alfred Crosby's book by that title, *Ecological Imperialism*, documents the impact that these imports had on the North American wilderness and its people. His contention is that European settlement was facilitated by the invasive modifications that plants, animals, and diseases of the Old World made on the New.

hunting, and expansion depended on—the forests, the wildlife, the wilderness. Hyperbole about the bounty and ferocity of North America was not intelligent commentary about the character of the place as they encountered it but the accumulating legend of how the settlers coped. It was glorification of their anxieties about the wild. The more that wilderness was dispensed with, the greater breathing room people had to consider, celebrate, and describe it—to describe their way with it. Regarding the cultural products of the white settlement of wilderness in the west, Snyder writes,

> For years the literature of the West was concerned with exploitation and expansion. This is what we mean when we talk about the "epic" or "heroic" period—a time of rapid expansion, of first-phase exploitation. This literature is not a literature of place. It is a history and a literature of feats of strength and of white, English-speaking-American human events. It's only about this place by accident (*A Place in Space* 154).

Just so the humor of these new Americans featured their heroics and was about place largely "by accident." It was, furthermore, about humans, placing little imaginative energy on the world as Coyote might see it—or as bear, wildcat, raccoon, and beaver might—and even less energy on how these creatures might perceive humans. Had the settlers been interested in becoming neighbors to the existing communities in the wild and had they been sensitive enough to know it to be an ecological household rather than unoccupied territory, then their attitude might have averted anxious heroism and instead been creative and accommodating. Their humor might have explored something more than their own psyches. Their impact on the continent might have been more benign, akin to the Native American experience here, thousands of years in the making, with no appreciable resource damage.

Yet contemporary Americans largely still pursue an outmoded heroics. From the beginning, there was no wilderness that could absorb our violence against it; that violence, Richard Slotkin argues, was the means used by our predecessors to take their place here and to make the nation (4). The very violence that undid the wild contributed to a national identity that depended greatly on the western frontier. Americans are heroic, the myth goes, for they have developed character by facing the hardships of the frontier. That frontier is gone. Snyder writes:

> The West ceases to exist (whether an area is geographically western or not) when the economy shifts from direct, rapid exploitation to a stabilized agricultural base. Heroics go with first-phase exploitation: the fur trade, then the cattle industry, then mining, then logging (*A Place in Space* 155).

The problem is that the heroics have become integral to a national myth, as Slotkin would have it, that perpetuates the violence of the "first-phase exploitation" and the self-reliant, ambitious individualism that accompanies it. Without the frontier, that violence is more glaringly misplaced than it was when it dismantled the wilderness. Slotkin writes, "A people unaware of its myths is likely to continue living by them, though the world around that people may change and demand changes in their psychology, their world view, their ethics, and their institutions" (4–5). Even though heroics can be destructive, Americans have been acculturated on it and esteem it to be indicative of success.

With such an attitude, we do not leave ourselves room to learn from the world around us. Our heroics have made us so thoroughly conquerors of our place that we have lost the great stretches of wilderness that fueled tall tales and established exaggeration as an American specialty. Heroics have meant that our wilderness is scattered in remnants, our virgin forests are gone, our topsoil is going, our aquifers are emptying, our waterways are polluted, our air quality is compromised, and our land is increasingly developed by shopping malls, subdivisions, and roads. Heroics have kept us from establishing a moral relation to the land and becoming native to North America. We have been an unsettled people, moving frequently enough to retard the affections and responsibilities that inspire moral relationships.

However, we can find native examples of an alternative to this mobility and ignorance. Keith Basso studied the Western Apache and found that the land has evolved in the Apache imagination as a moral teacher; he writes, "landscapes are always available to their seasoned inhabitants in other than material terms" (*Western Apache Language and Culture* 142). "Seasoned inhabitants" is Basso's precise shorthand for those with long-lived connections to a place—product of many generations. Stories about their homeplace and its history convey cultural wisdom and morality—to the extent that the Apache have come to connect their moral belief with the land. As Basso says, the land serves to remind people (127); it provides "indispensable mnemonic pegs on which to hang the moral teachings of their history"

(128); and so it is an "omnipresent moral force" (129). Since the natural world is inherent with power, according to Apache belief, the nexus of moral teachings with the land is no mere imposition of anthropocentric meaning on a passive backdrop. The land is an actor, forceful and necessitating respect. Specific powers include water, fire, thunder, rain, lightning, wind, moon, sun, changing woman, root, bear, eagle, snake, horse, cattle, mountain lion, deer, lizard, and coyote (Basso *The Cibecue Apache* 37–38). The etiquette is this:

> Apaches say that the surest way to maintain effective contact with a power is to accord it the same courtesies customarily extended to human beings. For example, instructions given by a power, however onerous, should be carried out without complaint or suppressed ill feeling. When making requests, the power should be addressed politely and spoken to in a low, unhurried key; it should never be bossed around. Having rendered a service, it should be given tangible payment, either with prayers of thanks, or by singing several of the chants associated with it. In short, viable and productive interaction with a power, like viable and productive interaction with other people, requires conscious effort and attention. It cannot be taken for granted. Failure to observe the appropriate social forms can engender hostility and this, in turn, can lead to termination of the relationship (*The Cibecue Apache* 39).

With such a status, the land and its creatures are not likely to be exploited. Nonhuman nature has a working relationship with people: it is sacred and ordinary. Having perceived that the miraculous presides in the familiar, the Apache have accorded the world around them due respect. Heroics have nothing to do with the calm and seemly attention that the Apache are culturally trained to give their place; in contrast, humor has a great role in this relationship. To credit Vine Deloria, Jr.'s statement that laughter and humor better illuminate "a group's collective psyche and values than do years of research" (140), we need only to look beyond the reasoning in Basso's chapter on Apache moral narratives to its emphasis on the humor of his Apache teacher, Nick Thompson. The old man's appetite for laughter infused everything he taught Basso. Infectious and communicative, his mirth shows the effect of his cultural heritage, for his world is rich with meaning, and he has learned to plumb it through concentration and play. Serious understanding requires the flexibility of perspective and insight that humor makes possible. In *Native American Renaissance*, Kenneth Lincoln discusses Indian expectations about how the world conveys meaning to them:

> The people hear and glimpse truths unexpectedly, out of the corner of the eye, as nature compresses and surprises with rich mystery. All things are alive, suggestive, sacred, and in common (46).

To acquire wisdom, according to this worldview, one must be adept at experimenting and coping with surprise. Humor advances one's moral education, in Native American experience, as ought to be vividly clear from Coyote's position as the original trickster, bungler, and cultural hero. Lincoln knows that Coyote manifests the playful style necessary to a Native American moral world—his "pratfalls emerge as comically inverse parables. He gambles with values in the breach; he stirs up original considerations, fringed with moral and epistemological concerns" (123). Coyote is a survivor, pervading the storytelling of native peoples and persistently accompanying them into contemporary times, where other folks, too, have picked him up in their poems and stories. Coyote has this charisma because he is a good psychological match to humans, who are forever in the ambiguous position between good and evil, and because his style of play, curiosity, and humor promotes survival. Lincoln identifies that style in Native American culture.

> No single mood corners nature's temperaments. No single curiosity exhausts the possibilities of surprise. Given a respect for nature's range, tribal peoples are free to experiment with natural rules, to discover inherent truths and error, to carry on their own investigation of traditions and moralities. Trusting tribal boundaries and a local sense of origin frees the people to explore their heritage and environment (51).

Knowledge of the limits of a local place and culture gives people a place within which to play. It safeguards them to experiment, in turn giving them skills to adapt to the present and thus to survive. Change is not a threat to such traditions—it is built into them. Kimberly Blaeser makes the point that some contemporary Native American writers who revise the presumed historical record[99] are empowered by "an awareness of the real-

---

99. She names Carter Revard, Gerald Vizenor, and Gordon Henry.

ity of the place" (353), since that reality is the authority over contested versions of the past. Place sets the limits, then, making possible the humor that these writers use "to unmask and disarm history," Blaeser says (353). Grounded by a sense of place, these writers can be securely experimental—good literary examples of a cultural capacity for change.

Settlers not responsible to the New World as a home had no sensitivity for the guideposts it could offer in directing the cultural "play" they undertook to adapt and survive. Such play—or accommodation to the place—was overwhelmed by the newcomers' wholesale development of the country, changing its character rather than using its existing limits to change their own cultural ways. Settlement won out over the frontier—and eliminated it. It is easy to see the "Great American Joke," which Louis Rubin, Jr. calls the incongruity between the "cultural ideal" and "everyday fact" (12), as the trick we have carried out on ourselves by glorifying our conception of American experience. The heroics we enjoyed partly for their exaggeration have nevertheless been taken seriously, resulting in the actual loss of the kind of territory that we idealized. The joke is on us. Not only are we left without expansive wilderness or the original bounty of the country but we also have driven ourselves to the west coast (and back and forth) without developing an attitude that might secure more benign relations with our place in the future.

Much of contemporary American humor is bleak, as Jesse Bier would argue, for it has pursued a course of exaggeration and deflation with purposeless fervor, accepting no limits under the false impression that the greatest freedom is independence from all things. Bier remarks, "The final comic antithesis of all is having no thesis whatsoever, a direction in which the majority of our nethermost humorists are leading" (476). The power that humor provides to critique and explore has often been applied with nihilistic energy, since many Americans do not have meaningful connections to home and community. Rather than depending on a structure of natural limits to discover freedom, as the Apache do, most Americans believe that personal freedom means overriding other commitments: "liberation" from responsibility. Humorists make money by shocking their audiences with "liberated" talk, but shock value alone is their concern—it is meaningless rather than free. Bier describes it as our urge "to enjoy life's conquest over all particular systems of value" (1). This is frontier psychology, based on triumph and dominance instead of understanding. It destroys more bonds than it creates, and it displaces us further from learning to be at home in the ecological household.

But there is another direction, a way home, a way to pick up on the trail of Coyote. Garrison Keillor has found it in his radio monologues about Lake Wobegon, his fictional hometown, whose community of people inspires affection from listeners and establishes the grounds for extensive humor. Well-schooled by Keillor in the characteristics and limitations of Lake Wobegon, we are primed to be amused. From Norwegian bachelor farmers to the regulars at the Sidetrack Tap and Chatterbox Cafe, the denizens are unique and beloved. We laugh because we know them and can understand their troubles and joy. Taking part in the humor of Lake Wobegon is like joining the household: it is a familiar world spread out before us, and we delight in its surprises because there would seem to be none left. From Keillor, we learn that intimacy augments the possibilities of humor. The creatures or people or places best known afford the greatest comic potential. Thus it is that nature writers have been busy, writing us into a community larger than the human one we are conditioned to, making us familiar with nonhuman nature.

In *The Psychology of Laughter and Comedy* (1923), J.Y.T. Greig has told us that intimacy with a subject is prerequisite to our humor about it, but he understands this to mean that humor involves only humans.[100] The presumption is fading that humor exists only because of humans. The most significant contribution to the development of humor along these lines comes from an unusual source—American nature writing, a literary field known more for its moralism than its humor. It is a surprise, then, that nature writers have begun the groundwork for humor that will be an expression of our "reinhabitation" of North America.[101] How they have done so is twofold: they give their moral opinions practical application by affirming that the world has natural limits we ought not to supercede, and, second, they reestablish our sense of community through intimacy with nature.

---

100. His work shows the influence of Henri Bergson, whose essay on laughter in 1900 asserted that humor always has a human basis. Critical work since then has explored the evolution of laughter and play in humans as a process that is mirrored in animal behavior. Charles Gruner's *Understanding Laughter* and William Fry's *Sweet Madness: A Study of Humor* pursue that course. Freud's work on the unconscious highlights the physiological nature of humor, as does Arthur Koestler's *The Act of Creation*. Studies by Konrad Lorenz, W. C. Allee and Gregory Bateson look to animals for the lessons that their behavior and play have for human beings. Others, like Joseph Wood Krutch in *The Best of Two Worlds*, argue that animals' behavior exhibits consciousness as well as instinct.
101. "Reinhabitation" is a term that describes our conscious resettlement of a place—being aware of its ecological character, doing restoration work to repair environmental damage, and developing economies that suit it.

Both efforts have succeeded in illuminating a world (threatened though it may be) that is comforting because of the etiquette it implies for its members. The transport between the human and nonhuman realms must be mutual in order for us all to survive. That transport has thrilling potential. So the natural limits nature writers have reinstated are liberating—foundation for new explorations, much as the Apaches' freedom issues from their dwelling in a structured, powerful world. We, too, need to be decent members of the household because it supports us; our health depends on the ecological health of the world.

Thus it is through their moral convictions about the expansiveness of our home, harboring human and nonhuman, that nature writers give us new possibilities for humor: humor that can be at play with utmost abandon since it occurs within the security of a structured world. Surprise flourishes when there are standards to diverge from. Or, as Snyder says in *The Practice of the Wild*, "You first must be on the path, before you can turn and walk into the wild" (154). That humor need not be *about* nature, per se. Nick Thompson's humor with Keith Basso mostly concerned bawdy jokes at the scholar's expense, much to Basso's bafflement (for how does one respond with professional composure to such provocation?) and delight (for the old man was lavishing attention on him, accepting, including, and enjoying him). Nevertheless, it is humor that issues from an ecological worldview. It belongs because it is part of the play within the household, and, as such, it is neither despairing nor solipsistic. In fact, humor may be more fundamental to human ecological awareness than anyone has previously imagined, for it makes us skilled at perceiving and intuiting connections in the world. Humor helps satisfy our desire to be connected to something larger than ourselves. It achieves this through its characteristic shift (or multiplication) of perspective, which we experience in having the presence or practice of mind to perceive a new context or relationship without losing "sight" of the old. Such context-setting implies the existence of a greater community—or Mind—than ourselves. At play with perspectives, we can imaginatively scope out the neighborhood and see how we fit in. Furthermore, humor helps us be connected to something larger than ourselves by involving us in its leap of faith—the point at which the crux of humor is a little beyond explanation, invested in the epiphany of the moment, folded into laughter. At that point, humor is wild because it makes sense out of no logical sense. Participating in that moment results in an internal, momentary, physiological spree, or high, that feels good because it relaxes our inhibitions and makes us free. It enables us to accept mystery and paradox

—and live comfortably in an endlessly complicated world. Humor puts us in touch with the sense we suspect the world makes.

Nature writers' role in the extension of community and ethics into nonhuman nature has nurtured just such humor. A founder of ecological writing and the modern environmental movement, Rachel Carson began simply with the idea of making us familiar with the sea and its inhabitants. In her three ocean books, she used her literary skills built upon her curiosity and scientific training to inspire our imagination and sympathy. She wanted her readers to feel something about the ocean. Scientific fact as isolated data was insignificant, in her eyes, unless attached to the whole ecological scene, and she was convinced that that scene could be accessed fully only through emotional commitment to the subject. She launched that commitment in us by making the ocean a familiar place. In that effort, passing in a narrative sweep through the ocean as if we could be amphibian, she delivers that world to us in language that makes us able to imagine it. Thus she writes, "fish herds browsed in the blue twilight, on the edge of the deep sea" (*Under the Sea-Wind* 254). This is a close enough match to our knowledge of common ungulate herds browsing that we can believe we have a sense for what the fish would be doing in that vastly different territory. Carson directs us to perceive the familiar in what might otherwise be strange to us. She talks about the homes of sea creatures and their daily activities, their life cycles; we are graduated by these domestic details into intimacy with what is utterly foreign to our experience. Carson further maneuvers us into a close-up of nonhuman nature by taking the perspective of animals and birds. We go with the eel down from a freshwater pond into the ocean to breed and spawn—we join in that life and numerous others, getting to explore a larger household than we ever thought existed.

Carson herself knows that household well. She has accomplished this in part by using the techniques of humor, specifically in shifting perspective and empathetically imagining situations that are not accustomed human ones. She has laid out for us a comic way in which to look at the world. Not only can we use her example to cleave to the world around us but we also can benefit from the optimism of her comic worldview. Its faith is that ecological changes have a comic pattern—balance will be restored and equilibrium regained. Evolution itself has the vagrancies and settlements of comedy. With this worldview, she wrote *Silent Spring* to be an affirming book despite its documentation of the tragic results of pesticides. Human impact on the evolutionary comedy may yet be incorporated into its dynamic balance without destroying it, at least that is the hope. Carson gives us ample hope because she has shown us a seaward glimpse of the ecological household, strong by merit of its flexibility, and a long taste of her positive attitude. She secures us in a world that delighted her and that gives us alliances to nonhuman nature, which, in turn, give us a look at ourselves from the outside in. In every way but being humorous, which she was professionally careful to skirt, Carson educates us on the helpful and enlightening possibilities of humor.

Wendell Berry, whose well-publicized commitments are to the farming communities of rural America, also teaches us through the example of his affections and attitude. He has much to argue for and against, but his clearest message proceeds from how he handles himself. His literary comportment consistently evinces dignity, love, and hope. These positive qualities are significant because Berry is among those he counts as his imperiled subjects—he is a small farmer whose family and community still farm and all of whom face increasing difficulty in making a living by working on a small scale on the land. Despite local tragedies that have affected him, Berry has sustained his optimism. How? Because Berry has been able to pull himself imaginatively and intellectually back from the current threats (agribusiness, automation, economic globalization) and see the survival of the people and places he loves. His creativity buoys his faith in the comic order of the universe. That creativity includes Berry's humor, which succors him from despairing and keeps alive his capacity to shift perspective from the fighting mode that the situation seems to require and enter instead a celebratory mode that explores positive alternatives.[102]

Part of the way Berry forwards the survival of his beloved countryside is through his fiction.[103] In numerous novels and collections of short stories, he has led his readers through the imagined community of Port William from all directions: we learn how the families care for themselves and the land—and how those cares are interdependent. We learn repeatedly that this community includes all of its inhabitants, human and nonhuman alike. Our intimacy with it predisposes us to agree with Berry that it has boundaries and limits that the land imposes (it is hilly, Kentucky River terrain) and that ought not to be overrun if community health is to be maintained. In Port William and the farmland beyond, we see an example

102. How humor is part of creativity is outlined by Arthur Koestler, whose study *The Act of Creation* (1964) names three aspects of creativity—humor, discovery, art—and shows them to be interpenetrating (27).

103. He is also politically active in his home state, Kentucky. He is a public figure whose views on agriculture in particular are well known.

of people who are profoundly free because they have chosen to work within the natural limits of the countryside. The lively exchange of stories and jokes that goes on among these people manifests that freedom, as does the incident in Miss Minnie and Ptolemy Proudfoot's kitchen when he, eager and desperate to establish camaraderie with his solemn guests, pours buttermilk down his shirtfront (pointing out to the little boy which side of the glass not to drink from) and she exclaims, " 'Why, Mr. Proudfoot, you *are* the limit'" (*Watch With Me* 107). There is extensive fun within this highly ordered world, or so Berry's fiction reveals. In showing us that this life is a beautiful way to be, Berry wants to convince us to look for the natural limits of our places and find creative ways to live in accordance with them.

Edward Abbey's work has similar goals but takes a more belligerent stance than Berry's. In the effort to change the American public's self-aggrandizement and convince them to limit their acquisitive ways in order to protect nonhuman nature—wilderness in particular—he defies all social norms he encounters. He rebels. He shocks us. He jokes. Posing as a literary outlaw, he endows upon himself the freedom to question American culture beyond the pale of conventional critiques: Abbey would like to see the rights of nature in parity with the rights of humans. He ushers us into this politically charged arena first by giving us the view of wild nature that he has repeatedly sought. It is an intimate and sensory view—the sounds and sights and heat and delights of walking in a desert canyon; or the rush and tumult of white water, the quiet pull of calm water on a river-boat trip. It is Abbey's compassionate and sensual understanding of the world. Given his exquisite writing about places, we understand his fierce commitment to the wild, for we have tasted it with him—we know its immanent power to make us alert, responsive, and alive. Thus it makes us feel at home within ourselves, no matter how far afield we have traveled with Abbey or on our own. We know nonhuman nature better because of Abbey; however, because he wants to prove that wildness is within ourselves too, he goes far beyond the usual scope of nature writing. His instinct for wildness through humor is substantiated by Koestler's analysis of the physiological origins of humor. Koestler's theory is that the attitude or emotion that is necessary to finding incongruity funny is begat by the adrenaline of the sympathetic nervous system, which has a full-body effect, unlike the quick action of the cerebral cortex. Emotion has inertia, as Koestler describes it, and the mind can outrace it. When our thinking diverges from the visceral response it had participated in, we experience the incongruity of our two modes of perception (55–58). Laughter results because there has been a "collision" between two ways of perceiving, which is the "bisociative" act that Koestler says underlies all creativity, including humor (35–36, 45). Since our reflexes and emotional faculties are "anachronistic," conditioned by surviving in the Paleolithic Age, our laughter has become a way of diffusing instinctive responses that are often unnecessary in the civilized world (Koestler 62).[104] Conversely, Koestler's work may be viewed to explain that humor gives us a chance to activate those limbic system responses that may be languishing because they are not socially sanctioned. Such is the function of Abbey's humor. He wants us to experience the thrill that our old brain, conditioned in the wild, can provide, and he introduces that charge to the social world by admitting it via humor. Abbey teaches us that our wildness is a way to celebrate wilderness and work for its security.

Perhaps never before considered a nature writer, Louise Erdrich writes her way into synchronicity with that tradition through her kaleidoscopic vision of one imagined place in North Dakota. She is concerned with how the human community there interacts and how it fits in that place. Her work is not prescriptive, for she considers her role as a mixed-blood Native American to be that of a storyteller, passing on accounts of survival. It is in her presentation of the community's family ecology and in her understanding of the place as both ordinary and magical that she falls best into the nature-writing tradition. Erdrich is a chameleon of perspective. She takes on the individual stories of her characters so that we learn about the events of Argus and the reservation from multiple angles: shifting with her among them, we sense the exchange of energy and power that binds the community together. We intuit that the network of friendships, blood relations, alliances, and even animosities is responsible for this group's continued survival. Erdrich's style thus points to the "ecological" character of her fictional population. Furthermore, her people have long-lived connections to their place, with its tempestuous weather, fertile soil, and mythical forces. In developing Lake Matchimanito as a locus of legendary power that defies anyone's grasp, and in associating the Pillager family with the lake's wildness and magic, Erdrich acknowledges the biological knot between people and nature that gives us significance and meaning, though it may remain forever ineffable, bound up in a physical, spiritual realm.

104. For instance, our agitation in modern-day "danger" situations such as taking exams or being interviewed does not warrant either violent action or flight to escape. Instead, laughter can diffuse our tension and prepare us for more appropriate action.

Erdrich expresses the ineffable through humor. Her comic talent for maintaining touch with multiple narrative perspectives is part of her larger capacity to create humor. With it, she transforms the ordinary and the tragic into events imbued with redemptive power; her humor shows that such events contribute to a comic world, whose beauty issues from its adaptability and continuance. So Erdrich has Fleur and the wind play a joke on the loggers to shake their presumption that they control anything. The wildness of the Matchimanito area is elusive and transcendent because it is immanent to the land. Hence, it appears again in the skunk who gives Lipsha his vision. From Erdrich we know that the characters participate in a much more expansive world than their human one and that they can access it through humor. By making us laugh, she gives us that step through ourselves to go beyond, partaking of the magical world that inhabits the ordinary one we know.

Humor is as multifarious as Coyote. It is instinctive, innate, and biological, and it is also socially and culturally conditioned. Writers who use humor to help us see that we belong in the natural world are fighting the contemporary course of destructive development while keeping themselves from becoming bitter. Their use of humor accomplishes resistance through celebration. They not only direct our focus to nature, they give us a brush with Coyote, replicating through the jolt of humor a responsive and alert state of wildness in us. They use humor to educate us about wildness, since it is primary to the ecological health of the world that they hope to protect. The limits that such a world entails are the lineaments of nature writers' moralism. And that moral conception of the world is their most profound contribution to the development of American humor because it establishes responsibilities and limits that make our explorations meaningful. If Coyote were not present at Creation in Native American tradition, and if he did not perform so many good deeds for humans, his role as a deviant and trickster would be one-dimensional and mean very little. He could hardly be bad were he not coming from something good. His endless education reflects human negotiation with the facts of the world. Nature writers are reestablishing among those facts environmental realities so that we may be better members of the household, that we may survive, and that we may be playful and delighted within our place. Humor is a way of sustaining ecologically conscious cultural evolution.

Like laughter, which is a reflex and can be conditioned (Frye *Anatomy of Criticism* 168), our humor is play that can be modified. There is evidence to suggest that we can create our own good humor. Konrad Lorenz has posited that the ritualized habits of animals can acquire the characteristics of an autonomous instinct just as human morality and humor can (58–67, 297). Since humor is an instinct and a habit of mind, it can propel changes in our character. Research shows that habits of visual perception have neurological consequences in the structure of the visual cortex: developing one's mind by focusing attention in certain ways means that the brain becomes physically suited to perceive in those ways (Sewall 206–7). How we practice our humor and direct our attitude may thus also direct our biological evolution. We can be creatures of creativity. Our play and laughter can make us becoming to nature, and so we may, at last, be at home.

Abbey, Edward. *Abbey's Road*. New York: E.P. Dutton, 1979.

———. *The Best of Edward Abbey*. San Francisco: Sierra Club Books, 1984.

———. *Beyond the Wall: Essays From the Outside*. New York: Holt, Rinehart, & Winston, 1984.

———. *Cactus Country*. New York: Time-Life Books, 1973.

———. *Confessions of a Barbarian: Selections from the Journals of Edward Abbey, 1951–1989*. Ed. David Peterson. Boston: Little, Brown, & Co., 1994.

———. *Desert Solitaire: A Season in the Wilderness*. New York: McGraw-Hill, 1968.

———. *Down the River*. New York: Penguin, 1982.

———. *The Fool's Progress: An Honest Novel*. New York: Avon Books, 1988.

———. *Good News*. New York: E.P. Dutton, 1980.

———. *The Hidden Canyon: A River Journey*. Photographs by John Blaustein. New York: Viking Press, 1977.

———. *The Journey Home: Some Words in Defense of the American West*. New York: E.P. Dutton, 1977.

———. *The Monkey Wrench Gang*. Philadelphia: J.B. Lippincott, 1975.

———. *One Life at a Time, Please*. New York: Henry Holt & Co., 1978.

———. "The Poetry Center Interview." By James R. Hepworth. In *Resist Much, Obey Little: Remembering Ed Abbey*, eds. James R. Hepworth & Gregory McNamee. 48–60. San Francisco: Sierra Club Books, 1996.

———. *A Voice Crying in the Wilderness (Vox Clamantis in Deserto): Notes from a Secret Journal*. New York: St. Martin's Press, 1989.

After Silent Spring: The Unsolved Problems of Pesticide Use in the United States. Washington D.C.: Natural Resources Defense Council, June 1993.

Allee, W.C. *Cooperation Among Animals, with Human Implications*. 1938. Rev. ed. New York: Henry Schuman, 1951.

Allen, Paula Gunn. *The Sacred Hoop: Recovering the Feminine in American Indian Traditions*. Boston: Beacon Press, 1986.

Aprile, Dianne. "The Good Life." *The Courier-Journal SCENE* November 27 (1993): 17–19.

Basney, Lionel. "Five Notes on the Didactic Tradition, in Praise of Wendell Berry." In *Wendell Berry*, ed. Paul Merchant. 174–83. Lewiston, ID: Confluence Press, 1991.

Basso, Keith H. *The Cibecue Apache*. New York: Holt, Rinehart, & Winston, 1970.

———. *Western Apache Language and Culture: Essays in Linguistic Anthropology*. Tucson: University of Arizona Press, 1990.

Bateson, Gregory. *Mind and Nature: A Necessary Unity*. London: Fontana, 1985.

———. *Steps to an Ecology of Mind*. New York: Ballantine, 1972.

Beard, Mary Ritter, and Martha Bensley Bruere. *Laughing Their Way: Women's Humor in America*. New York: Macmillan & Co., 1934.

Bergson, Henri. "Laughter (1900)." In *Comedy: Meaning and Form*, ed. Robert W. Corrigan. 471–77. San Francisco: Chandler Publishing Co., 1965.

Berry, Wendell. *Another Turn of the Crank*. Washington, D.C.: Counterpoint, 1995.

———. "The Art of Place." Interview with Marilyn Berlin Snell. *New Perspectives Quarterly* 9.2 (1992): 29–34.

———. *A Continuous Harmony: Essays Cultural and Agricultural*. San Diego: Harcourt Brace & Co., 1970.

———. *The Discovery of Kentucky*. Frankfort, KY: Gnomon Press, 1991.

———. *Entries*. New York: Pantheon, 1994.

———. *Fidelity: Five Stories*. New York: Pantheon, 1992.

———. "Field Observations: An Interview with Wendell Berry." By Jordan Fisher-Smith. *Orion* 12.4 (Autumn 1993): 50–59.

———. *The Gift of Good Land: Further Essays Cultural and Agricultural*. San Francisco: North Point Press, 1981.

———. *The Hidden Wound*. 1970. San Francisco: North Point Press, 1989.

———. *Home Economics: Fourteen Essays*. San Francisco: North Point Press, 1987.

———. *The Long-Legged House*. New York: Harcourt Brace & World, 1969.

———. *The Memory of Old Jack*. San Diego: Harcourt Brace & Co., 1974.

———. *Nathan Coulter*. 1960. Rev. ed. New York: North Point Press & Farrar, Strauss & Giroux, 1985.

———. *A Place on Earth*. 1967. Rev. ed. San Francisco: North Point Press, 1983.

———. "A Question a Day: A Written Conversation with Wendell Berry." By Mindy Weinreb. In *Wendell Berry*, ed. Paul Merchant. 27–43. Lewiston, Idaho: Confluence Press, 1991.

———. *Recollected Essays: 1965–1980*. San Francisco: North Point Press, 1981.

———. *Remembering*. New York: North Point Press, 1988.

———. *Sex, Economy, Freedom & Community*. New York: Pantheon Books, 1992.

———. *Standing by Words*. San Francisco: North Point Press, 1983.

———. *Two More Stories of the Port William Membership*. Frankfort, KY: Gnomon Press, 1997.

———. *The Unsettling of America: Culture & Agriculture*. San Francisco: Sierra Club Books, 1977.

———. *Watch With Me: And Six Other Stories of the Yet-Remembered Ptolemy Proudfoot and His Wife, Miss Minnie, Nee Quinch*. New York: Pantheon, 1994.

———. *What Are People For?* San Francisco: North Point Press, 1990.

———. *The Wild Birds, Six Stories of the Port William Membership*. San Francisco: North Point Press, 1986.

———. *A World Lost*. Washington, D.C.: Counterpoint Press, 1996.

Beston, Henry. "Miss Carson's First." *The Freeman* 3.3 (1952): 100.

———. *The Outermost House: A Year of Life on the Great Beach of Cape Cod*. New York: Viking Press, 1962.

Bier, Jesse. *The Rise and Fall of American Humor.* New York: Holt, Rinehart, & Winston, 1968.

Blaeser, K.M. "The New Frontier of Native American Literature: Disarming History with Tribal Humor." *Genre* 25.4 (1992): 351–64.

Blair, Walter. *Native American Humor.* New York: American Book Co., 1937.

Blair, Walter, and Hamlin Hill, eds. *America's Humor, From Poor Richard to Doonesbury.* New York: Oxford UP, 1978.

Briggs, Shirley. Letter to the author, 3 July 1997.

Bright, William. "The Natural History of Old Man Coyote." In *Recovering the Word: Essays on Native American Literature*, eds. Brian Swann and Arnold Krupat. 339–87. Berkeley: University of California Press, 1987.

Brooks, Paul. *Rachel Carson At Work: The House Of Life.* Boston: G.K. Hall & Co., 1985.

Brown, Carolyn S. *The Tall Tale in American Folklore and Literature.* Knoxville: University of Tennessee Press, 1987.

Bruchac, Joseph. *Native American Stories.* Golden, Colorado: Fulcrum, 1991.

Buell, Lawrence. *The Environmental Imagination: Thoreau, Nature Writing, and the Formation of American Culture.* Cambridge: Belknap Press of Harvard UP, 1995.

Burrison, John A., ed. *Storytellers: Folktales & Legends from the South.* Athens: University of Georgia Press, 1989.

Cahalan, James M. "Edward Abbey: Appalachian Easterner." *Western American Literature* 31.3 (1996): 233–53.

Carey, Drew. *Dirty Jokes and Beer: Stories of the Unrefined.* New York: Hyperion, 1997.

Carrighar, Sally. *One Day on Beetle Rock.* 1943. New York: Knopf, 1966.

Carson, Rachel. *Always, Rachel: The Letters of Rachel Carson and Dorothy Freeman, 1952–1964.* Ed. Martha Freeman. Boston: Beacon Press, 1995.

———. *The Edge of the Sea.* Boston: Houghton Mifflin Co., 1955.

———. *The Sea Around Us.* Reprint (1951) New York: Oxford UP, 1979.

———. *The Sense of Wonder.* New York: Harper & Row, 1965.

———. *Silent Spring.* Boston: Houghton Mifflin, 1962.

———. *Under the Sea-Wind.* Reprint (1941) New York: Penguin, 1969.

Castillo, Susan Perez. "Postmodernism, Native American Literature, and the Real: The Silko-Erdrich Controversy." *The Massachusetts Review* 32.2 (Summer 1991): 285–94.

Chavkin, Allan, and Nancy Feyl Chavkin, eds. *Conversations with Louise Erdrich and Michael Dorris.* Jackson: University Press of Mississippi, 1994.

Chawla, Louise. "The Ecology of Environmental Memory." *Children's Environments Quarterly* 3.4 (1986): 34–42.

———. "Ecstatic Places." *Children's Environments Quarterly* 7.4 (1990): 18–23.

Cobb, Edith. "The Ecology of Imagination in Childhood." In *The Subversive Science: Essays Toward an Ecology of Man*, eds. Paul Shepard and Daniel McKinley. 122–32. Boston: Houghton Mifflin Co., 1969.

Cohen, Sarah Blacher, ed. *Comic Relief: Humor in Contemporary American Literature*. Urbana: University of Illinois Press, 1978.

Cousins, Norman. *Anatomy of an Illness*. New York: Bantam, 1979.

Corrigan, Robert W., ed. *Comedy: Meaning and Form*. San Francisco: Chandler Publishing Co., 1965.

Crosby, Alfred W. *Ecological Imperialism: The Biological Expansion of Europe, 900–1900*. Cambridge: Cambridge UP, 1986.

Deloria, Jr., Vine. *Custer Died For Your Sins: An Indian Manifesto*. New York: Macmillan Co., 1969.

Devall, Bill, and George Sessions, ed. *Deep Ecology: Living As If Nature Mattered*. Salt Lake City: Gibbs Smith, Inc., 1985.

DeVoto, Bernard. *Mark Twain's America*. Boston: Little, Brown, and Co., 1935.

Dobie, J. Frank. *The Voice of the Coyote*. Curtis Publishing Co., 1947.

Dodge, Jim. "Living By Life: Some Bioregional Theory and Practice." In *Home! A Bioregional Reader*, eds. Van Andruss, Christopher Plant, Judith Plant, and Eleanor Wright. 5–12. Philadelphia, PA: New Society Publishers, 1990.

Dorson, Richard M. *American Folklore*. Chicago: University of Chicago Press, 1959.

———. *Folklore, Selected Essays*. Bloomington: Indiana UP, 1972.

———, ed. *Handbook of American Folklore*. Bloomington: Indiana UP, 1983.

Dresner, Zita Z. "Domestic Comic Writers." In *Women's Comic Visions*, ed. June Sochen. 93–114. Detroit: Wayne State UP, 1991.

Dunlap, Thomas R. *DDT: Scientists, Citizens, and Public Policy*. Princeton: Princeton UP, 1981.

Eastman, Max. *The Sense of Humor*. New York: Octagon Books, 1972.

Erdoes, Richard, and Alfonso Ortiz, eds. *American Indian Myths and Legends*. New York: Pantheon, 1984.

Erdrich, Louise. *The Beet Queen*. New York: Henry Holt & Co., 1986.

———. *The Bingo Palace*. New York: HarperCollins, 1994.

———. *The Blue Jay's Dance, A Birth Year*. New York: HarperCollins, 1995.

———. *Grandmother's Pigeon*. Illus. Jim LaMarche. New York: Hyperion Books for Children, 1996.

———. *Love Medicine*. Rev. ed. New York: HarperCollins, 1993.

———. *Tales of Burning Love*. New York: HarperCollins, 1996.

———. *Tracks*. New York: Henry Holt & Co., 1988.

———. "Where I Ought to Be: A Writer's Sense of Place." *New York Times Book Review* (July 28,1985) 1, 23–24.

Esbjornson, Carl D. "*Remembering* and Home Defense." In *Wendell Berry*, ed. Paul Merchant. 155–70. Lewiston, ID: Confluence Press, 1991.

Evernden, Neil. *The Social Creation of Nature*. Baltimore: Johns Hopkins UP, 1992.

Freud, Sigmund. *Wit and Its Relation to the Unconscious*. Trans. A.A. Brill. London: Fisher & Unwin, 1916

Foreman, Dave, *Confessions of an Eco-Warrior*. New York: Harmony Books, 1991.

Foreman, Dave, and Bill Haywood, eds. *Ecodefense: A Field Guide to Monkey-wrenching*. 2nd ed. Tucson, Arizona: Ned Ludd, 1987.

Fry, William F. "The Biology of Humor." *Humor: International Journal of Humor Research* 7.2 (1994): 111–26.

———. *Sweet Madness: A Study of Humor*. Palo Alto, Calif.: Pacific Books, 1963.

Frye, Northrop. *Anatomy of Criticism*. Princeton: Princeton UP, 1957.

———. "The Argument of Comedy." In *English Institute Essays, 1948*, ed. D.A. Robertson, Jr. 58–73. New York: Columbia UP, 1949.

Gartner, Carol B. *Rachel Carson*. Literature and Life Series. New York: Frederick Ungar Publishing Co., 1983.

Gleason, William. "'Her Laugh an Ace': The Function of Humor in Louise Erdrich's *Love Medicine*." *American Indian Culture and Research Journal* 11.3 (1987): 51–73.

Graham, Jr., Frank. *Since Silent Spring*. Boston: Houghton Mifflin Co., 1970.

Greig, J.Y.T. *The Psychology of Laughter and Comedy*. 1923. New York: Cooper Square Publishers, Inc., 1969.

Gruner, Charles R. *Understanding Laughter: The Workings of Wit & Humor*. Chicago: Nelson-Hall, 1978.

Harrison, Robert Pogue. *Forests: The Shadow of Civilization*. Chicago: University of Chicago Press, 1992.

Hepworth, James R. "*Canis Lupus Amorus Lunaticum*." In *Resist Much, Obey Little: Remembering Ed Abbey*, eds. James R. Hepworth and Gregory McNamee. 117–37. San Francisco: Sierra Club Books, 1996.

Hepworth, James R., and Gregory McNamee, eds. *Resist Much, Obey Little: Remembering Ed Abbey*. San Francisco: Sierra Club Books, 1996.

Hicks, Jack. "Wendell Berry's Husband to the World: *A Place on Earth*." In *Wendell Berry*, ed. Paul Merchant. 118–34. Lewiston, Idaho: Confluence Press, 1991.

Hobbes, Thomas. "Leviathan," *Works*. Ed. Molesworth. London, 1840.

Huizinga, Johan. *Homo Ludens: A Study of the Play-Element in Culture*. Boston: Beacon Press, 1950.

Hyde, Dayton O. *Don Coyote: The Good Times and the Bad Times of a Much Maligned American Original*. New York: Arbor House, 1986.

Hyde, Lewis. *The Gift: Imagination and the Erotic Life of Property*. New York: Random House, 1983.

Hyers, Conrad. *Zen and the Comic Spirit*. Philadelphia: Westminster Press, 1973.

Hynes, H. Patricia. *The Recurring Silent Spring*. New York: Permagon Press, 1989.

Inge, M. Thomas, ed. *The Frontier Humorists*. Hamden, Connecticut: Archon Books, 1975.

Jones, Loyal, and Billy Edd Wheeler, eds. *Laughter in Appalachia: A Festival of Southern Mountain Humor*. Little Rock: August House, 1987.

Kaufman, Gloria, and Mary Kay Blakely, eds. *Pulling Our Own Strings: Feminist Humor & Satire*. Bloomington: Indiana UP, 1980.

Kenney, W. Howland. *Laughter in the Wilderness: Early American Humor to 1783*. Kent State: Kent State UP, 1976.

Koestler, Arthur. *The Act of Creation*. New York: The Macmillan Co., 1964.

Krutch, Joseph Wood. *The Best of Two Worlds*. New York: W. Sloane Associates, 1953.

LaChapelle, Dolores. *Earth Wisdom*. Los Angeles: Guild of Tutors Press, 1978.

———. *Sacred Land, Sacred Sex: Rapture of the Deep*. Silverton, Colo.: Finn Hill Arts, 1988

Lear, Linda. *Rachel Carson: Witness for Nature*. New York: Henry Holt & Co., 1997.

Le Guin, Ursula. *Buffalo Gals and Other Animal Presences*. New York: Penguin Books, 1987.

Leopold, Aldo. *A Sand County Almanac*. 1949. New York: Ballantine Books, 1966.

Lincoln, Kenneth. *Native American Renaissance*. Berkeley: University of California Press, 1983.

Lorenz, Konrad. *On Aggression*. Trans. Marjorie Kerr Wilson. New York: Harcourt Brace and World, 1966.

Lynn, Kenneth S. *Mark Twain & Southwestern Humor*. Boston: Little, Brown, & Co., 1959.

Lynn, Kenneth S., ed. *The Comic Tradition in America*. Garden City, New York: Doubleday Anchor, 1958.

Lyon, Thomas J, ed. *This Incomperable Lande: A Book of American Nature Writing*. New York: Penguin, 1989.

Marco, Guio, J., et al. *Silent Spring Revisited*. Washington D.C.: American Chemical Society, 1987.

Marshall, Ian. "Humor and the Techniques of Humor in William Bradford's *Of Plymouth Plantation*." *Studies in American Humor* 5 (1986): 158–67.

Marx, Leo. *The Machine in the Garden: Technology and the Pastoral Ideal in America*. New York: Oxford UP, 1967.

McCann, Garth. *Edward Abbey*. Western Writers Series (29) Boise, Idaho: Boise State University, 1977.

McGhee, Paul E. "The Role of Laughter and Humor in Growing Up Female." In *Becoming Female: Perspectives on Development*, ed., Claire B. Kopp. 183–206. New York: Plenum Press, 1979.

McKenzie, James. "Lipsha's Good Road Home: The Revival of Chippewa Culture in *Love Medicine*." *American Indian Culture and Research Journal* 10.3 (1986): 53–63.

McNamee, Gregory. "If It's Not One Dam Thing, It's Another." *Utne Reader* March-April (1998): 20–21.

———. "Wendell Berry and the Politics of Agriculture." In *Wendell Berry*, ed. Paul Merchant. 90–102. Lewiston, ID: Confluence Press, 1991.

Meeker, Joseph. *The Comedy of Survival: Studies in Literary Ecology*. New York: Charles Scribner's Sons, 1974.

Meine, Franklin, J. "Tall Tales of the Southwest." In *The Frontier Humorists*, ed. Thomas M. Inge. 15–31. Hamden, CT: Archon Books, 1975.

Merchant, Paul, ed. *Wendell Berry*. The Confluence American Authors Series. Lewiston, Idaho: Confluence Press, 1991.

Miller, David L. *Gods and Games: Toward a Theology of Play*. New York: The World Publishing Co., 1970.

Mills, Stephanie. "The Wild and the Tame." In *Place of the Wild*, ed. David Clarke Burks. 43–57. Washington, D.C.: Island Press, 1994.

Mintz, Lawrence E., ed. *Humor in America: A Research Guide to Genres and Topics*. New York: Greenwood Press, 1988.

Momaday, N. Scott. "An American Land Ethic." In *Ecotactics: The Sierra Club Handbook for Environmental Activists*, eds. John G. Mitchell and Constance L. Stallings. 97–105. New York: Simon and Schuster, 1970.

Monro, D.H. *Argument of Laughter*. Australia: Melbourne University Press, 1951.

Muir, John. *The Mountain of California*. Berkeley: Ten Speed Press, 1977.

Nash, Roderick. *The Rights of Nature: A History of Environmental Ethics*. Madison: University of Wisconsin Press, 1989.

———. *Wilderness and the American Mind*. New Haven: Yale UP, 1967.

Nibbelink, Herman. "Thoreau and Wendell Berry: Bachelor and Husband of Nature." In *Wendell Berry*, ed. Paul Merchant. 135–51. Lewiston, Idaho: Confluence Press, 1991.

Norwood, Vera. *Made From This Earth: American Women and Nature*. Chapel Hill: University of North Carolina Press, 1993.

Oates, Joyce Carol. "Against Nature." In *On Nature: Nature, Landscape, and Natural History*, ed. Daniel Halpern. 236–43. San Francisco: North Point Press, 1987.

Oelschlaeger, Max. *The Idea of Wilderness, From Prehistory to the Age of Ecology*. New Haven: Yale UP, 1991.

O'Grady, John P. *Pilgrims to the Wild*. Salt Lake City: University of Utah Press, 1993.

Orr, David W. *Ecological Literacy: Education and the Transition to a Postmodern World*. New York: State University of New York Press, 1992.

Ortiz, Simon. *A Good Journey*. Tucson, Arizona: Sun Tracks and University of Arizona Press, 1977.

Piaget, Jean. *Play, Dreams and Imitation in Childhood*. Trans. C. Gattegno and F.M. Hodgson. New York: W.W. Norton & Co., 1962.

Pinsker, Sanford. "The Urban Tall Tale: Frontier Humor in a Contemporary Key." In *Comic Relief: Humor in Contemporary American Literature*, ed. Sarah Blacher Cohen. 249–62. Urbana: University of Illinois Press, 1978.

Radin, Paul. *The Trickster: A Study in American Indian Mythology*. London: Routledge and Kegan Paul, 1956.

Ramsey, Jarold, ed. *Coyote Was Going There: Indian Literature of the Oregon Country*. Seattle: University of Washington Press, 1977.

Rexroth, Kenneth. "The Decline of American Humor." *The Nation* 184 (1957): 374–76.

———. "Humor in a Tough Age." *The Nation* 188 (March 7, 1959): 211–13.

Roessel, Jr., Robert A. and Dillon Platero, eds. *Coyote Stories*. Rough Rock, Arizona: Navaho Curriculum Center, DINE, Inc., 1968.

Rolston, III, Holmes. *Environmental Ethics: Duties to and Values in the Natural World*. Philadelphia: Temple UP, 1988.

Ronald, Ann. *The New West of Edward Abbey*. Albuquerque: University of New Mexico Press, 1982.

Rothman, David J. "'I'm a humanist': The Poetic Past in *Desert Solitaire*." In *Coyote in the Maze: Tracking Edward Abbey in a World of Words*, ed. Peter Quigley. 47–73. Salt Lake City: University of Utah Press, 1998.

Rourke, Constance. *American Humor: A Study of the National Character*. New York: Doubleday & Co., 1931.

Rovit, Earl. "College Humor and the Modern Audience." In *Comic Relief: Humor in Contemporary American Literature*, ed. Sarah Blacher Cohen. 238–48. Urbana: University of Illinois Press, 1978.

Rubin, Jr., Louis D., ed. *The Comic Imagination in American Literature*. New Brunswick, NJ: Rutgers UP, 1973.

Rudd, Robert L. *Pesticides and the Living Landscape*. Madison: University of Wisconsin Press, 1964.

Ryden, Hope. *God's Dog*. New York: Coward, McCann & Geoghegan, Inc., 1975.

Schopenhauer, Arthur. *The World as Will and Idea*. Trans. Haldane and Kemp. 5th ed. London, 1906.

Sewall, Laura. "The Skill of Ecological Perception." In *Ecopsychology: Restoring the Earth, Healing the Mind*, eds. Theodore Roszak, Mary E. Gomes, and Allen D. Kanner. 201–15. San Francisco: Sierra Club Books, 1995.

Shelton, Richard. "Creeping Up on *Desert Solitaire*." In *Resist Much, Obey Little: Remembering Ed Abbey*, eds. James R. Hepworth and Gregory McNamee. 100–116. San Francisco: Sierra Club Books, 1996.

Shepard, Paul. *Nature and Madness*. San Francisco: Sierra Club Books, 1982.

Slotkin, Richard. *Regeneration Through Violence: The Mythology of the American Frontier, 1600–1860*. Middletown, CT: Wesleyan University Press, 1973.

Smith, Patricia Clark. "Coyote Ortiz: Canis latrans in the Poetry of Simon Ortiz." In *Studies in American Indian Literature: Critical Essays and Course Designs*, ed. Paula Gunn Allen. 192–210. New York: Modern Language Association of America, 1983.

Snyder, Gary. *The Back Country*. New York: New Directions, 1957.

———. *Left Out in the Rain*. San Francisco: North Point Press, 1986.

———. *No Nature, New and Selected Poems*. New York: Pantheon Books, 1992.

———. *A Place in Space: Ethics, Aesthetics, and Watersheds*. Washington, D.C.: Counterpoint, 1995.

———. *The Practice of the Wild*. San Francisco: North Point Press, 1990.

———. *Turtle Island*. New York: New Directions, 1974.

Sochen, June, ed. *Women's Comic Visions*. Detroit: Wayne State University Press, 1991.

Steffens, Ron. "Abbey, Edward: Hellraiser." In *Resist Much, Obey Little: Remembering Ed Abbey*. James R. Hepworth and Gregory McNamee, eds. 81–88. San Francisco: Sierra Club Books, 1996.

Stegner, Wallace. "A Letter to Wendell Berry." In *Wendell Berry*, ed. Paul Merchant. 47–52. Lewiston, Idaho: Confluence Press, 1991.

Sterling, Philip. *Sea and Earth: The Life of Rachel Carson*. New York: Thomas Y. Crowell Co., 1970.

Sully, James. *An Essay on Laughter: its forms, its causes, its development and its value*. London: Longmans, 1902.

Thoreau, Henry David. *Walden*. New York: The New American Library, 1960.

Toelken, Barre. "Life and Death in Navajo Coyote Tales." In *Recovering the Word: Essays on Native American Literature*, eds. Brian Swann and Arnold Krupat. 388–401. Berkeley: University of California Press, 1987.

Torrance, Robert M. *The Comic Hero*. Cambridge: Harvard University Press, 1978.

Trimble, Stephen, ed. *Words from the Land: Encounters with Natural History Writing*. Reno: University of Nevada Press, 1995.

Urrea, Luis Alberto. "Down the Highway with Edward Abbey." In *Resist Much, Obey Little: Remembering Ed Abbey*, eds. James R. Hepworth and Gregory McNamee. 40–47. San Francisco: Sierra Club Books, 1996.

Vygotsky, Lev. *Thought and Language*. Ed. Alex Kozulin. Cambridge: MIT Press, 1986.

Wakoski, Diane. "Joining the Visionary 'Inhumanists.'" In *Resist Much, Obey Little: Remembering Ed Abbey*, eds. James R. Hepworth and Gregory McNamee. 168–74. San Francisco: Sierra Club Books, 1996.

Walker, Alice. *The Color Purple*. New York: Pocket Books, 1982.

Walker, Nancy A. "Nineteenth-Century Women's Humor." *Women's Comic Visions*. Ed. June Sochen. 85–92. Detroit: Wayne State UP, 1991.

———. *A Very Serious Thing: Women's Humor and American Culture*. Minneapolis: University of Minnesota Press, 1988.

Watts, Alan. *Nature, Man, and Woman*. 1958. New York: Vintage Books, 1970.

White, Jonathan. *Talking on the Water: Conversations about Nature and Creativity*. San Francisco: Sierra Club Books, 1994.

Whitman, Walt. *Poems of Walt Whitman: Leaves of Grass*. New York: Thomas Y. Crowell Co., 1964

Whorton, James. *Before Silent Spring: Pesticides and Public Health in Pre-DDT America*. Princeton: Princton UP, 1974.

Wild, Peter. *Pioneer Conservationists of Western America*. Missoula: Mountain Press, 1979.

Wilkinson, Todd. *The Track of the Coyote*. Minocqua, Wisconsin: NorthWord Press, 1995.

Williams, Terry Tempest. "A Eulogy for Edward Abbey." In *Resist Much, Obey Little: Remembering Ed Abbey*, eds. James R. Hepworth and Gregory McNamee. 199–203. San Francisco: Sierra Club Books, 1996.

Winnicott, D. W. *Playing and Reality*. London: Tavistock, 1971.

Wonham, Henry B. "In the Name of Wonder: The Emergence of Tall Tale Narrative in American Writing." *American Quarterly* 41 (1989): 284–307.

Worster, Donald. *Nature's Economy: A History of Ecological Ideas*. 2nd ed. New York: University of Cambridge, 1994.

Yates, Norris. *The American Humorist: Conscience of the Twentieth Century*. Ames: Iowa State University Press, 1964.

INDEX